The Florida Keys Cookbook

The Florida Keys Cookbook
Recipes and Foodways of Paradise

Victoria Shearer

INSIDERS' GUIDE®

GUILFORD, CONNECTICUT
AN IMPRINT OF THE GLOBE PEQUOT PRESS

INSIDERS' GUIDE®

Copyright © 2006 by Victoria Shearer

Insiders' Guide is a registered trademark of Morris Book Publishing, LLC.
Three Forks is a trademark of Morris Book Publishing, LLC.

Spot art ©JupiterImages unless otherwise stated
Design by LeAnna Weller Smith

Library of Congress Cataloging-in-Publication Data
Shearer, Victoria.
The Florida Keys cookbook : foodways of paradise / Vicki Shearer.—1st ed.
p. cm.
Includes bibliographical references and index.
ISBN-13: 978-0-7627-3546-4 (alk. paper)
ISBN-10: 0-7627-3546-5 (alk. paper)
1. Cookery, American—Southern style. 2. Cookery—Florida—Florida Keys. I. Title.
TX715.2.S68S495 2005
641.59759'41—dc22   2005012547

Manufactured in the United States of America
First Edition/Second Printing

For Bob, who has made my life's journey such an incredible ride

Contents

Acknowledgments

The Beatles sang the words first, and they have rung true for every writing project I have tackled in the past ten years: "I get by with a little help from my friends!" For this labor of love, *The Florida Keys Cookbook: Recipes and Foodways of Paradise*, so many people shared their time, recipes, and expertise to help me on my journey through the culinary history of the Florida Keys. And so many others bravely volunteered to eat the results of my recipe-testing endeavors, which occasionally turned out to be less than a remarkable dining experience. Thank you all.

My sincere thanks to the Keys restaurateurs who shared their talents by contributing some tantalizing recipes: Lance and Jan Hill, chef/owners Barracuda Grill, Marathon; CJ Berwick and Doug Pew, owners The Fish House, Key Largo; Eliot Barton, chef Mangia, Mangia, Key West; Jackie, George, and Johnny Eigner, chef/owners Fish Tales, Marathon; Rob Millner, chef The Pier House, Key West; Beth Maglione, Bagatelle, Key West; Graff Kelly, Conch Republic Seafood Company, Key West; and Donna Edwards, Sloppy Joe's Bar, Key West.

And, my enduring gratitude to the talented group of amateur cooking aficionados who augmented the scores of recipes I developed by contributing their closely guarded secret favorites: Margit Donaldson, Suzanne and John Tobey, Mary Moccia, Meg Nelson,

Adam Mink, Pat Key, Frank Afshari, Louise Skidmore, Lisa Shearer, Grace Beachum, Karen McCabe, Rose Adams, Anna Lockwood, Jeanne Lyon, Betsy Conrad, Beverly Gottschaulk, Jeannie and Kim Huffman, Diane Cannon, Bob Shearer, Melanie Winter, and Ilianna Flagg. And a special thank you to the ladies of Club Duck Key. I am sorry space allowed me to include only a handful of the great recipes you shared with me.

Thank you also to Jerry Wilkinson for sharing his fantastic Keys photography collection with me. My gratitude to Tom Hambright, historian at the Key West Public Library, who dug deep in the archives to help me research little known culinary and lifestyle anecdotes of old Key West. And a very special thank you goes to my friend Dick Adler, who for more than a year constantly blessed my e-mail inbox with great links to fascinating and often obscure Keys historical culinary connections.

And to three people who made this book possible: Mary Norris at The Globe Pequot Press and my editors Megan Hiller and Mimi Egan. Thanks for the opportunity.

And finally, thanks to my star tasters and loyal guinea pigs: my husband Bob, my mother June Harbort, my children Brian and Lisa, Kristen and John, and especially my most discerning critics, my grandkids—Bethany, Bobby, Christopher, Ashleigh, Nicholas, and Leia.

Introduction

Food Customs, Cultures, and Traditions of the Florida Keys

IN THE BEGINNING

A string of patch reefs at the edge of the continental shelf, the Florida Keys flourished under the sea until the last glacial period, the Wisconsin. At this time, the oceans receded and the seas dropped more than 150 feet. The landmass that emerged—coral bedrock interspersed with fossil remnants—encompassed all of Florida Bay and Hawk Channel, as well as the exposed patch reefs now considered the Keys.

The climate began to warm about 15,000 years ago at the beginning of the present interglacial period, the Holocene Epoch. Sea levels again rose, reclaiming Florida Bay and Hawk Channel to the watery realm. Spurred on by global warming, the waters continue to rise. In fact, with a mere 15-foot rise in sea level, the ocean will once again reclaim the Florida Keys.

THE NATIVE AMERICANS

Sand burial and rock mounds, freshwater sinkholes, and kitchen middens have been discovered all throughout the Florida Keys, suggesting tribal cultures began here as early as A.D. 800. Mounds of bones and shells found in the middens, or ancient campsites, suggest fish, crabs, sea turtles, lobsters, shellfish, and conchs were plentiful and that the Native Americans—Tequestas, Calusas, and Matecumbes—were seafood gourmands.

The tribes were hunter-gatherers, supplementing their predominantly seafood diet by killing deer and raccoon for meat and harvesting such wild fruits as sea grapes, palm berries, and cocoplums. From masses of discarded conch shells, the seafarers fashioned cooking vessels, implements, and tools. Small shells were used as cups, dippers, and spoons. The spiral *columellae*—center of the conch shell—was utilized as a primitive drill to make holes in large conch shells. Wooden sticks were stuck through these holes, thereby creating hammers and clubs. It appears no part of a sea creature's remains was wasted. The flaring lips of the conch shells served as gouges, scrapers, and axes. And sharks' teeth were outfitted with wooden handles to form knives.

THE SPANISH

Foreigners began coming to the shores of the Keys in 1511 during the Spanish conquest of Cuba, just 90 nautical miles south. When Ponce de Leon discovered Florida in 1513, he declared the island archipelago *Los Martires* (the

martyrs) and the outlying islands *Las Tortugas* (the turtles).

Havana was founded in 1517 and by 1519 Spanish ships began sailing past *Los Martires*, traveling the northern currents of the Gulf Stream laden with treasure bound for the mother country. Despite a few dustups between the Calusas and the Spanish, the Native American tribes were friendly with the white men they encountered, who appeared more interested in harvesting fish, sea turtles, and birds' eggs, looking for enemy ships, and converting the natives to Catholicism than in colonizing the islands.

During the next two centuries the tribes helped the Spanish catch fish in Keys waters, pirate passing English ships, and salvage cargo from vessels that wrecked on the reef. Cubans camped on the northwest shore of Key West (now Mallory Square) and brought their piscatory harvest back to Cuba. And the Spanish supplied the rum . . . and disease, causing the native population to dwindle dramatically.

THE ENGLISH

At the same time, England also had interests in the region, claiming the Bahamas for King Charles I. Experienced fishermen from the Bahamas harvested

LEFT: *Early Keys pioneers, ca. 1900.*
Credit: State Archives of Florida.
ABOVE: *Keys home surrounded by palms, ca. 1895.*
Credit: State Archives of Florida.

the waters of the Keys on a regular basis, developing a lucrative trade with Havana. By the 1600s, Cuban fishermen began referring to the Keys as *Los Cayos de Florida*, the little islands of Florida. The English adopted the word *cayo*, which came from the Taino tribes in Cuba, and changed it to "cay." Eventually the word was corrupted to "key," and by 1742 the English were calling the islands the Florida Keys.

Seeking a strategically located naval base, England attacked and captured Cuba in 1762, looting Havana. The

country remained under English control for nearly a year, until in 1763 Spain ceded Florida to England in return for regaining Cuba. (Spain never really acknowledged the Keys to be part of Florida, however, and continued to fish its waters.) Fearing retribution by the English, the remaining indigenous people of the Keys fled to Cuba.

THE UNITED STATES

Spain regained control of Florida in 1783, but neither the Spanish nor the English colonized the Keys in large

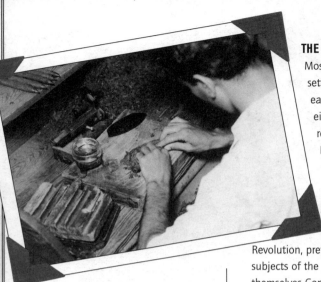

THE BAHAMIANS

Most of the Bahamians who settled in the Keys in the early to mid-1800s were either descendants of religious dissenters from England who settled Eleuthera in 1649 or Englishmen who left the American colonies for the Bahamas during the American Revolution, preferring to remain subjects of the English crown. Calling themselves Conchs, after the conch mollusk that was a staple of their diet, the Bahamian immigrants received homesteading rights from the U.S. government.

Initially, life in the Keys was lonely and secluded, but the hardy Conchs adjusted to life on the island with the valor and toughness of pioneers. The settlers respected the sea, earning their livelihood by fishing, turtling, sponging, and salvaging ships. They depended on their boats like western pioneers relied upon horses and covered wagons. No bridges existed between the islands, and foodstuffs other than what they harvested in their indigenous surroundings had to be supplied by passing ship.

numbers until 1821, when Spain ceded Florida to the United States. Salvage of ships wrecked along the coral reef off the coast of the Keys was big business by this time: According to the laws of salvage, the first captain who boarded a stranded ship became the wrecking master and was awarded the largest share of the recovered cargo. But the U.S. federal government began regulating the wrecking operations, issuing an edict stating that only U.S. citizens could engage in the salvage operations. Since this enterprise was of great interest to the Bahamians, they began to immigrate to the Keys in large numbers.

KEYS DAILY LIFE IN THE 1800s

These people were tough. They endured hurricanes, mosquitoes, sand fleas, extreme heat, isolation, no fresh water, no refrigeration, no electricity, no modern plumbing, and no medical aid. But along with an entrepreneurial spirit and a deep sense of religion, they did have clean air, warm sunshine, and the riches of the sea. Candles and oil lamps supplied light after the sun went down. Roof troughs carried rainwater during the rainy season to cisterns built near their homes. Outhouses in the back accommodated bodily ministrations. Except during the rainy season, bathing and laundry were done in the saltwater of the bay or ocean. Soap was home-made, and flat-irons heated on wood stoves in the yard were used for ironing clothing.

In spite of the tropical climate, women wore modest long dresses. They constantly battled roaches and ants in the kitchen-and-stove house, both of which were most often separated from the main house. All staples had to be stored in metal cans or tightly covered jars. These staples came in, only occasionally, by ship. Grits, rice, and flour were ordered by the barrel, pickled beef by the keg, canned milk—evaporated and sweetened condensed—by the case, dried beans in cloth sacks, and lard and butter in pails. Coffee came green and unroasted, salt was scarce, and molasses and honey were cheaper than sugar.

But much of the regular fare on the Keys pioneer table would be considered a delicacy today—lobsters, turtle steaks, conch chowder, oysters, quail, venison, dolphin, stone crab, snappers, grouper, and shrimp. Fresh fruits and vegetables—key limes, coconuts, mangos, papayas, sapodillas, tomatoes—were grown in dooryard gardens. True to its Bahamian roots, early Keys cuisine was decidedly English—dinner pies, roasts, stews, duffs, puddings, casseroles—with a touch of island spiciness that had evolved through successive waves of foreign conquerors and colonizers in the Bahamas.

KEY WEST

By 1822 Key West was a growing, thriving city. As island people, the Conchs remained firmly bound together by family ties and proximity. They regarded outsiders and mainlanders with reservation, calling them "strangers." The Conchs spoke with a southern lilt and a cockney accent—long "o's," dropping and adding "h's," substituting "v" for "w" were all part of the dialect. For instance: "The veather ain't no good fir fishin', an' the vater is too rough."

When the English left the United States for the Bahamas after the American Revolution, they brought along their slaves. The Emancipation Act of 1834 officially ended slavery within the British realm, and most Bahamian slaves were freed by 1838. From the 1830s to the 1850s, black Bahamians immigrated to Key West where jobs fishing, sponging, and in salt manufacture paid them cash

LEFT: *Cigar worker, late 1800s.* **Credit: State Archives of Florida. BELOW:** *Street scene in old section of Key West.* **Credit: State Archives of Florida.**

wages. Although racial and ethnic divisions were less rigid in Key West than in most of the American south, some wealthy landowners did keep slaves to do household chores. (Free blacks were restricted to living in what is now known as the Bahama Village section of Key West.)

When Florida seceded from the Union in 1861, Key West was the second largest and most cosmopolitan city in the state and the wealthiest city per capita in the nation. Key West sympathized with the Confederacy during the war, although Union soldiers were stationed at Fort Jefferson in the Dry Tortugas and Fort Zachary Taylor in Key West, and naval fleets regularly blockaded

supply ships in Keys waters that were heading toward the southern states.

A second wave of Bahamian immigration began after the Civil War. Pioneer families such as the Alburys, Lowes, Pinders, and Russells settled in the upper Keys, which was still a true wilderness. They began farming pineapples, key limes, and tomatoes in large plantations. Other pioneers, fleeing the American south after the abolition of slavery, settled in the Florida Keys as well.

THE CUBANS

Cubans began immigrating to Key West in a small, steady stream in the 1830s, when William H. Wall built a small

cigar factory on Front Street. But it was not until the Cuban Revolution of 1868 that the major influx of Cuban immigrants began arriving, forever changing the composition of the city . . . for the better. Accused of treason in

Cuba, Vicente Martinez Ybor moved his cigar factory and his entire family to Key West in 1869. Other prominent Cuban cigar manufacturers—such as E. H. Gato—followed. By 1878 Cubans made up one-third the population of Key West. By 1880, fifty-seven companies were making cigars in the city, making Key West the greatest clear-Havana cigar manufacturing city in the United States.

With the Cubans came their flavorful cuisine, which quickly became a part of Key West's food heritage. Traditional Cuban cuisine is a combination of Spanish (conquerors), African (West Indian slaves), and indigenous Indian (Taino and Siboney) ingredients and cooking techniques. Its basis has always centered on rice, beans, root vegetables, and plantains. Dishes are highly seasoned, but are not as fiery as other Latin American countries, and are often sweet as well as spicy. Pork, beef, and chicken dominate classic Cuban cuisine and are usually marinated in sour orange or lime juice and braised or roasted until they fall off the bone. And, surrounded by more than 2,000 miles of coastline, Cuba, like the Florida Keys, has always relied upon fish and seafood as dietary mainstays.

CONCH CUISINE OF THE 1900s

By 1900, Spanish was spoken as freely as English in Key West. As the decades passed, although Conchs were Conchs and Cubans were Cubans, they intermarried—both physically and culturally. The word Conch became redefined to mean any person descended from the original settlers of the Florida Keys and encompassed progeny of those who emigrated from the Bahamas, Cuba, and even the southern states of the U.S. All others were considered "strangers."

True Conch cuisine began evolving in the latter part of the nineteenth century, resulting in a unique blend of the English-Bahamian and Spanish-Cuban cultures. A combination of zesty Latin, spicy Caribbean, and traditional British influences wove their way through the bounty of indigenous foodstuffs of the Keys, forever changing the way either culture originally cooked. For instance, the Bahamians brought the English recipe for duff with them to the Keys, and the Cubans introduced guava fruit to the islands. What resulted was guava duff, one of the most popular Keys holiday desserts of the twentieth century.

Inherent differences in cooking approaches and traditions continued, however. Cubans preferred starchy side dishes more than leafy salads—plantains yucca, boniatos, calabaza, rice, and beans. Dishes were often cooked in a *sofrito*, a simmered sauce made of garlic, onions, bell peppers, tomatoes, and spices.

Conchs used Old Sour on their food after it was cooked. Cubans used it only during cooking; it never left the stove. Instead, Cubans preferred mojo (pronounced mo-ho)—a potent, garlicky sauce—to splash on meat, fish, and seafood at the table. Conchs, on the other hand, always kept a bowl of freshly cut limes on the table at mealtimes, liberally sprinkling it on everything.

Cubans spiced their food with oregano, cumin, and sweet basil, which grew in their dooryard gardens, and preferred cinnamon bark to ground cinnamon in their cooking. They imported capers and paprika from Cuba in bulk. Conchs put a bay leaf in nearly everything they cooked and cultivated fiery

LEFT: *Roof top view of Key West in 1898.* **Credit: State Archives of Florida. ABOVE:** *Butler and cook preparing meal in 1906.* **Credit: From the collection of Jerry Wilkinson.**

bird peppers (for Old Sour), chives, parsley, and mint in pots on their porches.

Cubans made fresh bread every day, a favorite repast in both cultures. For everyone in the Keys, dinner usually was eaten in mid-afternoon with a light meal taken in the evening. And for the Cubans at least, strong shots of coffee or café con leche were consumed all day long.

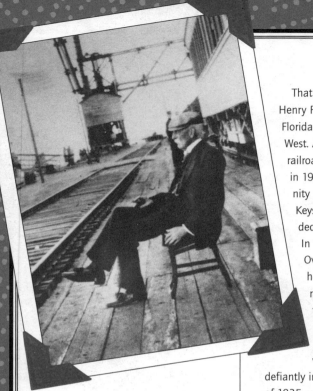

FLAGLER'S OVERSEAS RAILROAD— LINK TO THE MAINLAND

At the beginning of the twentieth century, Key West's prosperity began to wane. Government lighthouses had been constructed along the reef, so the wrecking industry died. Tarpon Springs cornered the sponge market. And cigar manufacturers—enticed by promises of lower taxes, moved up the Gulf coast to Tampa. Settlements in the rest of the Keys remained completely isolated except for boat transportation.

That changed, however, when Henry Flagler decided to extend his Florida East Coast Railroad to Key West. Against all odds, Flagler's railroad extension was completed in 1912, and a new day of modernity was predicted for the Florida Keys. That promise would take decades to materialize however. In 1923, construction of the Overseas Highway began, hopes being that the new road would bring tourism to the Florida Keys, even though the islands still were without an abundant fresh water source. Mother Nature defiantly intervened with the Hurricane of 1935, when 200-mile-an-hour winds smashed the railroad, the road construction, and the hopes of a more prosperous Florida Keys.

UNCLE SAM TO THE RESCUE

With the advent of the World War I and II, however, the U.S. Navy, utilizing Key West as a strategic military base, provided just the stimulus the Keys needed. The U.S. government constructed a freshwater pipeline from the mainland and commissioned the completion of the Overseas Highway. Hundreds of "strangers" moved to the Keys, and refrigerated truckloads of fresh perishable foodstuffs regularly made their way to the islands from Miami. By 1942, the Florida Keys finally had moved into the twentieth century.

The Conch cuisine of the 1940s and 1950s—using indigenous ingredients and foodstuffs imported from Cuba and the mainland—reflected the blended heritage of all the islands' residents. English dishes such as steamed turtle, crawfish soup, conch chowder, hopping john, queen of all puddings, guava jelly tarts, coconut duff, johnny cake, and grits and grunts, showed a definite assimilation of tropical ingredients.

And the "strangers," arriving in increasing numbers, introduced such "foreign" ideas as leafy salads, key lime pie, stuffed baked grouper, fried breadfruit, and baked avocados.

The Cuban influence showed most strongly in such dishes as boliche, picadillo, roast pork, ropa vieja, arroz con pollo, bollos, mollettes, and flan. By 1949, the majority of restaurants in Key West were owned by Cubans.

TOURISM—LINK TO THE WORLD

The Florida Keys began its metamorphosis into a desirable tourist destination in the second half of the twentieth century, when it became popular as a sportfishing destination. Fishing camps, such as writer Zane Grey's favorite Long Key Fish Camp, offered only basic amenities. Most restaurant food served to visitors—though very fresh—was often very plain as well. But by the 1980s, the Florida Keys emerged as a tourist-driven economy. "Strangers" had taken over the food scene, and restaurants opened up and down the Keys, featuring a "new" cuisine touted as Floribbean. Colorful, ethnic, and bursting with new flavors, it swept the nation.

Fresh tropical produce was the key ingredient in Floribbean cuisine. Ingredients and cooking styles unique to Central and South America and the islands of the Caribbean inspired tropical innovations of traditional dishes. For instance, curries became sweetly aromatic, incorporating sugar, allspice, and such local fruits as mangoes and bananas. Recipes reflected the rich cultural blend of people, ingredients, and food traditions of this new wave of settlers.

CONCHFUSION—THE TWENTY-FIRST CENTURY

With the dawn of a new millennium, forces of man and nature once again have combined to change the complexion of the Florida Keys. Technological advances connect the Keys to the rest

of the universe like never before. An unprecedented boom in tourism and settlement makes demands on fragile resources, however, threatening the ecological balance of surrounding waters while at the same time stimulating the economy.

A new wave of immigrants from Cuba, South America, the Caribbean, and Europe as well as settlement by scores of retiring baby boomers have joined cultures much as did the Conchs and Cubans of yesteryear. The new cuisine that has resulted, unofficially dubbed Conchfusion, takes advantage of the increased availability of unusual ingredients from around the globe, fusing them with the bounty of the sea and the tropical jewels of the dooryard garden.

One constant remains: Just as the riches of the sea first attracted pioneers

to the Florida Keys centuries ago, diversity of culture and cuisine continues to lure settlers and visitors to this watery world. But make no mistake: The sea is in charge here and always has been. As much as Human Nature plays with the islands' future, Mother Nature still holds all the cards.

LEFT: *Henry Morrison Flagler waiting for train, ca. 1912.* Credit: From the collection of Jerry Wilkinson. **BELOW:** *Opening of Seven Mile Bridge in 1983.* Credit: State Archives of Florida.

Cocktails, Coolers, and Finger Food 1

"Since Key West is both a navy town and a resort town, the chief demarcation between winter and summer lies in the crackling noise which sounds over the island in the winter. For some time this was attributed to the wind in the palms, until keener perceptions discovered that actually it was the crispy, crackling sound made by many people eating stuffed celery and crunchy crackers." Thus was life recorded, tongue in cheek, in 1949 by the Key West Woman's Club in their cookbook, *Key West Cook Book*.

Cocktail hour in the Florida Keys is no longer so bleak—finger food has improved immensely. And the party scene, especially in Key West, is alive and well. Apparently Key West was a pretty hopping place as far back as 1840: The small maritime frontier town sported thirty-two grog shops. By 1884, Key West's population was as diverse as its structures. A melting pot of Americans, Englishmen, Frenchmen, Germans, Spaniards, Cubans, Bahamians, Italians, and African Americans congregated at night, singing, dancing, and drinking in their own languages. Said a gentleman known only as Jack: "I learned to drink beer in seven languages while there . . ."

Things haven't changed much!

LEFT: *Guava, a mainstay of the Keys, ca. 1950.* **Credit: State Archives of Florida.**

Calamondin Brandy

Calamondin brandy or liqueur is the dooryard hooch of the Florida Keys. The tiny sour orange fruit is no longer grown commercially in Florida due to a raging outbreak of citrus cancer. Thus, calamondins are one of the true dooryard fruits still encountered only in the Florida Keys. Because they are so sour, calamondins require copious amounts of sugar in recipes to offset their tartness. But their flavor is so unique, no other fruit provides an adequate substitute.

50 whole ripe calamondins
1 quart (32 ounces) unflavored vodka
4 cups sugar

1. Pinch skin of each calamondin just enough to pop it slightly. Place whole calamondins in a gallon glass jar with a tight-fitting lid. Add vodka and sugar. Replace lid tightly on jar and shake back and forth, until sugar begins to dissolve. Shake contents of jar once a day for at least 2 weeks by turning jar upside down, then right side up, repeatedly for about 1 minute. (After a few days the sugar will dissolve into the vodka.)

2. After 2 weeks, remove fruit and strain liquid through coffee filters until the coffee filters are clear. Place brandy in a tall-necked glass bottle with a tight-fitting lid and store in refrigerator. Serve in chilled cordial or brandy glasses.

CHEF NOTE: When picking calamondins from the tree, be sure to use clippers or scissors. If you pull them off, the stem end of the fruit will tear and the calamondins will spoil more quickly. Once picked, calamondins should be refrigerated and used within a week.

Cuban Sunset

 SERVES 6

1 (12-ounce) can frozen lemonade, thawed

2 (12-ounce) cans lemon-lime carbonated soda

2 cups guava nectar

2 tablespoons grenadine

9 ounces Bacardi white rum

3 thin lemon slices, seeded and cut in half

1. Place lemonade, soda, guava nectar, and grenadine in a large glass or plastic pitcher. Stir well to combine. Refrigerate until needed.

2. To serve: Fill each of 6 tall glasses with ice. Add 1½ ounces rum to each glass. Pour guava mixture evenly into each glass (about ¾ cup each). Garnish each glass with a half lemon slice.

CHEF NOTE: You can omit the rum and serve this drink as a tangy breakfast beverage.

A *coctel* in old Havana was a pre-dinner cocktail party with finger food and a variety of rum drinks. Bacardi white rum had its birth in Cuba, so it is a natural pairing with the nectar of the guava or *guayaba,* one of the most popular and most widely used fruits in the Cuban culture (see sidebar in "Grand Finales" chapter).

Duck Key Snowbird

Duck Key remained uninhabited until the 1950s, when a man named Bryan W. Newkirk developed the island into one of the first planned communities in the Florida Keys. Although a saltworks briefly operated in low-lying areas in the 1830s, the island was mostly swamp and mangroves when Newkirk bought it. Now, more than half a century later, 2½ billion yards of fill, 4 miles of flow-through canals, and the vision of one man has turned Duck Key (mile marker 61) into one of the most desirable keys in the island chain.

1 quart (32 ounces) orange juice
¼ cup lemon juice
¼ cup sugar

¼ cup crushed mint leaves plus 6 whole sprigs
9 ounces dark rum
seltzer or club soda

1. Place orange juice, lemon juice, sugar, and crushed mint leaves in a large covered container. Stir to mix well. Refrigerate overnight.

2. In each of 6 large tulip glasses filled with ice, place 1½-ounces rum, 6 ounces orange juice mixture, and a splash of seltzer. Stir to mix. Garnish with a sprig of mint.

CHEF NOTE: You can make this drink with vodka instead of rum, for an equally tasty but different libation.

Frozen Margaritas Plus

 SERVES 3

1 (6-ounce) can frozen limeade
6 ounces Key West Pale Ale or any
  other beer
4 ounces tequila

1 ounce Triple Sec
1 key lime, quartered
margarita salt

1. Fill a blender half full with small ice cubes or crushed ice. Add limeade, beer, tequila, and Triple Sec. Blend until slushy.

2. Rub a key lime wedge around the rim of a wide-rimmed glass. Place a thin layer of margarita salt on a small plate. Dip glass into salt. Divide Margaritas among 3 glasses. Top each with a wedge of key lime.

CHEF NOTE: Beer in a margarita? Sounds absurd but wait until you taste these drinks. Smooth, sweet, and tangy, the libation is worthy of Jimmy Buffett himself.

The recorded music of Jimmy Buffett wafting out of his Key West Margaritaville restaurant permeates the honkytonk atmosphere on Duval Street. Buffett came to Key West in 1972, where he first per-formed in the Chart Room of the Pier House. Tourism had not yet boomed in the Keys. Instead, the 1970s was the decade of drug smuggling in the Florida Keys, attracting a rough and tumble array of characters. As in the days of Prohibition and immediately after its repeal, drinking was a favorite sport. Jimmy Buffett hit the big time during his Key West days, recording his first successful album in 1973—"A White Sport Coat and a Pink Crustacean." Although he no longer lives in the Keys, Buffett holds favorite-son status in Key West to this day.

Key Limes

The key lime holds a remarkable position of honor and respect in the Florida Keys: The main ingredient in our official dessert, key lime pie, as well as many of our tropical drinks, the key lime (*Citrus aurantifolia Swingle*) is actually a specific variety of lime that grows only in limited parts of the world. The species is very sensitive to the cold and thrives only in warm, moist climates.

Like the Bahamian and Cuban émigrés who settled the Florida Keys centuries ago, our signature key limes are naturalized, not native. Exactly how did these smooth-skinned sour yellow spheres, which range in size from a walnut to a golf ball, make it to the United States' southernmost island chain? No one knows for sure, but one thing is for certain: It was a long journey.

No record of the lime's introduction to the Florida Keys has been found, but the Spanish planted seeds of key limes wherever they landed, including Haiti by 1520 and Mexico after the fall of the Aztec Empire. It is a safe bet that the Spanish introduced the key lime to the Florida Keys as well. Ponce de León garnered credit for naming the Florida Keys *Los Martires* in 1513 during his exploration of the Gulf of Mexico.

Growing key limes in the Florida Keys was never easy. Finding limestone bedrock with no natural soil, early nineteenth-century pioneers resorted to rather unorthodox planting techniques, called jungle planting. They dug potholes in the limestone and placed a layer of soil in the bottom of each. Shortly before the rainy season, the farmers sowed a thick layer of key lime seeds in the soil. When the seedlings were a few inches high, during the rainy season, they transplanted each seedling into its own soil-filled pothole, fertilizing it with a mulch of cured seaweed. Because key lime trees are very thorny, growers collected the ripe yellow fruit from the ground twice a week, placing the fruit in wheelbarrows pushed along boards that were placed over the rough, rocky terrain.

Key limes were commercially grown on a small scale in the upper Florida Keys at the beginning of the twentieth century. Growers pickled the fruits in saltwater and shipped them to Boston, where they were popular as a snack food, especially loved by children. But the industry was short lived. The hurricane of 1926 wiped out all the citrus groves, forever terminating commercially grown key limes in the Florida Keys.

Today backyard key lime trees flourish here. Key lime aficionados stubbornly accept only limes grown in the Florida Keys as being authentic, but commercial key lime juice sold in the United States—such as Nellie and Joe's, bottled in Key West since the '70s—actually comes from commercial groves in Mexico and the West Indies, where they're called Mexican limes or West Indian limes.

RIGHT: *Young women pose with fruit during key lime festival in 1953.* **Credit: State Archives of Florida.**

Goombay Smash

This drink takes its name from a lively festival celebrated annually in the Bahamas, Key West, and other tropical islands. Originating in Africa and the West Indies, the festival featured dancers who used a skin-covered drum they called a "gombey," meaning rhythm. Traditionally dancers wore high, feathered headdresses, colorful costumes, and sometimes fanciful or bizarre masks.

3 ounces white rum
3 ounces coconut rum
3 ounces apricot brandy

3 tablespoons grenadine
3 cups pineapple juice
4 fresh pineapple spears

1. Put all ingredients except pineapple spears in a blender and process until frothy. Serve over ice in a tall glass and garnish with pineapple spear.

CHEF NOTE: This colorful drink, which is a frothy pink because of the grenadine, is so smooth you can easily get smashed!

Hibiscus Bagatelle

1 ounce light rum
½ ounce coconut rum
5 ounces pineapple juice

1 ounce cranberry juice
orange slice
maraschino cherry

1. Place all liquid ingredients in a cocktail shaker. Fill shaker with ice and shake vigorously. Transfer shaken drink and ice to a 12-ounce glass. Garnish with orange slice and maraschino cherry.

CHEF NOTE: White rum that has been flavored with coconut, either during fermentation or after it has been distilled, is called coconut rum.

Bagatelle restaurant presides over Key West's Duval Street like a queen on her throne. Situated in the ca. 1884 home built by sea captain Frederick Roberts, the island eatery is a maze of cozy rooms and sweeping verandas. Roberts and his family used to drink and dine on these very same verandas, cooled by the breezes wafting down Duval from the nearby Gulf of Mexico. Today the Hibiscus is one of Bagatelle's most requested drinks.

SERVES 2

Mango-Coconut Batido

Tropical fruits such as mangos, papayas, bananas, guavas, and coconuts are combined with milk, ice, and sometimes sugar to create a Cuban milkshake called a *batido*. This Key West shake is a cultural hybrid, however, because it also contains vanilla ice cream.

6 ounces skim milk
2 ounces cream of coconut
1 cup cubed mango

1 cup low-fat vanilla ice cream
1 teaspoon vanilla extract
2 tablespoons grated coconut, toasted

1. Place milk, cream of coconut, and mango in a blender. Pulse to mix well. Add ice cream and vanilla. Process on high until well mixed and frothy. Pour milkshake into 2 glasses. Sprinkle toasted coconut on top of milkshake.

CHEF NOTE: Grated coconut is unsweetened and available in the frozen food sections of Latin markets and many supermarkets. Cream of coconut is popularly marketed as Coco Lopez and is highly sweetened. You'll find cream of coconut in the supermarket drink mixer section. If instead you use coconut cream, such as that marketed by Ocho Rios, you should add 2 tablespoons of sugar to the milkshake. Coconut cream will be in the baking section of your supermarket.

Mojito

2 lime wedges

4 to 5 fresh mint leaves

2 ounces simple syrup (recipe in
Chef Note below)

2 ounces white rum

club soda

1. Place lime wedges and mint leaves in a pint glass. Muddle with the handle of a wooden spoon for 30 seconds. Add simple syrup and white rum. Fill glass with ice and top off with club soda. Shake or stir gently.

CHEF NOTE: To muddle means to simply bruise or gently pound the limes and mint leaves to release their juices and essence. (You can buy a muddler, which looks like a tiny baseball bat or billy club, at any good restaurant store.) To make simple syrup, in a small saucepan, combine 2 parts sugar to 1 part water. Heat until sugar is dissolved. Cool before using (keeps for weeks if refrigerated). For a fruity twist to your mojito, use flavored rum, such as mango, banana, or pineapple.

The Conch Republic Seafood Company in Key West makes the best mojito in the Florida Keys, and they offer this legend about the drink's origins: "The mojito (mo-hee-toe) was concocted in the seventeenth century by Sir Francis Drake. Sir Francis was crusading around the Caribbean when his stock of whiskey ran dry. He drank his whiskey with mint and a little sugar water. Being in 'rum country' and in need of a fortified beverage, he substituted rum for his whiskey and the mojito was born." Officially, however, Cuba claims to have invented the mojito in the teen years of the twentieth century. It was one of Ernest Hemingway's favorite libations when he visited La Bodeguita in Havana.

Orange Juice and Rum Sundowner

Made from sugarcane juice or molasses, all rums are distilled clear. They are then fermented for from 24 hours to 12 days, which accounts for variations in color. Myers's rum is a sweet, brown rum, which is aged in white oak barrels for at least five years. More like a rich cognac or brandy, this strongly flavored rum stands up well to pairings with fruit juices and other mixers in tropical concoctions.

1 ½ ounces Myers's dark rum
3 ounces orange juice
1 ½ ounces lemon-lime soda

key lime, cut in quarters
splash cranberry juice

1. Pour rum, orange juice, and soda in a tall glass filled with ice. Stir to mix. Squeeze piece of lime into glass. Mix again. Splash cranberry juice on top. Do not mix it into the drink. Garnish with a slice of key lime.

CHEF NOTE: This drink, which my husband concocted years ago, is the drink most requested by our houseguests for sunset celebrations.

Pomegranate Martini

 SERVES 1

2 ounces Absolut citron vodka

4 ounces POM Wonderful pomegranate
  juice

1 wedge fresh grapefruit

1. Place vodka and pomegranate juice in a cocktail shaker. Squeeze in juice from grape-fruit wedge. Add ice and shake until well chilled, about 1 minute. Pour into a 6-ounce martini glass.

CHEF NOTE: Wonderful is not an adjective for this brand of pomegranate juice, but rather the variety of pomegranate, which is available only from October through December. This drink is not really a martini, because it contains much more fruit juice than liquor, but it is shaken and served like a martini. The splash of fresh grapefruit juice is essential to this drink.

Welcome to the hippest new martini on the Key West club circuit: The pomegranate martini is now available to the masses at home, thanks to the increased availability of POM Wonderful pomegranate juice. Sold fresh in the refrigerated juice or organic food sections of most supermarkets, pomegranate juice is high in potassium, vitamin C, and antioxidants—almost making the martini good for you!

Buddy Act

The Writer and The Rumrunner

Bawdy and naughty, Key West in the 1920s paid little attention to the laws of Prohibition. Isolated from the mainland United States, the town bustled with speakeasies, honkytonks, bistros, brothels, home breweries, and gambling dens.

Charter-boat captain cum rumrunner Joe Russell ran an illegal little booze joint in his house during Prohibition, and Ernest Hemingway, an island newcomer in 1928, began buying bootleg scotch from him. The two men hit it off immediately, forming a fast friendship that lasted for decades. They shared interests and a mutual admiration.

For months at a time the men fished the Gulf Stream for sailfish and marlin aboard Russell's 32-foot boat *Anita,* or Hemingway's yacht *Pilar*. They sailed to Cuba, where they cruised the bars in Havana and drank mojitos at Sloppy Joe's and the Floridita. Hemingway immortalized their shared fishing adventures in *The Old Man and the Sea* and *Islands in the Stream*. He also used Russell as the model for Freddy in *To Have or Have Not*.

After the repeal of Prohibition in 1933, Russell leased a rundown bar on Greene Street for three dollars a week and made his liquor operation legitimate. The original name for the bar was The Blind Pig (present location of Captain Tony's Saloon), but Hemingway urged Russell to change the bar's name to Sloppy Joe's, after their favorite Havana haunt. A rowdy bar frequented by fishermen and unsavory characters, the dark, narrow establishment had no door. In fact the saloon never closed. This was the era of the Great Depression. Here a man could get 10 beers for a dollar, a shot of gin for 10 cents, or whiskey for 15 cents. If he had hit it lucky gambling in the backroom, he could afford a scotch at a whopping 35 cents.

Sloppy Joe's was Hemingway's favorite watering hole, which he frequented with a bunch of cronies he called "The Mob." The Old Master (Papa Hemingway) always drank at a discount. Serving the customers was bartender Al Skinner, an imposing African American who worked at Sloppy Joe's until his death in 1949.

Hemingway favored a sugarless daiquiri, a strong shaken drink made of a double shot of rum and a splash of lime, grapefruit, and maraschino cherry

juices. The drink, still served today, is named after Hemingway—Papa Dobles or Father Doubles, as in double shot.

In 1937 Joe Russell, irked that his rent was raised by $1 per month, moved Sloppy Joe's saloon to its present location on the corner of Greene and Duval Streets. For the move, which happened literally overnight, customers simply picked up their drinks, as well as the chairs and tables, and moved down the street.

Ernest Hemingway lived in his Key West mansion on Whitehead Street with second wife Pauline and his two sons from 1928 until 1939, when his marriage hit the rocks. Leaving Pauline behind, Hemingway headed for Cuba. He remained close friends with Russell, however, regularly fishing and carousing with him in Havana. In 1941, on one of their watery jaunts, Russell died of a massive heart attack at age 53, and Hemingway lost his best friend. By 1962, Hemingway himself was dead. Cause of death—a self-inflicted gunshot wound to the head.

In Key West, however, the legendary buddy act lives on at Sloppy Joe's—the infamous, and still doorless, saloon devoted to the entwined legacies of the writer and the rumrunner.

SLOPPY JOE'S Papa Dobles

Serves 1

Papa's favorite bar has their own version of the Papa Dobles, a lighter, fruitier concoction.

1¼ ounces Bacardi Silver Rum
fresh grapefruit juice
grenadine
sour mix
club soda
slice of key lime

1. Fill a 14-ounce cocktail shaker with ice cubes. Add rum and fill shaker almost to the top with grapefruit juice. Add a splash each of grenadine, sour mix, and club soda. Shake vigorously and pour ice and liquid into a tall glass. Garnish with a slice of lime.

Papa Dobles

Serves 1

Ernest Hemingway loved his libations strong. This drink, which contains a double shot of rum, was named for him, the father of the double shots, Papa Dobles. The drink, as with many Cuban cocktails, is strong, tart, and limey.

3 ounces white rum
2 ounces fresh grapefruit juice
1 ounce fresh key lime juice
1 ounce maraschino cherry juice

1. Place rum and juices in a cocktail shaker. Fill with ice and shake until frosty. Pour into a large wide-mouthed glass, such as a large daiquiri or martini glass.

Sangria

Originating in Spain, sangria also is a Cuban favorite. The basic ingredients of this red wine punch—wine, oranges, and lemons—grew abundantly in the coastal areas of Spain, which probably led to the drink's invention. In Spanish, *sangre* means blood, so the name sangria refers to the dark red-purple color of the wine used in its preparation.

1 quart Blackstone Merlot or any good dry red wine
1 orange, sliced thin with peel
1 lemon, sliced thin with peel

1 peach, skinned, pitted, and sliced
½ cup sugar
12 ounces club soda
½ cup vodka

1. Place all ingredients except 6 slices of orange or lemon in a large pitcher. Stir to mix well. Refrigerate overnight. Serve over ice in tall glasses. Garnish with lemon or orange slice.

CHEF NOTE: Be sure to use a quality bottle of wine when you make sangria. Spanish rioja is traditional, but I think the merlot is smoother.

Tobey's Wake-up Call

2 tablespoons cream of coconut

6 ounces papaya nectar

6 ounces pineapple nectar

3 small finger bananas or one large banana, peeled

12 ounces orange juice

1. Combine all ingredients in a blender until smooth. Chill in refrigerator for 30 minutes. Re-blend and serve.

CHEF NOTE: This tropical fruit drink evolved when I gave one of my dearest houseguests free access to my pantry and my blender. It proved a great addition to our morning brunch.

Canned or bottled nectar is made from fruit puree that is then mixed with corn syrup and water. Nectar, which is favored in Cuban culture, is sweeter than canned or bottled juice, which usually is made straight from fruit concentrate.

Black Bean-Chipotle Dip with Fresh Tortilla Chips

Chipotle peppers are actually ripe red jalapeno peppers that have been smoked over mesquite. They are considered medium on the heat scale. It is believed that the Aztecs were the first to smoke-dry jalapenos. The jalapeno is a fleshy chile that tends to rot before it completely air dries. Smoking hastens the drying process. Chipotles (pronounced che-pote-lays) are available dried whole, powdered, pickled, and canned in adobo sauce.

1 package (8) 8-inch flavored flour tortillas

1 teaspoon olive oil

½ cup chopped sweet onions, like Vidalia

2 garlic cloves, minced

½ cup diced plum tomatoes

⅓ cup bottled picante sauce

½ teaspoon chipotle chile powder

½ teaspoon ground cumin

1 (15-ounce) can black beans, drained

1 tablespoon fresh key lime juice

¼ cup finely shredded Colby-Monterey Jack cheese

1. Preheat oven to 350°F. Cut each tortilla into 8 wedges. Place tortilla wedges on an ungreased baking sheet. Toast in oven for 8 to 10 minutes, turning several times, until browned and crispy. Cool chips and store in an airtight container until needed.

2. Heat olive oil in a medium nonstick skillet over medium heat. Add onions and garlic, and sauté for 4 minutes or until tender.

3. Add diced tomatoes, picante sauce, chile powder, cumin, and black beans. Cook 5 minutes, stirring constantly, until thick. Remove skillet from heat. Partially mash black bean mixture with the back of a wooden spoon or a potato masher.

4. Stir in lime juice. Add cheese and stir until it melts. Serve warm or at room temperature with crispy tortilla chips.

CHEF NOTE: Ground chipotle chile powder, which adds a smoky-hot punch to this dip, is sometimes difficult to find. You can order it online from Penzeys Spices, www.penzeys.com. You can substitute regular chile powder for the chipotle if you like.

Bollos

1 pound dried black-eyed peas
10 cloves garlic, roughly chopped
3 small red serrano chiles or 2 bird
  peppers, seeded and minced

salt and freshly ground black pepper
canola oil for deep frying

1. **One day ahead:** Place dried black-eyed peas in a large bowl. Cover them by 2 inches with water and soak overnight.

2. Drain the peas in a colander. Place a couple of handfuls of peas between two paper towels and rub until husks fall off peas. Pick peas from husks and place them in a food processor. Repeat with remaining peas.

3. Pulse peas until ground. Remove to a separate bowl. Place garlic, chiles, and one-quarter ground peas back in food processor. Pulse until well mixed. Add another quarter of peas plus 1 teaspoon salt and ½ teaspoon pepper. Pulse until well mixed. Add remaining ground peas to food processor, a quarter at a time, pulsing until well mixed. Add 1 teaspoon salt and ½ teaspoon pepper. Pulse until mixed.

4. Transfer ground pea mixture to the bowl of an electric mixer. Beat on high speed until creamy, adding 1 to 2 tablespoons water if necessary. (Mixture can be transferred to a covered container and refrigerated for up to 1 day.)

5. Place oil in a deep fryer to manufacturer's recommended level. Preheat oil to 375°F. Form black-eyed pea mixture into small, round balls about 1½ inches in diameter. Deep-fry bollos for 3 minutes, until they are golden brown. Remove bollos and drain on paper toweling. Sprinkle liberally with salt. Serve hot.

CHEF NOTE: This method of peeling the black-eyed peas is faster than peeling them one at a time. The bollo batter should approximate the consistency of cookie dough. Bird peppers are tiny red, yellow, orange, and green hot chile peppers (heat 8–9).

The bollo (pronounced boy-ō), a Keys specialty in the early to mid-1900s, is a tiny, round, deep-fried fritter consisting mainly of finely ground black-eyed peas. Hawked as street food by vendors who cooked the fritters on site, these strange little spheres were the most popular between-meal snacks in Key West. Piping hot and laden with salt, bollos were sold by the baker's dozen and served in brown paper bags. During the Great Depression, bollos cost a penny apiece. Key Westers love to eat them with thick, sweet Cuban coffee.

Conch Ceviche in Endive Cups

Ceviche is an old-world dish that originated along the Pacific coast of Peru and Ecuador in pre-Columbian times. When the acid of the key lime juice comes in contact with the conch, the resulting chemical process turns the seafood opaque and firm, thus "cooking" it. Seafood markets in the Florida Keys most often sell whole or ground conch pre-tenderized and frozen in 1- or 2-pound packages. Gram per gram, conch contains more protein than chicken.

CHEF NOTE: If you have trouble finding the whole spices called for in this recipe, you can order online from CMC Company, www.thecmccompany.com. Gourmet Garden® has come out with a line of herb blend pastes that are becoming widely marketed today. You'll find lemongrass, hot red chile, gingerroot and more, already minced and ground, with a shelf life of several months. Look in the refrigerated section of your market's produce department. A real time saver!

2 tablespoons coriander seeds
1 tablespoon star anise pods
1 tablespoon Szechuan peppercorns
1 tablespoon minced fresh gingerroot
2 cloves garlic, minced
2 tablespoons minced lemongrass, white parts only, outer husk discarded
2 tablespoons fish sauce
¼ cup key lime juice
½ cup rice vinegar
1 tablespoon sesame oil
2 teaspoons chili garlic sauce

¾ to 1 pound tenderized conch, cut into ½-inch dice
¾ cup finely diced red onions
1 cup finely diced English cucumbers
½ cup finely diced red bell peppers
2 scallions, both white and green parts, sliced thin
¼ cup snipped fresh basil leaves
¼ cup snipped fresh mint leaves
¾ teaspoon salt
½ teaspoon cracked black pepper
2 endives, leaves separated, washed, and dried

1. **Up to 1 month ahead:** Place coriander seeds, star anise pods, and Szechuan peppercorns in a small skillet over medium heat. Cook them until they are lightly toasted, about 2 to 3 minutes. Allow spices to cool, then transfer to a spice or coffee grinder. Grind until smooth. Place in a tightly covered container and freeze until needed.

2. **One day ahead:** Place gingerroot, garlic, lemongrass, fish sauce, key lime juice, vinegar, sesame oil, and chili garlic sauce in a medium bowl. Whisk ingredients together until smooth. Set aside.

3. Place conch, red onions, cucumbers, red bell peppers, scallions, basil, mint, and 2 teaspoons of spice mix in a large bowl. Toss to mix. Add salt and pepper to taste. Pour marinade over the conch mixture and toss until all ingredients are well coated. Place in a covered container. Refrigerate overnight.

4. **To serve:** Remove ceviche from the marinade with a slotted spoon and drain in a colander. Place a heaping tablespoon of ceviche in each endive leaf and arrange on a serving platter.

Conch Fritters with Coconut-Lime-Curry Dipping Sauce

FOR THE FRITTERS:

1 cup chopped green bell peppers

½ cup chopped red bell peppers

1½ cup chopped yellow onions

12 ounces tenderized ground conch, fresh or frozen and thawed

½ teaspoon celery salt

½ teaspoon salt

1 teaspoon bottled hot sauce

2 eggs

1½ cups Bisquick

freshly ground black pepper

canola oil for deep frying

FOR THE SAUCE:

5 tablespoons fresh key lime juice

⅔ cup sweet cream of coconut, such as Coco Lopez or Coco Casa

1½ teaspoons curry powder

¼ teaspoon cayenne pepper

¼ teaspoon salt

½ cup minced scallions

1. **One day ahead:** Place bell peppers, onions, and conch in a food processor. Pulse until finely chopped. Add celery salt, salt, hot sauce, and eggs. Pulse until smooth. Add Bisquick, ½ cup at a time, pulsing until smooth and well mixed. Add black pepper to taste. Transfer to a covered container and refrigerate overnight.

2. Place key lime juice, cream of coconut, curry powder, cayenne pepper, and salt in a small bowl. Whisk to combine. Add scallions and stir with a spoon to combine. Cover and refrigerate until needed.

3. Place oil in a deep fryer to manufacturer's recommended level and preheat to 375°F. Using a small ice-cream-type scoop, drop balls of conch fritter batter into hot oil. Work in small batches; do not crowd fryer. When fritters are golden-brown on all sides, remove with tongs and drain on paper toweling.

4. Place dipping sauce in a small bowl in the middle of a serving platter. Surround with conch fritters.

Raw conch is tough as a rubber tire, so it must be tenderized before it is consumed. Early in Keys history, Conchs pounded the conch with a wooden mallet, a hammer, or the edge of a plate. Later, the mollusk was run through a household grinder. Today, most seafood markets tenderize and grind conch for the consumer. The conch does not come from Florida Keys waters anymore, however. This large sea snail joined the U.S. endangered species list in 1985. Conch is imported from the Bahamas, Belize, or the Turks and Caicos Islands.

CHEF NOTE: You can substitute fresh Persian lime juice if you don't have fresh key lime juice, but fresh juice is essential in this recipe.

Conch of the Keys

Long revered in many cultures as a symbol of peace, joy, and life, the queen conch has been adopted as the symbol of the Florida Keys as well. In fact, so important has the conch been in the islands' history, anyone born and bred in the Florida Keys is deemed a Conch, an appellation of distinction. Upon entering Key West harbor in the nineteenth century, foreign sailing vessels hoisted conch shells to their yardarms to signify their peaceful intent. And by the twentieth century, proud parents traditionally announced a new birth by posting a conch shell on a stick in front of their home.

The queen conch (*Strombus gigas*) is a large sea snail that lives near the coral reef on the ocean floor. Feeding off soft algae and bacterial debris, it is protected by a spindle-shaped shell that has a distinctive 12-inch flaring pink lip. Native to tropical waters, the conch is found from the Bahamas and the Florida Keys to Brazil. The word *conch,* pronounced konk, originates from the French word *conque*, meaning shell.

Queen conchs are strong but slow. They lead lives of isolation on the sea bottom, spread out from each other except during multiple two-week mating periods from late February through October. After mating, the female deposits banana-shaped strings of encapsulated eggs in a depression in the sand. (She can produce five to eight egg masses per season.)

A tiny hatchling emerges from each egg, drifting around in open water eating microscopic algae. If it manages to escape being eaten by a predator, the hatchling settles to the bottom and buries itself, where it remains hidden for a year, growing into a bottom-feeding snail about the size of a grain of sand.

The yearling slowly moves along the sea bottom, propelled by its single-clawed foot in search of turtle grass and other vegetation. The juvenile is still much at risk from predators, such as lobsters, crabs, and octopus, for the next three years. When sexually mature and grown to full size of 9 to 10 inches at about age four, the conch's only undersea predators are sharks, spotted eagle rays, and loggerhead turtles, which can break the mollusk's shell and eat its meaty foot.

Conch meat and shells have been important trade items for thousands of

LEFT: *Conch meat was once a major protein source in the Keys, ca. 1959.* **Credit: State Archives of Florida. RIGHT:** *Conch shell trumpet, ca. 1966.* **Credit: State Archives of Florida.**

Recipe for a Florida Keys Conch Trumpet

Long used by Caribbean natives to communicate from village to village and to initiate battles, horns or trumpets fashioned from conch shells became standard equipment on every small boat in the Florida Keys by the 1900s. They also were played at parties and celebrations. Accomplished conch blowers have been known to play complete melodies, even Beethoven's Fifth Symphony.

How to make: Purchase an imported conch shell from a local shell shop. Cut off the last three spiral rows of the shell's apex with a hacksaw (about 1 to 1¼ inches down). Chisel the center column, or *columella* to form a mouthpiece. Polish the edges with an emery cloth.

How to play: Curl your lips like you are playing a conventional trumpet and blow into the mouthpiece, allowing your lips to vibrate. (A large shell, with an opening of up to 12 inches, will create a deeper sound than a small shell, which has a higher pitch.) Learn a tune, then compete in the annual Key West Old Island Days Conch Blowing Contest in March.

---

years. When Christopher Columbus landed in the Bahamas in 1492, he noted the Arawak Indians used conch in many ways. Besides consuming the meat, they crafted hammers, chisels, and adzes—ax-like tools with thin, curving blades used to carve out log canoes—from the pearly shells. The Arawaks made currency from small pieces of shell, which they ground to a consistent size and shape. The shells also were carved into jewelry, decorative items, and trumpets.

Conchs were so plentiful in the early Keys settlement days of the 1800s, they could be harvested by the armful in shallow waters. Eaten daily, the meat was a major source of dietary protein. But, tough as rubber, conch has to be pounded with a mallet or the edge of a dinner plate. Once tenderized, its chewy, sweet flesh is reminiscent of abalone, scallops, or clams. (Young conch meat tastes better than that from old conchs. Called sambas, old conchs have thickened shells and bitter meat.) Some locals even believed raw conch was an aphrodisiac that would grant them eternal youth.

Once prolific in the shallow turtle-grass beds of Florida Keys' nearshore waters, conch was harvested to point of extinction by the 1970s. (In 1965 alone, 250,000 conchs were brought into Key West harbor.) Florida Department of Conservation banned commercial conch harvesting in 1975, but allowed a restricted number to be taken for home consumption. In 1985, however, the mollusk officially was declared endangered nationally, and all harvesting in U.S. waters became outlawed. Today, conch consumed in the Florida Keys is imported from the Bahamas, Belize, or the Turks and Caicos Islands.

Hot and Sour Chicken in Lettuce Wraps

Originating in India, lemongrass (*Cymbopogon citratus*) traditionally has been used in Thai and Vietnamese cooking, but recently has become popular in Caribbean cuisine as well. The aromatic herb, grown commercially in Florida and California, is a perennial that also can be cultivated in the home garden. Fresh lemongrass's light lemony flavor pairs well with hot chiles.

CHEF NOTE: Called *larb* in Thailand, these spicy chicken salad wraps make a great lunch or appetizer course. You can substitute ground turkey for the ground chicken if you like. The ground rice adds authentic Thai texture to this chicken dish, but you can eliminate this step. The fish sauce is very salty, so add additional salt only after you taste the dish. You can find fresh lemongrass in ethnic markets and some supermarkets.

1 tablespoon long-grain rice (optional)
1 pound ground chicken
⅓ cup chicken broth
2 tablespoons minced shallots
2 scallions, chopped
1½ tablespoons fish sauce
1 tablespoon dried lemongrass or 2 tablespoons fresh, white parts only
2 fresh red Thai chiles or 4 dried red chilies, seeded and minced

2 tablespoons snipped mint leaves, well packed
3 tablespoons fresh lime juice
salt (optional)
Boston, bib, or iceberg lettuce leaves, washed and dried
fresh mint leaves, washed and dried
1 lime, cut in thin wedges
½ English cucumber, cut in julienne slivers

1. Heat a small, nonstick skillet over medium heat. Add rice. Cook, stirring frequently, until rice is browned but not burned, about 5 minutes. Remove from heat and cool to room temperature. Grind rice in a blender or mortar and pestle and set aside.

2. Heat a 12-inch nonstick skillet over medium heat. Add chicken and broth and cook until chicken is no longer pink, about 8 minutes. Remove chicken with a slotted spoon and drain on paper toweling. Set aside to cool.

3. To the remaining broth in the pan, add the shallots, scallions, fish sauce, lemongrass, and chilies. Mix well and cook for 1 minute. Remove from heat. Stir in ground rice, mint, and lime juice. Add chicken and stir to mix well. (Add ⅛ teaspoon of salt if mixture is not salty enough.) Refrigerate for at least 1 hour or overnight to allow flavors to blend. Bring to room temperature or reheat in microwave before serving.

4. **To serve:** Place about ¼-cup chicken mixture in center of a lettuce leaf. Arrange filled lettuce leaves on a platter and garnish with fresh mint leaves, lime wedges, and cucumber slivers.

5. **To eat:** Add mint, a squeeze of lime, a sprinkling of cucumber slivers atop the chicken mixture if desired. Fold in the left and right edges of lettuce and roll into a cylinder. Eat with your fingers.

Mushroom Empanadas

2 tablespoons butter or margarine

8 ounces white button mushrooms, wiped clean and thinly sliced

12 ounces portobello mushrooms, wiped clean, fins removed, cut into ½-inch dice

1 cup minced scallions

1 tablespoon minced garlic

2 tablespoons minced fresh gingerroot

salt and freshly ground black pepper

1 (17.3-ounce) package Pillsbury Grands refrigerator biscuits

½ teaspoon fresh lemon juice

½ cup unsweetened coconut milk

1 teaspoon sugar

1 teaspoon soy sauce

½ teaspoon minced serrano chile

¼ cup finely chopped honey roasted peanuts

1. Preheat oven to 350°F. Place butter in a large, nonstick skillet over medium-high heat. When butter is melted, add mushrooms. Sauté, stirring frequently, until mushrooms release their liquid and are nearly cooked dry, about 5 minutes. Add scallions, garlic, gingerroot, and salt and pepper to taste. Continue cooking for 2 minutes more, stirring frequently. Remove skillet from heat and allow mushrooms to cool.

2. Cut each of 8 biscuits in half horizontally so that you have 16 rounds. Working 1 round at a time, pat or roll the dough into a 4-inch circle. Place 1½ measuring tablespoons mushroom mixture in the center of each round. Fold dough over filling to form a half-moon shape. With the tines of a fork, press the edges together to seal. Turn empanada over and press edges on other side with fork to seal. Place empanada on an ungreased baking sheet. When you have completed all 16 empanadas, bake for 12 to 15 minutes or until golden brown.

3. Meanwhile, in a small bowl place lemon juice, coconut milk, sugar, soy sauce, minced chile, and peanuts. Stir to mix.

4. **To serve:** Place empanadas on a serving platter. Drizzle each with a tablespoonful of sauce. Serve extra sauce on the side.

Spanish explorers and missionaries from the Galicia region brought the crescent-shaped turnovers known as *empanadas* to Cuba and Latin America. Cuban immigrants introduced the savory snacks to the Florida Keys. The *empanada*, which means "baked in pastry," traditionally contains meat, fish, sausage, or other savory ingredients, but the Cubanized versions add peppers, onions, and garlic as well.

CHEF NOTE: Traditional empanada pastry is made from scratch, but it is available frozen from South Florida supermarkets and some Latin markets elsewhere. But today's refrigerator dough makes a good-tasting, easy-to-prepare, flakier substitute. For miniature, bite-size turnovers, called *empanaditas*, use regular size refrigerator biscuits instead of the Grands. Place bowl of sauce in the middle of the platter of *empanaditas*. Dip each bite-size snack in sauce before devouring.

Pickled Pinks with Parmesan Pita Crisps

Shrimp found in the Gulf of Mexico and South Atlantic waters are categorized by color—brown, gray, pink, white—depending upon their species, diet, home waters, and environment. Shrimp inhabiting Florida waters are pink shrimp or *Penaeus duorarum*. Though named pink shrimp, the shrimp actually change colors to blend in with their environ-ment: Those found along the Atlantic coast are brown in color and in the northern Gulf coast they are a lemon yellow. Only in the Florida Keys are pink shrimp actually pink, reflecting their sandy bottom lives in coral reef waters.

FOR PITA CRISPS:

2 tablespoons grated Parmesan cheese

2 teaspoons dried Italian seasoning

1 teaspoon paprika

¼ teaspoon salt

4 tablespoons (½ stick) butter, melted

4 (6-inch) whole-wheat pita bread rounds, split open (8 in total)

FOR SHRIMP:

4 pounds medium Key West pink shrimp, unpeeled (21 to 25 count)

½ cup chopped celery, including some top leaves

¼ cup mixed pickling spices

3 teaspoons seasoned salt

1 large sweet onion, like Vidalia, thinly sliced

6 bay leaves

1 cup canola oil

¼ cup olive oil

¾ cup white wine vinegar

3 tablespoons capers with juice

2½ teaspoons celery seed

1 teaspoon paprika

¼ teaspoon dry mustard

⅛ teaspoon cayenne pepper

fresh parsley sprigs

1. **One day ahead:** Preheat oven to 350°F. Combine Parmesan cheese, Italian seasoning, paprika, and salt in a small bowl and mix well. Brush melted butter evenly over each pita round, then sprinkle with cheese mixture.

2. Cut each pita round into 8 wedges. Place on a nonstick baking sheet and bake for 8 minutes or until crisp. Allow crisps to cool thoroughly. Store in an airtight container and refrigerate until needed. Yields 64 crisps.

3. Place shrimp, celery, pickling spices, and salt in a large saucepan and cover with hot water. Cover and simmer just until the shrimp turn pink, 3 to 5 minutes. Drain and dis-card cooking liquid and seasonings. Run shrimp under cold water, then peel and devein them.

4. In a large glass or plastic bowl with an airtight lid, layer the shrimp with the onion slices. Place bay leaves on top. In a small bowl, combine oils, vinegar, capers, celery seed, paprika, mustard, and cayenne pepper and pour mixture over shrimp and onions. Secure the cover tightly and place in refrigerator for 24 hours, turning at least twice during the marinating time.

5. **To serve:** Remove shrimp and onions from marinade with a slotted spoon and drain in a colander. Arrange shrimp and onions on a serving platter and garnish with fresh parsley. Serve with Parmesan Pita Crisps.

CHEF NOTE: You can use any species of shrimp in this recipe. Key West Pinks are generally not marketed outside of Florida.

Poke Tuna Tartare

Poke (*poke-ee*) had its origins in Hawaii, where marinated raw yellowfin tuna is commonly served as a snack, appetizer, or luncheon salad. Reinterpreted in the Florida Keys, this exquisitely flavored dish is slightly "cooked" in the lime juice marinade. Looking and tasting more like beef than fish, the highest grade of filleted yellowfin—sashimi grade number one—is most coveted as a basic sushi ingredient.

CHEF NOTE: To make prepared wasabi, place 1 tablespoon wasabi powder in a small bowl. Add just enough water (about 1 tablespoon) to make a loose paste. To serve tartare as a dip, drain tuna as directed, then return it to bowl. Add vinaigrette, sesame seeds, scallions, and cilantro leaves and mix together with a spoon. Transfer tartare to a glass bowl and serve with crispy wonton chips.

¼ cup rice wine vinegar
¼ cup soy sauce, divided
2 tablespoons honey
2 tablespoons minced pickled ginger
¼ cup sesame oil, divided
12 ounces sashimi grade yellowfin tuna
¼ cup minced yellow bell peppers
¼ cup minced red bell peppers
1 jalapeno pepper, stemmed, seeded, and minced
¼ cup minced sweet onions, like Vidalia

¼ cup fresh lime juice
1 tablespoon prepared wasabi
kosher or sea salt
2 tablespoons black sesame seeds, toasted
2 tablespoons white sesame seeds, toasted
¼ cup scallions, green part only, cut on severe angle to make diamonds
¼ cup whole cilantro leaves

1. **Early in the day:** Place rice wine vinegar, 2 tablespoons soy sauce, honey, pickled ginger, and 2 tablespoons sesame oil in a small bowl. Whisk to combine. Cover vinaigrette with plastic wrap and refrigerate until needed.

2. With a sharp knife, cut tuna into ⅛-inch-thick slices. Cut each slice into ⅛-inch-wide strips. Then cut each strip into ⅛-inch dice. Transfer to a medium bowl. Add bell peppers, jalapenos, and onions. Toss with a spoon to mix. Add lime juice, 2 tablespoons soy sauce, wasabi, and 2 tablespoons sesame oil. Toss to mix well. Season with kosher salt to taste. Cover with plastic wrap and refrigerate. Chill four 6-inch plates in refrigerator.

3. **To serve:** Drain tuna mixture in a fine sieve, reserving vinaigrette. Line 4 small ramekins or molds with plastic wrap. Divide tuna mixture among the ramekins, pressing gently to pack into place. Invert each ramekin onto a chilled plate. Gently pull on the plastic wrap to unmold. Remove plastic wrap. Mix the black and white sesame seeds in a small bowl. Sprinkle one-quarter of the seeds atop each tartare mold. Stir vinaigrette, then spoon it around the tartare. Sprinkle scallion greens and cilantro atop the pool of vinaigrette. Serve with crispy wontons, rustic bread slices, or shrimp-flavored chips.

Savory Stuffed Breads

3 eggs

2 tablespoons oregano

2 tablespoons garlic powder

½ cup plus 1 tablespoon grated Parmesan cheese

2 loaves frozen bread dough, thawed in refrigerator overnight

6 ounces sliced pepperoni

¼ pound proscuitto, thinly sliced

¼ cup julienne-cut sun-dried tomatoes

2 (16-ounce) packages shredded mozzarella cheese

1. Preheat oven to 325°F. Place eggs, oregano, garlic powder, and Parmesan cheese in a small bowl. Beat with a wire whisk. Set aside.

2. Working one thawed loaf at a time with a rolling pin, roll dough into a rectangle approximately 12 x 9 inches. (Keep bread dough refrigerated until ready to roll; roll loaves one at a time.)

3. With a spoon, liberally coat the top of each dough rectangle with a little more than one-third the egg mixture. Cover one dough rectangle with a tight layer of pepperoni. Cover the other dough rectangle tightly with prosciutto slices. Cover prosciutto with an even sprinkling of sun-dried tomatoes. Divide mozzarella and sprinkle evenly over each rectangle of dough.

4. Coat your hands with vegetable cooking spray. Working from the long end, roll dough lengthwise, tucking in ends and pressing in the lateral seam. Baste exterior of both loaves with remaining egg mixture. Place both loaves on a large baking sheet, allowing adequate room for bread to expand. (You can prepare stuffed bread several hours ahead and keep in refrigerator until ready to bake. If left at room temperature before baking, dough will rise.)

5. Bake at 325°F for 30 to 40 minutes or until golden brown. Allow bread to rest for 10 minutes before slicing. With a serrated bread knife, cut loaves into 2-inch-wide slices.

Prosciutto is an air-cured ham most famously from the Italian regions of Parma, Tuscany, Modena, and San Daniele, although it is now also processed in North America. Lacking refrigeration, Keys pioneers sun-dried pork jerky and tomatoes, and could only make fresh bread when an occasional cargo ship brought flour and yeast to market.

CHEF NOTE: Experiment with other ingredient combos for these savory breads, such as spicy Italian sausage and fresh mushrooms, or a potpourri of sautéed fresh veggies. Be sure you drain ingredients well and blot out extra moisture with paper toweling before encasing in the bread dough.

Sesame Ginger Mussels

Mussels are not indigenous to the Florida Keys, but then, neither are a majority of today's residents—the "strangers" who have come from far and wide to enjoy the islands' tropical bounty. Mussels are popular appetizers in many of the upscale Keys restaurants, such as Morada Bay in Islamorada, and local fish markets will order the mollusks upon special request. Some markets, like Islamorada Fish Company, regularly offer frozen New Zealand mussels.

24 mussels, debearded and scrubbed
½ cup dry white wine
3 teaspoons chopped fresh gingerroot, divided
1 clove garlic, minced
½ cup soy sauce
½ cup peanut oil
5 drops sesame oil

1 teaspoon rice wine vinegar
pinch of sugar
1 teaspoon Dijon mustard
2 tablespoons chopped fresh cilantro
2 tablespoons chopped fresh parsley
1 red onion, finely diced
2 ounces pickled ginger

1. **Two hours ahead:** In a 4-quart saucepan over medium-high heat, place mussels, wine, 1 teaspoon chopped fresh gingerroot, and garlic. Cover and cook, shaking pan every few minutes, until all the mussels have opened, about 6 to 8 minutes. Cook the mussels only long enough to open the shells (overcooking will make the mussels tough). Remove pan from heat and allow mussels and liquid to cool.

2. Meanwhile, in a small glass or stainless steel bowl, place soy sauce, oils, vinegar, sugar, mustard, 2 teaspoons chopped fresh gingerroot, cilantro, parsley, and onions. Whisk until well blended. Set aside until needed.

3. Discard any mussels that have not opened. Remove mussels from their shells. Break the 2 sides of each shell apart and reserve 24 of the best looking shells. Place mussels in the marinade and stir to coat thoroughly. Cover with plastic wrap and allow mussels to marinate at room temperature for one hour.

4. **To serve:** Place 1 mussel in each shell and top with a little of the marinade and onion. Top each mussel with a slice of pickled ginger.

CHEF NOTE: The former owners of the Pilgrim's Inn in Deer Isle, Maine, shared this fantastic recipe with me many years ago when I visited during a summer escape from the Keys hurricane season. If you can't get mussels, you can substitute littleneck clams. Pickled ginger can be found in the Asian foods section of most supermarkets.

Sour Dough Jack Bread

1 unsliced round loaf sour dough bread
   (about 1 pound)
1 pound sliced Monterey Jack cheese

8 tablespoons (1 stick) butter, melted
½ cup chopped scallions
2 tablespoons poppy seeds

1. Preheat oven to 350°F. With a sharp bread knife, cut bread in a gridlike pattern, taking care not to cut through the bottom crust. Insert cheese slices between each deep cut (about 2 dozen).

2. Place melted butter, scallions, and poppy seeds in a small bowl. Stir to mix well. Make a blanket of aluminum foil large enough to totally encompass the bread. Place bread in the center of the foil. Drizzle butter mixture over bread and cheese.

3. Wrap foil tightly around bread and place it on a baking sheet. Bake for 15 minutes. Open foil and bake 10 minutes more, until cheese is melted.

4. **To serve:** Place unwrapped bread in a napkin-lined bread basket. Guests serve themselves by ripping pieces of cheese bread from the loaf.

CHEF NOTE: Substitute a flavored artisan bread, such as you'll find at Cole's Peace Bakery, 1111 Eaton Street, Key West, next to the Restaurant Store. Website: www.colespeace.com.

Food historians maintain that sourdough is one of the oldest forms of leavened bread. It is believed that Christopher Columbus and later European immigrants brought the sour dough starter—a fermented mix of grains and water—with them to the New World, and thus to the Florida Keys.

Yellowfin Sushi Summer Rolls

Rice papers are brittle, translucent, paper-thin sheets commonly used in Vietnamese cuisine. The papers—sold as 6-inch-rounds or as triangles each one-quarter of a round—are created from a mixture of rice flour, salt, and water that is dried in the sun on bamboo mats (that is why the papers have a faint bamboo-like imprint). Rice papers can be found in the supermarket's Asian food section or purchased over the Internet from such companies as The CMC Company, www.thecmccompany.com. Rice papers have joined crepes and tortillas as favored wraps used by Keys restaurant chefs.

FOR THE DIPPING SAUCE:

1 tablespoon sugar

1 Thai red chile or serrano chile, stemmed, seeded, and minced

2 teaspoons peeled and minced gingerroot

2 tablespoons fresh lime juice

2 tablespoons fish sauce

FOR THE SUMMER ROLLS:

12 ounces yellowfin tuna

1 cup rice stick noodles or rice vermicelli

16 round rice papers

2 cups grated carrots

4 scallions (white part with a little green), cut into slivers the long way

3 inches English cucumber, cut into thin julienne strips

1 avocado, seeded, peeled, and cut into thin strips

1/2 cup snipped fresh mint leaves

1/2 cup snipped fresh cilantro

1. **For the dipping sauce:** Combine sugar, chiles, gingerroot, lime juice, and fish sauce in a small bowl. Stir to combine ingredients. Set aside.

2. **For the summer rolls:** Place a small, nonstick skillet over high heat. Heat dry skillet until very hot. Sear tuna in skillet, 1/2 minute per side. Remove tuna from skillet and slice it into 8 pieces. Set aside.

3. Soak rice noodles in a medium-size bowl of hot tap water for 10 to 15 minutes or until soft. Drain noodles thoroughly in a colander. Set aside.

4. Working one wrap at a time, briefly immerse 2 rice papers in a shallow bowl of warm water, about 10 seconds. Remove rice papers from water and place one on top of the other on clean kitchen towel. (Don't leave papers in the water too long or they will tear. The papers may seem a bit stiff when you remove them from the water, but they will become more pliable as you work with them.) In the third of a round nearest to

you, place a heaping teaspoon of grated carrots, then 3 or 4 scallion slivers, 4 or 5 cucumber strips, a slice of avocado, and a piece of seared tuna. Top with a generous sprinkling of mint and cilantro leaves. Then place a small mound of rice noodles on top.

5. Working with the two papers as one, fold in the left and right side of the round and wrap the lower end of the rice paper tightly over the filling. Tightly roll the rice paper over the filling forming a cigar-shape (be care not to tear the rice paper). Place each wrap on a platter and cover with a damp kitchen towel until you are finished rolling all the wraps. The summer rolls are best served immediately but can be refrigerated, covered tightly with cling wrap, for up to 2 hours before serving.

6. **To serve:** Cut each roll in half on the diagonal and serve with dipping sauce.

CHEF NOTE: Rice stick noodles in various widths (also called dried rice sticks) are sold in looped skeins of brittle semi-transparent noodles in 8-ounce and 1-pound packages. You'll need only an 8-ounce package of thin or medium rice sticks for this recipe.

Spinach, parsley, basil, and garlic often carpeted a Keys dooryard garden. If families didn't have enough room to grow greens and herbs, they planted tin cans with seeds and grew the plants on their porch railings. Since water was scarce, it wasn't unusual for plants to be irrigated with leftover wash water.

Roquefort-Parmesan-Herb Terrine

8 ounces cream cheese, at room temperature

4 ounces Roquefort cheese, at room temperature

1 cup loosely packed fresh spinach leaves, rinsed and spun dry

¾ cup loosely packed fresh Italian flat-leafed parsley, rinsed and spun dry

¼ cup loosely packed fresh basil leaves, rinsed and spun dry

1 teaspoon minced garlic

¼ cup olive oil

¼ cup finely chopped walnuts, dry toasted

1 cup freshly grated Parmesan cheese

¼ cup slivered sun-dried tomatoes

1. Place cream cheese and Roquefort cheese in a small bowl. Beat with an electric mixer until smooth. Set aside until needed.

2. Place spinach, parsley, basil, and garlic in a food processor. Pulse until coarsely chopped. With motor running, slowly add olive oil, processing until mixture is smooth. Add walnuts and Parmesan cheese and pulse until well mixed.

3. Line a loaf pan with plastic wrap, allowing excess wrap to hang over sides of the pan. Spread one-third cheese mixture across bottom of pan. Then spread half the herb mixture atop cheese layer. Sprinkle one-half sun-dried tomato slivers over herb mixture and press into place. Repeat layers—cheese, herb, tomato—then spread remaining one-third cheese mixture to form final layer. Cover tightly with excess plastic wrap and refrigerate overnight.

5. **To serve:** Uncover plastic wrap from top of loaf pan. Invert on serving platter. Remove plastic wrap covering terrine. Allow terrine to come to room temperature before serving. Serve with crackers.

CHEF NOTE: For a fancier presentation, layer terrine in a decorative mold. This red, white, and green appetizer is great for an Italian-themed dinner party or a Christmas buffet.

Wild Salmon Mousse

 **SERVES A CROWD**

2 pounds fresh wild salmon fillets

1 cup cream sherry

canola or olive oil

1 tablespoon unflavored gelatin

2 tablespoons water

4 ounces cream cheese, softened

1 egg white

1 tablespoon lemon juice

salt and freshly ground black pepper

1 large English cucumber plus ⅓ cup diced, seeded English cucumber

¼ cup finely chopped scallions

2-3 dashes hot sauce, to taste

¾ cup heavy cream

1 lemon, halved and sliced

1. **One day ahead:** Place salmon fillets and sherry in a large skillet over medium-low heat. Cover and poach for 15 minutes or until fish is cooked through and flakes when tested with a fork. Remove salmon from skillet, cover and let it cool. When cool, flake salmon into bite-size pieces. Place salmon in a large mixing bowl and set aside.

2. With a small brush or a piece of paper toweling, oil a large fish mold. Place gelatin and water in a small bowl and stir until it is dissolved. Set aside.

3. Add cream cheese to salmon. Beat with an electric mixer for 1 minute or until well combined. Add egg white, lemon juice, and salt and pepper to taste. Mix on low speed to thoroughly combine ingredients. With a large wooden spoon or spatula, fold in gelatin, ½ cup diced cucumber, and scallions. Add hot sauce and fold to mix well.

4. Whip cream in a small bowl with an electric mixer until thick and fold it into salmon mixture. Pour mixture into oiled mold and refrigerate overnight.

5. **At least 1 hour before serving:** Cut cucumber into very thin slices. (Slices should be thin but not so thin that they are difficult to handle.) Place cucumber slices in a bowl. Pour 1 cup boiling water over cucumber, blanching cucumber for 1 minute, then drain and cool. Unmold salmon mousse onto a large platter. Place cucumber slices in overlapping rows on salmon mousse, so that they resemble fish scales. Garnish with lemon slices and serve with crackers.

Wild Pacific salmon, according to a 2004 study reported in *Science Journal*, contains significantly fewer PCBs (dangerous, potentially cancer-causing chemicals) than do farm-raised salmon. Farm-raised salmon, on the other hand, feed on a concentrated fishmeal made from fish that may have consumed ocean pollutants. The U.S. Food and Drug Administration disputes the study's recommendation to eat farm-raised salmon only once a month, however, maintaining the pollutant levels in farm-raised salmon are too low for serious concern.

CHEF NOTE: Salmon is widely available from most fishmongers, even in the Keys. You can substitute 2 (14-ounce) cans red salmon for the wild salmon, but if you can find and afford fresh wild salmon, it really is superior.

Soups, Bisques, and Chowders 2

The Conchs who immigrated to the Florida Keys—Bahamians and Cubans—brought with them a culinary heritage rich in soups. The Bahamians' ancestors were British pilgrims who settled in the Bahamas in the 1600s or British loyalists who fled their U.S. plantations with their slaves in the 1700s. Incorporating the unique seasonings brought to the Bahamas by waves of European conquerors and colonizers and African slaves, the Bahamians developed a spicy yet decidedly English cuisine. The Cubans developed a less fiery cuisine than their Spanish conquerors, preferring mild green chile peppers to the red hot peppers of other Spanish colonies. Since sugarcane was Cuba's largest crop for centuries, dishes were often sweet as well as spicy.

The collision of cultures in Key West engendered a distinctive breed of soups. A true Conch soup was a heavy one-pot meal, thick with root vegetables and potatoes, and loaded with seafood, chicken, or the occasional cut of beef, often seasoned with little more than salt and pepper. The soups were served hot, testifying to the old adage that in a warm climate, food that is hot in temperature and seasoning is actually cooling, since it stimulates perspiration.

With ensuing generations, "strangers"—a Conch term for anyone not born in the Keys—introduced lighter, first-course-style luncheon soups that utilized fruits and vegetables from their dooryard gardens. But one tradition has always accompanied a good bowl of soup in the Florida Keys: crisp, freshly baked Cuban bread.

LEFT: *The Wanderer guided barges loaded with cypress water tanks to the Keys, ca. 1910.*
Credit: State Archives of Florida.

Bahamian Conch Chowder

British pilgrims arrived in the Bahamas in the 1600s, finding a host of indigenous ingredients to spice up their traditional English cuisine.

True Bahamian soups were one-pot meals, and conch chowder is no exception. The Bahamians held the conch in mystical regard, believing its consumption enhanced male potency. Traditionally seasoning the soup with tomatoes, chile peppers, thyme, and other spices, the Bahamians brought their culinary creation with them when they immigrated to the Florida Keys. Conch chowder is ubiquitous in the Keys today, with endless variations such as the addition of cubed potatoes or the substitution of heavy cream for the classic tomato base.

1 teaspoon olive oil
2½ cups chopped sweet onions, like Vidalia
1 large bell pepper, chopped (about 1 cup)
1 cup lean ham, cut into small dice
2 large cloves garlic, minced
2 (14.5-ounce) cans chopped tomatoes
1 (6-ounce) can tomato paste
½ cup tomato juice
1 cup hot water
1 bay leaf

1 tablespoon barbecue sauce
1 teaspoon marjoram
½ teaspoon sage
¼ teaspoon thyme
1 teaspoon parsley
½ teaspoon oregano
¾ teaspoon salt
½ teaspoon cracked black pepper
¼ teaspoon cayenne pepper
1 pound tenderized ground conch
Busha Browne's Spicy & Hot Pepper Sherry (optional)

1. Place olive oil, onions, bell peppers, ham, and garlic in a large soup pot over medium-high heat. Sauté, stirring occasionally, for 5 minutes or until onion is translucent. Add tomatoes, tomato paste, tomato juice, hot water, bay leaf, barbecue sauce, marjoram, sage, thyme, parsley, oregano, salt, cracked and cayenne peppers. Stir to combine ingredients and bring mixture to a boil.

2. Add conch to the pot. Reduce heat to low and simmer, covered, for 5 to 6 hours or until conch is tender. Lace each individual serving of soup with hot pepper sherry to taste.

CHEF NOTE: Busha Browne's Spicy & Hot Pepper Sherry adds an additional kick to the chowder. But, since the chowder is already spicy, you may want to opt for just a splash of sherry instead.

Caldo Gallego (Spanish Bean Soup)

 **SERVES 8 TO 10**

1 pound dried northern beans
1 pound smoked ham hocks
1 pound beef shank bone
4 small, uncooked chorizo sausage links (about ½ pound)
1 medium sweet onion, like Vidalia, chopped

2 large cloves garlic, minced
3 medium potatoes (about 1¼ pounds), peeled and cut into small dice
¼ teaspoon salt
freshly ground black pepper

1. **One day ahead:** Sort through beans, discarding broken ones. Rinse and drain beans. Place beans and 2 quarts water in a large soup pot. Cover and allow beans to soak overnight.

2. Add ham hocks and shank bone to beans and soaking water. Add enough water to cover by an inch (about 2 cups). Place soup pot over high heat and bring to a boil. Skim off foam. Reduce heat to low and simmer for about 4 hours, until beans are plumped and tender.

3. Remove ham hocks and beef bone from soup pot. With a fork, separate any lean, cooked meat from the bones. Shred meat and add to the soup pot.

4. Remove chorizo sausage from casings. In a large nonstick skillet over medium-high heat, crumble sausage and cook, stirring frequently, for 5 minutes. Add onions and garlic and cook 5 minutes more, stirring frequently.

5. Increase heat under soup pot to medium-high. Add sausage mixture, diced potatoes, and salt to pot. Bring to a boil, then reduce to medium-low and cook, stirring frequently, until potatoes are tender, about 15 minutes. Adjust salt and pepper to taste.

CHEF NOTE: Since I used smoked ham hocks, I opted for the raw Mexican chorizo in this recipe. If you'd like to make this soup with classic Spanish smoked chorizo, substitute an uncooked, unsmoked ham hock instead. Cut the smoked chorizo into thin slices and add them to the soup at the same time you add the potatoes. You'll need 2 teaspoons olive oil in which to sauté the onions and garlic if you use this method.

This hearty soup made its way to Cuba with Spanish colonists centuries ago and traveled on to the Keys when many Cubans emigrated in the 1800s. The Conchs and Cubans created many variations over the years—such as using dried garbanzos/chickpeas—but chorizo sausage has always been a constant ingredient. Chorizo is a pork sausage, highly seasoned with chili powder, garlic, and other spices. Two distinct types of chorizo are available: smoked and soft cured. Spanish chorizo is a smoked sausage and requires no cooking. Soft-cured chorizo, also known as Mexican chorizo, is raw. Most often sold as links, it comes in a casing that must be removed before cooking.

Green Turtle Steam

In the Florida Keys of the 1800s, nothing beat a good, old-fashioned green turtle steam. What's a green turtle steam? Neither an emerald-colored facial nor a slow sauna, a steam is a vintage Conch culinary staple, commonly known as stew in the rest of the country. The well-to-do might steam a chicken or an occasional rare cut of beef, but most folks put a turtle in their pot, so plentiful were these creatures in Keys waters in those days.

Turtle season was April, May, and June, when the green turtles crawled up on the beach to lay their eggs. They were most abundant during the full, or turtle, moon in June, when it's been said that a man could walk for quite a distance stepping only on turtle shells. After the turtles deposited their eggs and headed back to the water, opportunists would turn the creatures over onto their backs, pilfering their eggs, taking them home, and tying the turtles up in the water like cows.

Commercial turtle hunters loaded their catch into skiffs, keeping the turtles on their backs so they couldn't move (hence the phrase "turn turtle," meaning flip upside down), then transferred them to 80-foot vessels and headed for the docks in Key West. The men carved their initials in each turtle's soft undershell to ensure they got proper credit for their bounty. The men received between $30 and $50 per turtle. An adult female green turtle weighed about 300 pounds and averaged about 3 feet in length.

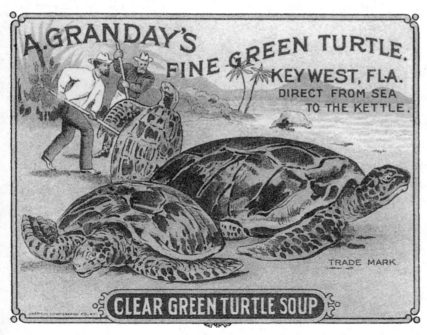

A. GRANDAY'S FINE GREEN TURTLE.
KEY WEST, FLA.
DIRECT FROM SEA TO THE KETTLE.

TRADE MARK.

CLEAR GREEN TURTLE SOUP

LEFT: *Green Turtle Soup Label.* **Credit: State Archives of Florida.**

Green turtles were so named because of the layers of green fat that lie just under their upper and lower shells. (The shells themselves are black, gray, olive, or brown with streaks or spots.) Once at the docks, the men would push the turtles, still on their backs, down a ramp to the kraal, an Afrikaans word meaning "holding pen." The turtles lived in these in-water corrals for up to two weeks before being hauled, with flippers tied together, to the slaughterhouse. Employees butchered several turtles each afternoon about 3:30 P.M.—skins went to leather, meat to steaks and soups, and shells to jewelry.

Armand Granday, a Frenchman who was once chef to a New York millionaire financier, is credited with starting the wildly successful turtle canning business in the Keys, when in 1849 he established the Key West Turtle Cannery along with a turtle kraal next to the slaughterhouse. Granday's belief—the faster the turtle was cooked after leaving its natural habitat the better the flavor of the meat—made him a fortune. The cannery operated under a succession of owners until the 1970s, producing green turtle soup and turtle steak—thought to taste like young veal. These delicacies were much in demand in Europe and the mainland. The Key West Turtle Cannery supplied 80 percent of all turtle products in the United States for years. (Today, Turtle Kraals is a popular Key West seafood grill. Adjacent to the eatery, on the site of the original cannery, is the Turtle Kraals Museum. The exhibits and photographic displays in this museum depict the history of the turtling industry in Key West and the plight of all of Florida's sea turtles.)

In 1948, Sid and Roxie Siderius opened Sid & Roxie's Cannery up the Keys in Islamorada, where they canned green turtle soup for decades. Next door they opened a roadside inn called Green Turtle Inn, serving fresh turtle and seafood specialties and providing nightly lodging. The cannery trucked several 200- to 500-pound live turtles from Key West every week, using about 6,000 pounds of meat per month. The soup was brewed in 60-gallon vats and then processed in 1-pound cans and shipped worldwide. The Green Turtle Inn operated as a popular seafood restaurant under a variety of owners until 2005, at which time it finally closed its doors.

Green turtles flourished in the waters between Key West and the Dry Tortugas, as well as in Caribbean and South Florida waters, from around 1500 throughout the 1800s. By 1878 turtle hunters were shipping 15,000 green turtles from the Caribbean waters—deemed the best turtling area of the world—to

...
Since 1993, the only turtle soup now legal in the United States is mock turtle soup.
...

Europe per year. But nearly a century later, in the 1970s, the green turtle population was so decimated that the U.S. federal government took action.

The Endangered Species Act of 1973 prohibits the taking of green turtles in U.S. waters. A sighting of a green turtle in the wild here now is a rare occurrence.

And what has become of green turtle soup? Since 1993, the only turtle soup now legal in the United States is mock turtle soup.

Crab Claw Bisque

Crabmeat is graded according to which part of the crab the meat comes from and by the size of the pieces. Jumbo lump, comprised of large pieces of white body meat, is most expensive, followed by lump (medium pieces of body meat) and flake (small pieces). Deluxe is a combination of flake and lump. Claw meat, which is darker, is the least expensive. In days gone by, Keys cooks would use indigenous stone crab in this bisque. But today stone crabs are so expensive that they are rarely used in soup preparations.

2 tablespoons butter or margarine
1 cup seeded, chopped tomatoes
¾ cup snipped fresh basil, divided
2 teaspoons minced garlic
1 pound fresh crab claw meat
½ cup flour
2 cups Clamato juice
1½ cups heavy cream
⅓ cup ketchup

⅓ cup bottled clam juice
3 teaspoons Old Bay seasoning
½ teaspoon hot pepper sauce
½ teaspoon salt
1 teaspoon sugar
1 cup water
3 tablespoons fresh lemon juice
Busha Browne's Spicy & Hot Pepper
   Sherry (optional)

1. Melt butter in a large pot over medium heat. Add tomatoes, ½-cup basil, garlic, and crabmeat. Sauté 2 minutes. Sprinkle in flour, mixing well. Whisk in Clamato juice, heavy cream, ketchup, clam juice, Old Bay seasoning, hot pepper sauce, salt, and sugar. Cook, stirring constantly, for 2 minutes. Reduce heat to low and simmer for 10 minutes.

2. Remove from heat and puree soup in batches in blender until smooth. Return soup to pot. Stir in water and lemon juice and simmer for 1 minute, until heated through. (Soup can be made the day ahead and chilled in refrigerator until serving. Place in a pot and heat to a simmer before serving.)

3. **To serve:** Divide soup among soup bowls and sprinkle with remaining ¼-cup basil. Top bisque with a couple of drops of hot pepper sherry if desired.

CHEF NOTE: Fresh crabmeat perishes quickly. Be sure raw crabs are alive before you cook them. Never cook a dead crab. Both fresh-cooked crabmeat and commercially packed pasteurized crabmeat should be refrigerated in the coldest part of the refrigerator, just above 32°F. At this temperature fresh-cooked will last up to 10 days, pasteurized (which is treated for longer shelf life) for up to 6 months.

Ginger-Anise Butternut Squash Soup

2 tablespoons butter

⅔ cup minced shallots

1 large clove garlic, minced

3 whole star anise

1 tablespoon finely grated gingerroot

1 butternut squash (about 1¾ pounds), peeled, seeded, and cut into 1-inch pieces

4 cups chicken broth

2 cups water

¼ teaspoon salt

1. Melt butter in a large soup pot over medium heat. Add shallots, garlic, star anise, and gingerroot and cook, stirring occasionally, until shallot is softened, about 3 minutes.

2. Add squash, broth, water, and salt. Simmer, uncovered, until squash is tender, about 20 minutes.

3. Puree soup in small batches in a blender until very smooth, about 1 minute per batch. Place pureed batches in a large bowl. Blend soup in small batches a second time, returning soup to the pot. Keep soup warm over low heat until serving. (Soup can be refrigerated in a covered container up to one day. Gently reheat on low before serving.)

CHEF NOTE: This bell-shaped winter squash has a thin skin, which easily can be removed with a vegetable peeler. The squash's gold-orange flesh is sweet and nutty, the perfect foil for the ginger and anise in this recipe. You can substitute Cuban calabaza squash in this recipe (see Index, Calabaza Mash).

Grown in the Far-East countries of China, Indonesia, and Japan, star anise is the unusual fruit of a small Asian evergreen tree in the magnolia family. Star-shaped, the fruit is picked before it ripens, then dried. Star anise can be used whole or ground to a reddish-brown powder. This licorice-flavored spice, stronger and more pungent than aniseed, is a popular ingredient in Conchfusion recipes.

Hot Black Bean Chili

Believed to have originated in Mexico and Central America more than 7,000 years ago, black beans made their way to the Florida Keys several centuries ago with Cuban immigrants. Also known as turtle beans because of their smooth, black, shell-like appearance, black beans taste mildly sweet, exude an earthy flavor reminiscent of mushrooms, and hold their shape when cooked.

2 tablespoons olive oil

¼ cup minced garlic

2½ cups chopped yellow onions, divided

2½ pounds lean ground beef

¼ cup chili powder

2 tablespoons paprika

1 tablespoon chopped, seeded jalapeno pepper

1½ teaspoons ground cumin

¾ teaspoon ground coriander

1 cup merlot or cabernet sauvignon

1 (14-ounce) can chicken broth

1 (14-ounce) can beef broth

1 (14.5-ounce) can garlic-and-olive-oil petite-cut tomatoes, drained

3 tablespoons Asian hot chili sauce

¼ cup tomato paste

2 (15-ounce) cans black beans, drained

1 cup sour cream

1. Place olive oil in a large pot over medium heat. When hot, add garlic and 2 cups chopped onions. Sauté until tender, about 5 minutes. Add ground beef and sauté until cooked through, about 5 minutes. Add chili powder, paprika, jalapeno, cumin, and coriander. Stir to mix well with beef and onions.

2. Add wine and simmer until most of liquid has evaporated, about 5 minutes. Add broths, chopped tomatoes, chili sauce, and tomato paste. Stir to mix well. Bring mixture to a boil, stirring frequently. Reduce heat to medium-low and simmer uncovered for 45 minutes, until liquid thickens slightly. (At this point chili can be cooled and refrigerated in a covered container for up to 2 days.)

3. Add black beans and cook on medium-low heat until heated through, about 15 minutes. (If reheating base soup, bring soup to a simmer before adding beans.) Ladle soup into shallow soup bowls and top each serving with a dollop of sour cream and a sprinkling of chopped onions.

CHEF NOTE: Canned black beans work fine in this recipe, but if you want to make your black beans "from scratch" using dried beans, use the Cuban Black Beans recipe (see Index). Drain liquid from beans and substitute 3 cups of these beans for the 2 cans black beans called for in the chili recipe.

Indonesian-style Pumpkin-Mango Soup

 SERVES 6

32 ounces fat-free chicken broth

1 (15-ounce) can pumpkin puree

1 (12-ounce) can mango nectar

¼ cup chunky peanut butter

2 tablespoons rice vinegar

2 tablespoons minced scallions

1 teaspoon peeled, grated fresh gingerroot

½ teaspoon grated orange peel

¼ teaspoon crushed red pepper

1 clove garlic, crushed

chopped fresh cilantro (optional)

1. Place chicken broth, pumpkin, and mango nectar in a large pot over medium-high heat. Stir to combine and bring mixture to a boil. Reduce heat to low, cover, and simmer for 10 minutes.

2. Combine 1 cup pumpkin mixture with peanut butter in a blender or food processor and process until smooth. Return mixture to pot. Stir in vinegar, scallions, gingerroot, grated orange peel, crushed red pepper, and garlic. Simmer over low heat for 10 minutes, stirring frequently. (If you want to make soup ahead and refrigerate in a covered container overnight, reduce simmer time to 5 minutes. Reheat soup on low heat, covered, for 5 minutes or until heated through.) Remove crushed garlic and serve. Sprinkle with fresh cilantro if desired.

CHEF NOTE: You can find mango nectar in the international aisle of most supermarkets. Rich in vitamins A and C, mango nectar is also a good source of potassium and beta carotene.

Although peanuts and hot chile peppers are essential components of many authentic Indonesian recipes, these ingredients were actually introduced to Indonesia by the New World. After the Dutch colonized the entire Spice Island archipelago, trading ships circling the globe brought to the islands chiles from Mexico, peanuts from the Americas, and exotic vegetables from the Caribbean and South America. Making these ingredients their own, Indonesian cooks have exported their techniques around the globe, and by the twenty-first century, even to the Florida Keys.

Water, Water Everywhere and Not A Drop To Drink

For most of pioneer America, making soup was as simple as filling a pot with fresh water, throwing in some vegetables and fresh herbs, and, on a lucky day, adding a chicken or a ham hock. Not so in the Florida Keys. Living only a scant few feet above sea level, in houses anchored deep in coral rock, Conchs survived without fresh ground water. The adventuresome tried digging wells but reached brackish, unpalatable water, which rose and fell with the ocean's tides.

Thus, settlers relied on rainfall to supply their freshwater needs. They built their houses with two to three broad, sloping roofs, which directed the rainwater into pipes leading to cisterns. The cisterns, built of wood held together with wooden pegs, collected the water. To kill larvae and bacteria and to keep the water fresh, Conchs poured kerosene on the surface water of the cistern.

Later on the settlers used porous brick to filter the water. In an effort to make the water more nutritious, they tossed stick sulphur and old iron spikes into the cisterns. It's a wonder their fresh water didn't kill them.

Fresh water was always a problem for Keys settlers. The cisterns were full during the rainy season, but during periods of drought, which is much of the year, the cisterns often became nearly dry. It was then that families cleaned their cisterns. First, using a broom, they scrubbed the inside of the cistern with dehydrated lime and water. Then they waited for rain.

of the dooryard gardens—coconut milk, juices from tomatoes, citrus, mangoes, and vegetables—as the foundation of their soup creations.

With an increasing military presence in Key West in the 1930s, the need for fresh water became crucial. Wells were dug in the area of what is now Homestead and Florida City at the top of the Keys, and the U.S. Navy began constructing an 18-inch pipeline from those wells to Key West. The Florida Keys Aqueduct Commission was created in 1941 with a mandate to supply fresh water to the residents of the Florida Keys. Completed in 1942 at a cost of $6 million, the 125-mile pipeline became a vital life-sustaining link to the mainland.

Now brought from the mainland in huge pipes suspended from the four-lane concrete Overseas Highway (U.S. Hwy. 1) that was completed in the 1980s, fresh water is still a precious resource in the Florida Keys. Residents must pay for this commodity by the ounce. And though it has become easier to put water in the soup pot, the Keys tropical bounty still permeates the islands' soup creations.

LEFT: *The Wanderer with a water barge in the Keys.* Credit: State Archives of Florida.
ABOVE: *Cypress tanks were used to transport fresh water to the Keys; each tank held 7,000 gallons.* Credit: State Archives of Florida.

The Conchs parsimoniously meted out this coveted, scarce resource. No drop was wasted. Wash days were also bath days. In his document "History Talk of the Florida Keys," historian Jerry Wilkinson quotes Bertram Pinder, son of one of Islamorada's founding fathers as saying: "The maddest I ever saw my Daddy was once when one of us left the top off the cistern and a cat fell in and drowned. All that precious water wasted."

Over the decades, cisterns evolved into massive cement structures, which kept the water between 70 and 80 degrees in the summer. Pitcher pumps in the kitchen simplified the task of fetching the water. But fresh water remained scarce, and Conch cooks continued to rely on the bounty

Completely isolated from the rest of the world except by boat, pioneer homesteaders in the upper Keys during the mid-1800s relied upon their pineapple crop and the harvest of their dooryard gardens for fresh fruits and vegetables. During the dry season, fresh water had to be hauled long distances by boat from the mainland in wooden barrels and demijohns, so many pioneer soups were fruit or vegetable based.

Pistachio-laced Pineapple-Cucumber Soup

1 seedless English cucumber (about 12 ounces), peeled and chopped into small dice

2 cups diced fresh pineapple (peeled, cored, and 1-inch dice)

1 yellow bell pepper, seeded and cut into 1-inch dice

¼ cup water

1 teaspoon hot sauce

1 teaspoon Worcestershire sauce

½ teaspoon salt

¼ teaspoon black pepper

½ cup finely chopped shelled pistachios

6 sprigs mint

1. Place cucumber, pineapple, and bell pepper in a medium bowl. Stir with a wooden spoon to mix. Place half the cucumber mixture in a blender. Add water. Process until smooth. Add remaining cucumber mixture. Process until smooth. Add hot sauce, Worcestershire sauce, salt, and black pepper. Pulse until combined.

2. Place a food mill over a large bowl. Add soup to food mill and process until only solids are left in the food mill. Discard solids. Transfer soup to a covered container and refrigerate overnight to combine flavors.

3. **To serve:** Serve soup in chilled martini glasses. Sprinkle each serving with 1½ tablespoons chopped pistachios and garnish each with a sprig of mint.

CHEF NOTE: Look for shelled, unsalted pistachios for this recipe. Unsalted, the nuts are low in sodium, in addition to being a good source of protein, potassium, and vitamin E.

Spicy Herbed Gazpacho

 **SERVES 8 TO 10**

3 tablespoons olive oil
¾ cup finely diced red onions
¾ cup finely diced red bell peppers
¾ cup finely diced green bell peppers
3 large cloves garlic, minced
2 cups tomato juice
2 cups spicy V-8 juice
1 cup Clamato juice

1 cup chicken broth
3 tablespoons snipped fresh parsley
3 tablespoons snipped fresh basil
3 tablespoons snipped fresh chives
salt and freshly ground black pepper
2 cups seeded, diced fresh tomatoes
1 English cucumber, peeled, sliced thin, then diced (about 1½ cups)

1. **One day ahead:** Place olive oil in a 5-quart saucepan over medium heat. When oil is hot, add onions, red and green peppers, and garlic. Sauté until soft, about 7 minutes. Add tomato juice, V-8 juice, Clamato juice, chicken broth, parsley, basil, and chives. Season with salt and pepper to taste. Raise heat to high and bring mixture to a boil. Immediately remove from heat and add tomatoes and cucumber. Stir to combine.

2. Transfer soup to a covered container and refrigerate overnight to marry flavors.

CHEF NOTE: The secret of a good gazpacho is the harmonious marriage of flavors. This soup is best at peak harvest season, when vine-ripened tomatoes, peppers, and cucumbers are available.

The soup we know as gazpacho originated in Spain's southern region of Andalusia. Farm harvesters traditionally prepared their lunches in the fields by pounding garlic, stale bread, water, olive oil, and salt in a large wooden bowl, forming a sort of nourishing paste to which they added cold water. Legend maintains that Christopher Columbus took barrels of this paste on his first voyage to the New World. Discovering tomatoes, cucumbers, and bell peppers in the Andes, he added them to the mix, creating the liquid salad we still call gazpacho.

Thai-fired Mushroom-Orange Soup with Shrimp

Thailand's bounty of land and sea mirrors the Florida Keys in many ways. It is little wonder that given today's global outlook and with increased availability of once-exotic ingredients, Keys chefs—professional and amateur alike—adapt Thai-inspired recipes to indigenous resources. Thai soups are often served for breakfast, may be a whole meal at lunch, and are an integral part of any traditional Thai-style dinner.

1 cup chicken broth

1 cup coconut milk

1 cup freshly squeezed orange juice

1 heaping tablespoon finely grated orange peel

1 tablespoon fish sauce

1 teaspoon sambal oelek (Thai chile paste)

2 serrano chiles (about 1 1/2 inches long), seeded and minced

3 cups thinly sliced white button mushrooms

2 ounces enoki mushrooms

1 tablespoon honey

1/2 pound medium shrimp (about 14), peeled and deveined

1/3 cup snipped fresh basil

1. Place broth, coconut milk, orange juice, grated orange peel, fish sauce, sambal oelek, and minced chiles in a 4-quart saucepan over high heat. Bring to a boil, stirring frequently, then reduce heat to medium-low and simmer, uncovered, for 2 1/2 minutes. Add sliced white mushrooms and cook until tender, about 3 minutes. Add all but 12 enoki mushrooms and cook for 1 minute. Stir in honey. Add shrimp and cook just until shrimp turn pink, about 3 minutes. Stir in basil and remove from heat. Ladle into small soup bowls. Sprinkle 3 enokis over each serving.

CHEF NOTE: Before slicing the button mushrooms, trim stem ends and wipe the mushrooms clean with a damp paper towel. To get 2 ounces usable enoki mushrooms, buy a 3.5-ounce package and trim off the stem ends just to where the individual stems can be separated. Fresh orange peel and freshly squeezed juice are absolutely essential in this recipe. Sambal oelek is a paste made from ground fresh chilies. You'll find it in the international aisle of most supermarkets. A staple in Thai recipes, it lasts forever in the refrigerator.

Lemony Asparagus-Dill Soup

 **SERVES 6 TO 8**

3 pounds thin asparagus, washed

4 cups chicken broth

salt and freshly ground black pepper

3 tablespoons butter

1½ cup chopped celery

1½ cup finely chopped sweet onions, like Vidalia

1 cup chopped leeks, (cleaned well) white parts only

3 eggs

¼ cup plus 2 tablespoons fresh lemon juice

¼ cup snipped fresh dill weed

dill sprigs for garnish (optional)

1. Break off the woody ends of asparagus and reserve. Cut tips off asparagus spears and reserve. Cut asparagus stalks into 1-inch pieces.

2. Place asparagus ends and chicken broth in a saucepan over high heat. Cover, bring to a boil, and then immediately remove mixture from heat and allow it to rest for 15 minutes. Strain broth and reserve. Discard asparagus ends.

3. Place several cups of water and ½ teaspoon salt in a small saucepan. Bring to a boil, then blanch the asparagus tips until bright green and barely cooked through. Remove from heat, drain, then refresh tips in a bowl of ice water. Drain again and reserve.

4. Melt butter in a large soup pot over medium heat and add chopped celery, onions, and leeks. Sauté until softened, about 6 minutes. Season with salt and pepper to taste. Add asparagus pieces and mix together well. Add infused chicken broth and 2 cups water. Increase heat to high and bring to a boil, then reduce heat to medium-low and simmer, covered, about 5 minutes, until asparagus is tender.

5. Puree soup in batches in a blender. Return pureed soup to the pot and allow to cool about 5 minutes, or until lukewarm.

6. In a small bowl that can withstand heat, whisk together eggs and ¼ cup lemon juice until creamy and well mixed. Slowly add 1 cup of the slightly cooled soup, whisking constantly, then slowly add this egg mixture to the remaining soup in the pot, whisking constantly.

7. Cook soup over low heat, whisking constantly, until soup is thickened slightly. Do not allow soup to boil. Whisk in snipped dill and 2 tablespoons lemon juice. Add salt and pepper to taste. Garnish with asparagus tips just before serving.

Originating in the eastern Mediterranean, asparagus, a member of the lily family, grows wild in many parts of the world but has never been cultivated in the Florida Keys. Asparagus actually are gendered. The female stalk is plumper than the male. This recipe treats asparagus to a classic Greek egg and lemon soup technique, known as *avgolémono*.

CHEF NOTE: This is not really a bisque, because it does not contain any heavy cream. Nevertheless, this asparagus soup is thick, rich, and creamy, thanks to the addition of eggs and lemon.

Salads *and* 🌴 **3**
Vegetables

Until the influx of U.S. Navy families to the Florida Keys during the two world wars, fresh salads didn't really have much of a place at either the Conch or Cuban dining table. In all fairness, the early Key West pioneers only had access to perishables that grew in their dooryard gardens. The "strangers," as the locals referred to the newcomers, however, were used to eating fresh leafy produce "up North" and introduced the concept of salads to Conch cooking.

Initially a Conch salad consisted simply of lettuce, tomato, onion, and cucumber, with an oil and vinegar dressing. Or, when in season, an avocado was sliced and eaten raw with a splash of Old Sour. Salads evolved over the decades with improvements in transportation to the Keys and between the Keys, which brought a potpourri of produce heretofore unavailable. Today, salad possibilities are as vast as the imagination.

Key Westers relied on a stable of cooked vegetables for the bulk of every meal—tomatoes, okra, eggplant, and plantains, which they cooked in myriad concoctions. Harvesting their dooryard gardens or buying from lower Keys vegetable farmers who sold their produce in town, they referred to the decades before refrigerated shipping as "B.B—Before Birdseye."

LEFT: *Fresh fruit for a Key West cut-up, ca. 1960.* **Credit: State Archives of Florida.**

Arugula and Watercress with Orange-Poppy Seed Dressing

Oranges are thought to have originated between the Tigris and the Euphrates Rivers in what is now Iraq. It takes an orange tree up to five years to produce fruit, but then it can produce a staggering 1,000 pounds of oranges or more a year, for up to 50 years. Orange trees grace many contemporary Florida Keys dooryard gardens.

¼ cup honey

1 heaping tablespoon grated orange peel (peel from 1 large orange)

3 tablespoons fresh orange juice

1 tablespoon rice wine vinegar

¼ cup light olive oil

1 tablespoon poppy seeds

1 bunch watercress, washed and lower stems removed (about 3 packed cups)

1 bunch arugula, washed and lower stems removed (about 1½ packed cups)

1. Combine honey, orange peel, orange juice, and vinegar in a glass container with a tight-fitting lid. Shake to mix well. Slowly stir in olive oil, then poppy seeds. Refrigerate for up to three days. (Bring to room temperature before serving and shake to mix.)

2. **To serve:** Place watercress and arugula in a large bowl and toss. Add enough dressing to coat greens and toss to mix well.

CHEF NOTE: This orange-poppy seed dressing is light as a sea breeze. It is equally tasty tossed with baby greens. Divide tossed greens into 4 portions and top with grilled shrimp, scallops, or chicken for a light-bite entrée.

Caesar Salad

 **SERVES 4 TO 6**

3 tablespoons fresh lemon juice

1 large clove garlic, crushed

1 teaspoon Worcestershire sauce

dash salt

½ teaspoon freshly ground black pepper

4-6 oil-packed anchovy fillets, finely minced

1 teaspoon capers

1 teaspoon Dijon mustard

1 coddled egg (see Chef Note below)

⅓ cup virgin olive oil

2 heads romaine lettuce hearts, torn into bite-size pieces

¾ cup grated Parmesan cheese, divided

1 cup croutons

¼ cup shredded Parmesan cheese

1. Place lemon juice, garlic, Worcestershire sauce, salt, pepper, anchovies, capers, and mustard in a medium bowl. Mix together with a wire whisk. Add coddled egg and whisk until mixture is smooth. Slowly drizzle the olive oil into the dressing mixture, whisking constantly until smooth.

2. Place one-half the dressing in a large salad bowl. Add romaine and toss. Taste a leaf of romaine to determine if salad needs more dressing. Add more dressing to taste and toss to combine. (Do not overdress.) Add ½ cup grated Parmesan cheese and croutons and toss again. Divide salad among individual plates. Sprinkle each portion with 1 tablespoon shredded Parmesan.

CHEF NOTE: To coddle an egg: Bring a small saucepan of water to boil over high heat. Add egg and boil for exactly 45 seconds, no more. Remove egg, run under cold water, and allow it to cool.

Having absolutely nothing to do with Julius Caesar, the Caesar salad was named for its inventor, Caesar Cardini, owner/chef of a Tijuana, Mexico, restaurant, who purportedly concocted it for the Prince of Wales and his entourage in the 1920s. The original salad contained no anchovies. How they became part of this legendary dish remains a mystery. The ubiquitous Caesar salad turns up on literally every restaurant menu in the Florida Keys, most often overdressed and topped with chicken or shrimp. This salad wears a light, lemony Caesar dressing, perfectly suited for our tropical climate.

Classic Tomato and Mozzarella with Tangy Goat Cheese Dressing

Fresh milk was a scarce commodity in the early days of Key West, so cheese didn't factor into the daily diet of the settlers. Grazing land was nearly nonexistent on the tiny island, but some families kept a goat or two; it is possible that they may have made goat cheese. France is the world's leading producer of goat cheese, which, because it contains no beta-carotene, is whiter than cheese made from cow's milk.

4 ounces goat cheese, at room temperature
2 teaspoons white wine vinegar
1 teaspoon Dijon mustard
1 tablespoon sugar
2 tablespoons low-fat buttermilk
1 tablespoon minced red onions

2 tablespoons water
salt and freshly ground black pepper
2 large beefsteak tomatoes
2 rounds mozzarella cheese
¼ cup snipped fresh basil

1. Place goat cheese, vinegar, mustard, and sugar in a small bowl. Stir until smooth. Add buttermilk and red onions and stir until smooth. Add up to 2 tablespoons water, stirring constantly, until dressing is the consistency of heavy cream. Season with salt and pepper to taste. Transfer to a covered container and refrigerate for up to 3 days. (Makes 1 cup.)

2. Cut tomatoes into 1-inch slices. Thinly slice mozzarella. Arrange tomatoes on a serving plate. Place a slice of mozzarella atop each tomato slice. Top each with a dollop of goat cheese dressing. Sprinkle with snipped basil.

CHEF NOTE: You can use this tasty dressing as a topper for steamed fresh vegetables or baked potatoes. For a thicker consistency, do not add the 2 tablespoons water called for in this recipe.

Dilly Corn and Black Bean Salad

5 ears sweet corn, husks and silks removed

1 tablespoon sugar

1 (14.5-ounce) can black beans, rinsed and drained

½ cup finely chopped sweet onions, like Vidalia

½ cup finely chopped red bell peppers

2 tablespoons fresh snipped dill

1 large clove garlic, finely minced

¼ cup olive oil

3 tablespoons apple cider vinegar

salt and freshly ground black pepper

1. Place a large pot of water over high heat and bring to a boil. Add sugar and corn. Reduce heat to medium and cook 5 minutes. Drain corn, refresh with cold water, and drain again. Set aside to cool.

2. When cool enough to handle, cut kernels from cobs. Place corn kernels, black beans, onions, bell peppers, dill, and garlic in large bowl. Stir to mix well.

3. Whisk together oil and vinegar in small glass measuring cup. Pour over corn mixture. Toss dressing with corn mixture and season with salt and pepper to taste. Cover and refrigerate at least 1 hour until chilled. Salad can be prepared 1 day ahead and served either cold or at room temperature.

CHEF NOTE: When sweet corn is left at room temperature for 6 hours or more, 40 percent of its sugar turns to starch and the corn loses much of its sweetness. Look for corn whose husks are bright green and tight. Take a look at the kernels. Kernels at the tip should be smaller than the rest. Large tip kernels mean the corn is overly mature.

A staple of Native American civilizations, corn can be traced back to 3400 B.C. in Mexican and Central American cultures. Evidence of black beans in these same cultures goes back 7,000 years. The two have commingled in Spanish culinary circles for centuries and are paired in Conchfusion cooking as well. Black beans are a favorite in the Cuban culture, and sweet corn is grown in Homestead truck farms at the top of the Keys.

The Dooryard *Garden*

Vegetables played but a minor role in the culinary theater of early Key West. The limestone bedrock of the island, which was covered by a scant few inches of soil, proved an inhospitable medium for extensive farming. In the 1800s, fresh produce arrived only occasionally, by boat, from the truck farms in the upper and lower Keys or from the island of Cuba, 90 miles to the south. By the early 1900s, commercial farming in the Keys had ceased completely, and only pineapples, malangas, and plantains came in from Cuba. So until the advent of the Flagler's East Coast Railroad Extension in 1912 and then the Overseas Highway in 1938, when produce was finally imported in refrigerated trucks from the mainland, Key West cooks relied on their own ingenuity and the friendly tropical climate in which they lived to grow their own fruits and vegetables.

Virtually every backyard in Key West sported a dooryard garden. (Those who didn't have a large enough yard planted a tin can garden on their porch railing or steps.) Here grew tropical fruit trees, herbs, peppers, tomatoes, and a few heat tolerant vegetables, such as okra. Coconut trees covered the yards, the nuts of which provided such staples of Conch cuisine as coconut meat, coconut water, and coconut milk.

Short, plump Cuban bananas, called hog bananas (far tastier than the over-hybridized bananas we get today), and plantains were usually

Three trees reigned as dooryard royalty— guava, mango, and papaya . . .

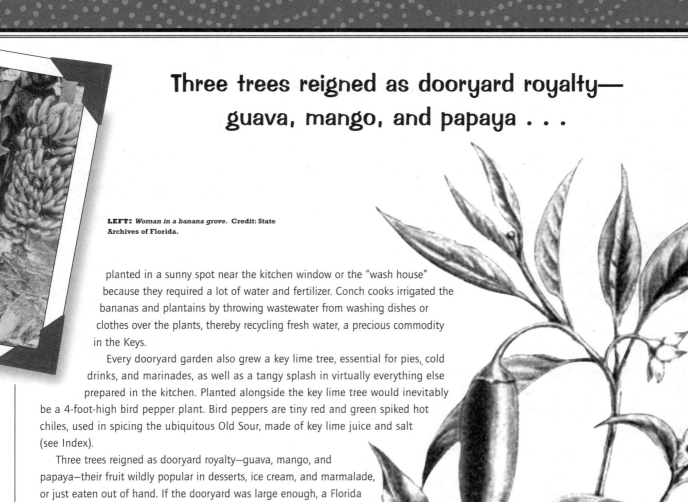

planted in a sunny spot near the kitchen window or the "wash house" because they required a lot of water and fertilizer. Conch cooks irrigated the bananas and plantains by throwing wastewater from washing dishes or clothes over the plants, thereby recycling fresh water, a precious commodity in the Keys.

Every dooryard garden also grew a key lime tree, essential for pies, cold drinks, and marinades, as well as a tangy splash in virtually everything else prepared in the kitchen. Planted alongside the key lime tree would inevitably be a 4-foot-high bird pepper plant. Bird peppers are tiny red and green spiked hot chiles, used in spicing the ubiquitous Old Sour, made of key lime juice and salt (see Index).

Three trees reigned as dooryard royalty—guava, mango, and papaya—their fruit wildly popular in desserts, ice cream, and marmalade, or just eaten out of hand. If the dooryard was large enough, a Florida avocado tree, whose fruit resembles a smooth, green-skinned ostrich egg, might share its turf with a sour orange tree (essential for many Cuban marinades), a sugar apple or soursop (good in ice cream), a Barbados cherry, and a carpet of basil, chives, cilantro, parsley, and mint.

The sapodilla and the tamarind were much coveted for their fruit, but these trees grew so huge that even a family with a substantial plot of land had to choose between them.

Green Bean, Feta, and Walnut Salad

Authentic feta is a curd cheese originally made of unpasteurized sheep's milk by shepherds in the mountains of Greece. Milk curdled with rennet is separated and drained in a cloth bag or specially designed mold. The cheese is then cut into large slices, salted, and packed into barrels containing brine or whey. The feta found in U.S. markets today is most often made with pasteurized cow's milk and is much firmer than that made with sheep's milk. The name feta means "slice."

FOR THE DRESSING:

¼ cup white wine vinegar

1 tablespoon chopped fresh dill

1 teaspoon minced garlic

¼ teaspoon salt

¼ teaspoon freshly ground black pepper

¾ cup olive oil

FOR THE SALAD:

1 cup coarsely chopped walnuts

1½ pounds green beans, cut into thirds

1 small red onion, thinly sliced, then quartered

4 ounces herbed feta cheese

1. **Up to 1 day ahead:** Place vinegar, dill, garlic, salt, and pepper in a small bowl. Whisk to combine. Slowly add olive oil, whisking constantly. Place dressing in a covered container and refrigerate until needed. (Bring dressing to room temperature and shake well to mix before using.)

2. Place chopped walnuts in a small nonstick skillet over medium heat. Toast nuts, stirring occasionally, until they are fragrant and browned slightly. Remove walnuts from heat and cool. (If not using immediately, refrigerate in a small zipper bag.)

3. Place a vegetable-steamer rack and two inches water in a large pot over medium-high heat. Add green beans to steamer. Steam beans until crisp-tender, about 5 minutes. Drain beans in a colander. Rinse with cold water and drain again. Pat beans dry with paper toweling. Transfer beans to a large bowl. Add walnuts, red onion, and feta cheese. Toss to mix well. Cover bowl with plastic wrap and refrigerate for at least 1 hour to chill. Pour dressing (without tossing) over bean mixture one hour before serving, re-cover with plastic wrap, and return bowl to refrigerator. Do not toss ingredients with dressing until just before serving.

CHEF NOTE: When I first made this recipe, which was given to me by a friend, my husband said simply: "Wow!" And, given that he is a meat-and-potatoes man, that said a lot. The flavors in this salad transcend its ingredients. You can use fat-free herbed feta in this recipe without sacrificing any of its wonder.

Mangia Mangia Balsamic Vinaigrette on Baby Greens

½ cup red wine vinegar

¼ cup balsamic vinegar

2 tablespoons water

¾ teaspoon dried oregano

¾ teaspoon dried basil

¼ teaspoon coarsely ground black pepper

2¼ teaspoons finely minced garlic

½ cup extra virgin olive oil

½ cup pure olive oil

mixed baby greens

1. **Up to 3 days ahead:** Place vinegars, water, oregano, basil, pepper, and garlic in a large glass jar. Shake to mix well. Slowly add olive oils, stirring constantly to mix well. Refrigerate until needed. (Bring to room temperature before serving and shake to mix.)

2. **To serve:** Place desired amount of mixed baby greens in a large bowl. Add dressing to coat and toss to mix well.

CHEF NOTE: You can use this tangy dressing on any mixed green salad. The recipe makes enough dressing for several occasions. Try drizzling the vinaigrette on steamed asparagus or toss with steamed julienne zucchini.

Says Chef Eliot Barton of Mangia Mangia restaurant in Key West: "This is the only dressing available at Mangia Mangia. Though simple to make, it is delicious and through the years many customers have requested that we sell the dressing. Well, the mystery is now revealed." He recommends using high quality vinegars and olive oils and adds: "The little bit of water reduces acidity but retains the fine flavor of the vinegar. Inexpensive vinegars are already too diluted. Look for vinegars in the range of 6 percent acidity."

Nutty Cabbage Slaw

English cucumbers are the "burpless," gourmet variety of cukes. Their seeds are so small they don't need to be removed. The cucumbers are thin and about a foot long. They are shrink-wrapped in plastic to retain moisture because they are not waxed like other cucumbers.

5 cups shredded green cabbage

1 seedless English cucumber, peeled, then halved lengthwise, and thinly sliced

1 cup thinly sliced, quartered red onions

½ cup snipped fresh cilantro

½ cup chopped salted peanuts

6 tablespoons red wine vinegar (3 ounces)

4 teaspoons sugar

1 teaspoon salt

1. Place cabbage, cucumber, onions, cilantro, and peanuts in a large bowl. Toss to mix well.

2. Place vinegar, sugar, and salt in a small bowl. Whisk until sugar is dissolved. Add vinegar mixture to cabbage slaw and toss well to combine. Cover slaw and refrigerate for at least 1 hour or overnight so that flavors mingle.

CHEF NOTE: Snipping fresh herbs may sound like a real pain, but don't be tempted to substitute dried in this recipe. Here's what I do: choose a rainy Saturday, buy a wide selection of fresh herbs, wash and dry them thoroughly, turn on a favorite movie, and snip away. Place snipped herbs in a freezer-weight zipper bag and label them. Then pop them in the freezer and when a recipe calls for fresh herbs, you're ready to go. The color will be a bit darker, but the frozen herbs will taste just like fresh.

Pineapple-Carrot Slaw with Blue Cheese and Bacon

5 cups shredded cabbage

2 cups shredded carrots

½ cup golden raisins

2 cups fresh pineapple, cored and cut in small dice

2 ounces blue cheese

2 tablespoons honey-Dijon mustard

1 tablespoon chopped garlic

½ cup white wine vinegar

¾ cup canola oil

5 slices bacon

salt and freshly ground black pepper

1. Place cabbage, carrots, raisins, pineapple, and blue cheese in a large mixing bowl. Toss to combine. Set aside.

2. Place mustard, garlic, and vinegar in a blender. Process until smooth. On lowest speed, slowly add oil, processing constantly.

3. Meanwhile, cook bacon in a large skillet until crispy. Remove bacon and place on paper toweling to absorb grease. Remove skillet from heat. Slowly stir dressing into bacon grease. Crumble bacon and add to dressing mixture. Stir to mix well. Pour dressing over cabbage mixture and toss to combine. Season with salt and freshly ground black pepper to taste. Chill for at least 1 hour before serving.

CHEF NOTE: If you aren't a fan of blue cheese, substitute one of the crumbled, seasoned feta cheeses now on the market.

Given the unforgiving lime-stone bedrock that blankets the Florida Keys, carrots were never able to be cultivated here. But the oft-taken-for-granted staple vegetable has enjoyed a colorful voyage to our shores. First cultivated in Afghanistan in the seventh century, the carrot had yellow flesh and a purple exterior. The Dutch developed the orange carrot, while the French crossbred an elongated version. English colonists brought carrots to the Americas. Those that escaped into the wild became Queen Anne's Lace.

The papaya, called *fruta bomba* by the Cubans because its shape resembles a hand grenade, is as common in the Florida Keys and the American tropics as apples are in the rest of the country. The large fruit hangs from the leafy top of a small spindly tree that is actually a giant herb. The skin of the papaya turns yellow when ripe and its flesh becomes a bright orange. Tiny black edible seeds, which taste a little like watercress, fill the inner cavity of the papaya. Rob Millner, executive chef at the Pier House in Key West, developed this tasty dressing.

Sliced Avocados Dressed with Papaya Seed Vinaigrette

⅔ cup pureed fresh papaya

⅓ cup rice wine vinegar

½ cup olive oil

½ teaspoon coarse sea salt or kosher salt

½ teaspoon ground white pepper

⅓ cup papaya seeds

2 teaspoons snipped mint leaves

3 small Florida avocados or 3 Hass avocadoes, peeled, pitted, and thinly sliced

1. Whisk together papaya puree and vinegar in a medium mixing bowl. Add oil in a slow steady stream, whisking to emulsify into the papaya mixture. Whisk in salt and pepper. Add papaya seeds and mint and whisk to combine. Refrigerate in a covered container until needed. (Bring dressing to room temperature and shake to mix before using.) Makes 2 cups.

2. Arrange avocado slices on each of 6 glass salad plates. Drizzle vinaigrette over avocado slices.

CHEF NOTE: The amount of papaya seeds called for in this recipe generally equals the amount in the center of a large papaya. Serve the remaining papaya in wedges, for breakfast, with just a splash of lime juice.

Snow Pea and Mango Salad

¼ cup lemon juice

¼ cup orange juice

¼ cup honey

1 tablespoon balsamic vinegar

2 cups snow pea pods, washed and trimmed

2 mangos, seeded, peeled, and thinly sliced up to 2-inch lengths

1 cup thinly sliced red peppers, cut in 2-inch pieces

1 cup thinly sliced red onions, cut in 2-inch pieces

The French name for snow peas is *mange tout*, or "eat it all." These flat, crisp pods secret 5 to 7 tiny immature sweet peas inside. Snow peas can be kept in the refrigerator for up to 2 weeks.

1. **Up to 2 days ahead:** Whisk together lemon juice, orange juice, honey, and balsamic vinegar in a small bowl. Place citrus dressing in a covered container and refrigerate until needed. (Bring dressing to room temperature and shake to mix before using.)

2. Bring a large pot of water to boil. Place snow pea pods in a vegetable steamer. Blanch snow pea pods for 1 minute. Drain pea pods and rinse with cold water. Drain and rinse again. Drain a final time, and then place snow pea pods in a medium bowl. Add mangos, red peppers, and onions. Toss to mix. Add dressing. Toss to combine. Place salad in a covered container and refrigerate until serving.

3. **To serve:** Drain snow pea mixture in a colander and place in serving bowl.

CHEF NOTE: When buying fresh mango, look for fruit blushed with red, yellow, and orange. Next take the sniff test. Choose only fruit with a rich, sensuous aroma. Ripen the fruit at room temperature on a windowsill. When flesh gives a little under thumb pressure, it is ripe. A ripe mango can be stored in the refrigerator for up to 2 days.

Spinach is believed to have originated in ancient Persia, now Iran. Europeans discovered the nutritious vegetable in the fifteenth century. Americans have been eating spinach since the 1800s, but cookbooks from that era called for cooking spinach for 25 minutes! Baby spinach grows prolifically in the Keys dooryard gardens.

Spinach Salad with Strawberries and Blue Cheese

½ cup sugar

¼ cup apple cider vinegar

dash Worcestershire sauce

1 tablespoon chopped sweet onions, like Vidalia

¼ cup olive oil

1 (10-ounce) package fresh baby spinach, washed and spun dry

1 pint strawberries, cleaned and thinly sliced

1 medium red onion, diced

½ cup crumbled blue cheese

¼ cup sliced almonds

¼ cup shredded Parmesan cheese

1. Up to 2 days ahead, place sugar, vinegar, Worcestershire sauce, and chopped sweet onions in a small bowl and whisk until sugar is dissolved. Slowly whisk in olive oil. Place in a covered container and refrigerate until needed. (Bring to room temperature and shake to mix well before using.)

2. Place spinach, strawberries, red onions, blue cheese, almonds, and Parmesan cheese in a large salad bowl and toss to combine. Add dressing to coat and toss. Serve on individual plates.

CHEF NOTE: Spinach contains the chemical oxalic acid, which binds with the vegetable's iron and calcium and reduces the body's absorption of these minerals. To improve absorption of the vegetable's beneficial iron and calcium, spinach should be eaten with foods rich in vitamin-C, such as strawberries, which help release the minerals.

"The" Salad

3 tablespoons sugar

2 tablespoons red wine vinegar

2 tablespoons minced red onions

¼ teaspoon salt

¼ teaspoon dry mustard

¼ cup olive oil

1 (10-ounce) package mixed greens, washed and spun dry

3-4 scallions, chopped

½ red pepper, chopped

½ carrot, shredded

¼ cup finely slivered fennel

¼ cup chopped honey roasted peanuts

2 ounces crumbled blue cheese

1 cup chow mein noodles

1. **Up to 1 week ahead:** Place sugar, vinegar, onions, salt, and dry mustard in a small bowl. Whisk until sugar is dissolved. Slowly add olive oil, whisking constantly. Transfer to a tightly covered container. Refrigerate until needed. (Bring dressing to room temperature and shake well to mix before using.)

2. Place salad greens, scallions, red peppers, shredded carrots, fennel, peanuts, and blue cheese in a large bowl. Toss to combine. Just before serving, toss with enough dressing to coat. Add chow mein noodles and toss again.

CHEF NOTE: I call this "The" Salad, because it is my guests' favorite. When they come to dinner they ask, "Did you make *the* salad?" While the potpourri of veggies and crunchies combine interesting flavors and textures, I think what everyone really loves is the light, sweet dressing.

In the mid-1800s former Maryland slave Sandy Cornish carved an oasis from the limestone wasteland that was his meager yard, creating the most renowned garden in Key West. Uncle Sandy, as he was called, always had a bountiful harvest. Uncle Sandy may have had "The" Garden, but this is "The" Salad, a winning showcase for the harvest of any dooryard garden.

Baked Pineapple

Grown only in the New World tropics, pineapples belong to the bromeliad family. Bromeliads are epiphytes, or air plants, which means they absorb water and nutrients from their environment through microscopic hairs at the base of their leaves. Their roots function only as an anchoring support. It takes 13 to 18 months for a pineapple to mature.

1 ripe pineapple
8 tablespoons (1 stick) butter
1 Persian lime, peeled and separated into segments

2 tablespoons sugar
¼ teaspoon red pepper flakes
½ cup fresh breadcrumbs

1. Preheat oven to 425°F. Remove all but about 1 inch of green leaves from top of pineapple. Cut pineapple in half lengthwise. With a serrated knife, carefully cut around the perimeter of each half pineapple. With a large serving spoon, carefully scoop out pineapple, separating it from the shell. (Be sure to keep the shell intact.)

2. Cut the flesh of each half pineapple in half again, lengthwise. Cut out the tough inner core. Cut the pineapple in 1-inch, bite-size pieces (about 3 cups). Drain one pineapple shell on paper toweling. Discard the other shell.

3. Melt 4 tablespoons butter in a large skillet over medium-high heat. Add pineapple, lime segments, sugar, and red pepper flakes. Cook for 5 minutes, stirring frequently. Transfer pineapple mixture, including all butter, to pineapple shell. Set aside.

4. Melt remaining 4 tablespoons butter in a medium skillet over medium-high heat. Add breadcrumbs and sauté, stirring frequently, until crumbs are toasted and browned. Top pineapple with toasted breadcrumbs.

5. Place pineapple shell in an appropriately sized baking dish. Bake for 12 to 15 minutes. (Can prepare this recipe early in the day, cover with plastic wrap, and refrigerate until baking. Bake for 20 to 25 minutes.)

CHEF NOTE: In the tropics, fruit is quite often cooked like a vegetable and served as a side dish. If you want an even more peppery kick to this dish, add ⅛ teaspoon cayenne pepper to the breadcrumb-butter mixture.

Balsamic Mushrooms and Roasted Onions

4 large sweet onions, like Vidalia

¼ cup plus 1 tablespoon balsamic vinegar

¼ cup plus 1 tablespoon olive oil

1 teaspoon dried thyme

½ teaspoon dried basil

¾ teaspoon salt, divided

⅝ teaspoon pepper, divided

1 pound white button mushrooms, cleaned and stems removed

4 ounces shiitake mushrooms, cleaned and stems removed

12 ounces portobello mushrooms, cleaned and stems removed

4 cloves garlic, crushed then minced

⅓ cup chopped fresh parsley

1. Preheat oven to 450°F. Peel onions, leaving roots intact. Cut each onion into 8 wedges. Place onions in an 11 x 7-inch baking dish that has been coated with vegetable cooking spray. Place ¼ cup vinegar, 1 tablespoon olive oil, thyme, basil, ¼ teaspoon salt, and ⅛ teaspoon pepper in a small bowl and whisk well to combine. Pour vinegar mixture over onions. With a spatula, turn onions over and over, coating all sides with vinegar mixture. Cover with aluminum foil. Bake for 25 minutes. Uncover and, with a spatula, turn onions. Bake 45 minutes more, turning occasionally.

2. Meanwhile, cut button and shiitake mushrooms into quarters. Halve portobellos and cut into thick slices. Place ¼ cup olive oil and garlic in a large skillet over medium-high heat. Sauté for 1 minute. Add mushrooms and sauté for 5 minutes, stirring frequently. Add 1 tablespoon balsamic vinegar, ½ teaspoon salt, and ½ teaspoon pepper, and sauté for 2 minutes more. With a slotted spoon, remove mushrooms to a medium bowl. Toss with parsley.

3. Remove onions from oven. Add mushrooms and toss them together with onions. Transfer mushrooms and onions to a serving bowl.

Fresh provisions were a rare treat in the Florida Keys of the mid-1800s. As part of a military family assigned to Fort Jefferson in the Dry Tortugas in 1892, Emily Holder longed for fresh vegetables. In her journal she wrote: "Captain Wilson returned from Key West, sixty miles away, with the word that there was nothing in Key West but a few onions, which were quoted at one dollar per small bunch."

CHEF NOTE: Since mushrooms are about 90 percent water, do not wash them under running water. Instead, clean them with damp paper toweling or brush them lightly with a vegetable brush. Be sure to always discard the stems of shiitakes and portobellos because they are tough.

Pineapple Plantations

Captain Ben Baker, a former Key West wrecker, started the first Keys pineapple plantation on Key Largo in 1866. Importing 6,000 pineapple suckers from Cuba and impoverished blacks from the Bahamas to plant, cultivate, and harvest the fruit, Baker pioneered an industry that flourished until 1906. Other homesteaders followed, such as Amos and Eliza Lowe and the six Johnson brothers, forming the settlement of Planter (later named Plantation Key after these pineapple plantations). Others planted large tracts of pineys or pines, as the sweet, juicy fruit was called, on the Matecumbe Keys and Elliot Key. By 1870 in the Keys, the human population outside Key West had increased fourfold, to 300. And, 60,000 pineapples were harvested annually in the upper Keys.

 typical plantation used a slash and burn method to clear the dense wooded hammock that encompassed the upper Keys. At about 10,000 to the acre, suckers were planted in the ashes of the burned foliage, wherever soil was found. The Bahamian cutters harvested the pineapples about two weeks before

...

By 1915 commercial pineapple farming in the Keys was history.

...

they were ripe, wearing heavy clothing to protect their skin from the poisonous spines of the leaves. Balancing huge baskets woven from coconut palm fronds on their heads, the Bahamians toted fruit to the waterfront docks. Here they loaded the pineys into small sloops and sailed the fruit out to schooners anchored in deeper waters.

ABOVE: *Repacking Cuban pineapples in Key West, ca. 1920.* **Credit: From the collection of Jerry Wilkinson.**

The schooners then headed north, where 5½ days later, in good weather, the fruit was marketed in such cities as Baltimore, Boston, and New York.

Conch farmers harvested about 7,000 pineapples per acre and could get a second and third crop from the same roots. But they never fertilized, nor did they rotate their crops. After four to five harvests, the meager nutrients in the thin Keys soil layer were depleted, and one by one the fields were exhausted and ultimately abandoned. To complicate matters, a plant blight hit the fields in 1906, closely followed by a devastating hurricane, which destroyed most of the pineapple crop. The final nail in the industry's coffin was the completion of Flagler's East Coast Railroad Extension in 1912. Pineapples grown more cheaply in Cuba were shipped to Key West, then loaded onto boxcars and transported by train to the northern markets, bypassing the plantations of the upper Keys altogether. By 1915 commercial pineapple farming in the Keys was history.

Key West Cut-Up

One of the most popular after-dinner gatherings in the early 1900s was known as a Key West cut-up. Whereas today you might expect to nosh on chips and dip or nachos, Conchs feasted on fruit. Today's slang might dub the occasion a B.Y.O.F—Bring Your Own Fruit.

Each guest brought a different fruit, cut into bite-size pieces. Papaya, called paw-paw by the Conchs, was a cut-up staple because it was available all year round. Bananas, mango, avocado, and guava came from dooryard gardens. Apples and oranges were purchased from the store. The host mixed all the fruit in a large bowl and squeezed fresh key lime juice over the top. The fruit steeped in the lime juice for several hours, as guests socialized. When the cut-up was deemed ready, each person picked a piece of fruit from the bowl in turn, until all the fruit was eaten. Anticipation rose as the bowl emptied, because the person who ate the last piece got to drink the juice, always considered the very best part.

Kids loved to do their own cut-ups, often creating a strange mixture of raw fruits and vegetables. The children brought whatever they could find at home—tomatoes, onions, sweet potatoes, peppers, avocados, as well as fruit. After adding the key lime juice, the kids mixed the cut-up with their hands.

...

> **Anticipation rose as the bowl emptied, because the person who ate the last piece got to drink the juice, always considered the very best part.**

...

Calabaza Mash

3 pounds calabaza, seeded, peeled and
  cut into 2-inch chunks
½ cup mayonnaise
¾ cup chopped sweet onions, like
  Vidalia
1 egg, beaten
1 teaspoon brown sugar

¼ teaspoon salt
¼ teaspoon freshly ground black pepper
½ cup Japanese breadcrumbs, like
  Panko
¼ cup grated Parmesan cheese
2 tablespoons butter, melted

A member of the squash family also known as West Indian pumpkin, calabaza has bright orange flesh and a mottled green and tan skin. Native to the American tropics, calabaza was a staple in the diets of Florida Keys Indians and early settlers and a chief ingredient in Caribbean and Latin American cuisine as well. Calabazas are very large, so they are often cut into 1- to 3-pound chunks before being offered for sale. Fibrous and watery, calabaza is best used in combination dishes like stews, soups, and gratins.

1. Preheat oven to 350°F. Place calabaza in a large pot and fill with water to cover by 2 inches. Place pot over high heat, bring to a boil, then reduce heat to medium-low and simmer until calabaza is tender when pierced with a fork, about 10 minutes. Drain calabaza in a colander. Return it to pot and mash with an electric mixer for 1 minute.

2. With a spoon, mix together mayonnaise, onions, egg, brown sugar, salt, and pepper in a small bowl. Add mayonnaise mixture to calabaza and stir with a spoon to combine ingredients well.

3. Coat a 2-quart baking dish with vegetable cooking spray. Transfer calabaza mixture to dish and set aside.

4. Place breadcrumbs and Parmesan cheese in a small bowl and mix with a fork. Pour in melted butter and mix with a fork until crumbs are well coated with butter. Sprinkle buttered crumbs atop calabaza mixture.

5. Bake uncovered for 35 to 45 minutes or until topping is lightly browned and squash is heated through.

CHEF NOTE: If you are lucky enough to find calabaza in your market you can use it in most recipes calling for pumpkin, butternut, acorn, buttercup, or Hubbard squash. If you can't find it, substitute one of these vegetables in the recipe above.

Cheesy Tomato Pie

After the demise of the Keys pineapple industry in the early 1900s, tomatoes were planted in the plantation plots of Upper Matecumbe and Key Largo. It often rained for weeks on end in October before the young plants were set out in the fields. The mosquitoes were so bad that workers wore mosquito nets over their heads and around their necks when planting tomato seedlings. A packing-house operated near today's location of the Islander hotel in Islamorada. The Key Largo tomato crop netted $250,000 in 1929.

CHEF NOTE: Store tomatoes stem side down at room temperature to ripen fully. Keep them out of direct sunlight or they will ripen unevenly. Never refrigerate tomatoes; cold temperatures damage the fruit. To easily snip basil: Stack four or five basil leaves at a time and roll them into a cigar shape. Cut narrow strips with a kitchen scissors. Separate strips with your fingers.

1 pound bacon
½ cup thinly sliced scallions
¼ teaspoon minced garlic
4 large tomatoes, peeled and cored
½ teaspoon salt
1 teaspoon dried oregano
¼ teaspoon crushed red pepper flakes
2 prepared deep-dish (9-inch) piecrusts
1 cup snipped fresh basil
6 ounces Gruyère cheese, shredded
¼ cup mayonnaise
1 egg, lightly beaten

1. In separate batches, microwave 6 slices bacon between paper toweling for 5 minutes or until crispy. Crumble bacon into a small bowl. Add scallions and garlic. Mix well and set aside.

2. Cut each peeled tomato in half. Gently scoop out seeds with your fingertip. Cut each tomato half into 3 thick slices. Drain slices on paper toweling.

3. Mix together salt, oregano, and red pepper flakes in a small bowl.

4. **To assemble:** In one piecrust, place ½ of the tomato slices and sprinkle with ½ the spice mixture. Layer with ½ the bacon mixture and ½ the basil. Repeat layers: tomato slices, spices, bacon mixture, basil. (Mixture will be mounded.)

5. With clean hands, mix shredded cheese and mayonnaise in a medium bowl. Press cheese mixture evenly onto tomato mound.

6. Invert second piecrust, in tin, over tomato and cheese mound. Gently loosen edges of crust and remove tin. Gently crimp the edges together to form a seam. Cut four 1-inch slits in the top of crust. Brush beaten egg generously over the entire piecrust, including the seamed edges. (Pie will hold for up to 2 hours in the refrigerator before baking.)

7. **To bake and serve:** Preheat oven to 375°F. Place pie on a baking sheet. Bake for 30 minutes or until crust is golden brown. Remove pie from oven and allow it to rest 5 minutes before serving. (Pie can rest for up to 30 minutes and be served at room temperature.)

Eggplant Parmesan

4 medium purple eggplants
salt
1 tablespoon olive oil
2 large garlic cloves, minced
2 (14.5-ounce) cans whole tomatoes
2 tablespoons tomato paste
⅛ teaspoon freshly ground black pepper

1 tablespoon chopped fresh oregano
2 tablespoons chopped fresh flat-leafed parsley
½ cup flour
1 cup canola oil
1 (8-ounce) package shredded part-skim mozzarella cheese
1 cup grated Parmesan cheese

1. Cut eggplants into ½-inch slices. Sprinkle both sides of each slice with salt and place in a colander. Allow eggplants to drain for 1 hour.

2. Meanwhile, place olive oil and garlic in a large saucepan over medium heat and cook for 1 minute or until aromatic. Add tomatoes, tomato paste, ¼ teaspoon salt, pepper, oregano, and parsley. Bring to a boil. Reduce heat to low, cover, and simmer for 30 minutes.

3. Pat eggplant slices dry. Place flour in a strainer and dust both sides of eggplant slices with flour and place dusted slices on paper toweling. Working in batches, coat a large nonstick skillet with canola oil and fry eggplant slices over medium-high heat until they are lightly browned on both sides. (Add oil in small increments, per batch, as eggplant will immediately soak up available oil.) Place cooked eggplant slices on paper toweling to drain.

4. **To assemble:** Coat a 13 x 9-inch baking dish with vegetable cooking spray. Place one-third tomato sauce mixture evenly on bottom of pan. Place one-third eggplant slices in a layer atop tomato sauce. Place one-third mozzarella atop eggplant slices. Place ⅓ cup Parmesan cheese atop mozzarella. Repeat these layers two more times, ending with Parmesan cheese. (Eggplant Parmesan can be covered at this point and refrigerated for up to 2 days.)

5. **To cook:** Preheat oven to 400°F. Place baking dish in oven, covered with aluminum foil, for 15 minutes. Remove foil and bake for 15 minutes more.

Native to India, eggplant now ranks as one of the world's most popular vegetables. But centuries ago, in parts of Europe, eating eggplant was blamed for everything from madness and leprosy to bad breath and cancer. This may explain why the vegetable didn't become popular in much of England or the United States until the twentieth century. Isolated from Europe and the mainland, early Key West settlers weren't influenced by these myths and legends. Eggplant was one of the few vegetables that thrived in their dooryard gardens, and families loved it.

CHEF NOTE: Scars or bruises on the exterior of an eggplant indicate decay. Look for those with firm, smooth, unwrinkled skin that quickly bounces back when pushed with a fingertip. Eggplants should be symmetrical and heavy, not over 6 inches in diameter. Oversize eggplants could be tough and very bitter.

Elizabeth Russell Pinder said of her family's hardscrabble existence in the upper Keys in 1905: "With no refrigeration, keeping food was a problem. We'd buy salt by the 100-pound sacks and butter in 10 pound tubs, then bury the butter in the salt and keep it until it was gone or the next freight shipment. The butter always had a salty taste." Today we harvest our dooryard gardens to season our butter.

Green Beans with Citrus-Parsley Butter

8 tablespoons (1 stick) butter, room temperature
1 teaspoon finely grated orange peel
1 teaspoon finely grated lemon peel
1 teaspoon finely grated Persian lime peel

3 tablespoons snipped fresh parsley
¼ teaspoon salt
¼ teaspoon white pepper
2 pounds baby green beans

1. **To make citrus-parsley butter:** Place butter, grated citrus peels, parsley, salt, and pepper in a small bowl. Mix well with a spoon. Transfer butter mixture to a 15-inch piece of plastic wrap. Fold plastic wrap over butter mixture and roll, forming a log. Twist ends and place underneath log. Wrap butter log in another piece of plastic wrap and freeze until needed.

2. **To make green beans:** Add 2 inches of water to a large pot and place steamer rack with baby green beans over water. Bring water to boil over high heat and steam beans for 3 to 5 minutes, or just until crisp tender. Drain, rinse with cold water, and drain again. Place beans in a serving dish.

3. Cut a 3-inch piece from the frozen butter log. (Reseal log and return to freezer for future use.) Place butter in a small bowl and microwave for 30 seconds to melt the butter. Toss butter with green beans.

CHEF NOTE: Baby green beans or *haricot verte* are often difficult to find and always very pricey. This recipe works just as well with snap beans, but hand-choose the thinnest, youngest beans you can find.

Grilled Portobello with Gorgonzola

½ cup crumbled Gorgonzola cheese

½ cup light sour cream

4 large portobello mushrooms, about 4 to 5 inches in diameter

2 tablespoons olive oil

4 ½-inch–thick tomato slices, cut from a large tomato

4 ½-inch–thick onion slices, cut from a large sweet onion

seasoned salt

salt and freshly ground black pepper

1. Preheat gas grill. Place Gorgonzola cheese and sour cream in a small bowl. Stir to mix. Cover and refrigerate until needed.

2. Scrape black fins from the undersides of the mushrooms with a teaspoon. Wipe mushrooms clean with a damp paper towel. Brush both sides of mushrooms, tomatoes, and onions generously with olive oil. Sprinkle mushrooms with seasoned salt to taste. Season tomato and onion slices with salt and pepper to taste.

3. **Grill vegetables:** mushrooms, 4 minutes per side; onions, 3 minutes per side; tomatoes, 1 minute per side.

4. **To assemble:** For each mushroom, place portobello on plate. Spread with a thin layer of Gorgonzola sauce. Top with onion and spread with sauce. Crown with tomato and place a dollop of sauce atop. Sprinkle with salt and pepper to taste.

CHEF NOTE: Penzey's 4/S seasoned salt is a wonderful addition to this recipe but you can use your own favorite seasoned salt if you like. You can order Penzey's brand on their website: www.penzeys.com. Crumbled blue cheese or Roquefort can be substituted for the Gorgonzola. To make portobello sandwiches, while vegetables are cooking, toast 4 large sesame buns on grill for 30 seconds. Remove vegetables and buns from grill. Divide Gorgonzola sauce into 8 equal portions, spreading the top and bottom of each bun with 1 portion. Place Portobello mushroom on the bottom bun. Top with onion and then tomato. Place top bun on sandwich and cut into half. Repeat with other 3 sandwiches.

Unavailable in the Florida Keys until the second half of the twentieth century, Gorgonzola cheese was named after a town outside of Milan where it was first made. Gorgonzola is a rich, creamy Italian cow's milk cheese. Dating back to the ninth century, Gorgonzola was aged in caves, where naturally occurring spores caused the cheese's blue veining to develop. Today, meeting strict production standards, the mold spores are mixed in with the curds during the cheese-making process.

Originating more than 5,000 years ago in India, where it looked like a plum and tasted like turpentine, the mango has evolved into one of the sweetest, most sought-after fruits in the world. Called the "peach of the tropics," the mango is widely grown in the Florida Keys. Nearly every yard showcases a mango tree, which can grow up to 60 feet tall. And as any local will tell you, absolutely nothing tastes as good as a tree-ripened fresh mango.

Mango-Sesame Sautéed Spinach

½ cup cider vinegar
1 teaspoon minced garlic
¼ teaspoon hot pepper sauce
½ cup pureed mango
1½ tablespoons sugar
1 tablespoon fresh lime juice
¼ cup extra virgin olive oil

½ tablespoon black sesame seeds
½ tablespoon white sesame seeds, dry toasted
salt and freshly ground black pepper
1 tablespoon olive oil
2 pounds baby spinach, washed and spun dry

1. **Up to 2 days ahead:** Place vinegar, garlic, hot pepper sauce, mango, sugar, and lime juice in a blender. Pulse until mixed. Slowly add olive oil, processing at blender's slowest speed. Add sesame seeds and pulse once or twice to mix. Season to taste with salt and freshly ground black pepper. Refrigerate vinaigrette in a covered container. (Bring dressing to room temperature and shake well to mix before serving.)

2. Place 1 tablespoon olive oil in a large skillet over medium-high heat. When oil is hot add spinach and sauté, stirring and tossing spinach leaves constantly, until spinach has just wilted. Remove from heat immediately. With a slotted spoon, transfer spinach to serving dish. Drizzle spinach with mango-sesame vinaigrette. Fill a small pitcher with additional vinaigrette and offer with spinach.

CHEFS NOTE: White sesame seeds have a nutty flavor that is especially enhanced when dry-toasted in a skillet for a few minutes. Black sesame seeds are more bitter than white. Some feel black sesame seeds should not be toasted because it accentuates the bitter taste, but it really is a matter of individual preference. If you buy sesame seeds in bulk, freeze them or keep them in the refrigerator because they contain a high percentage of oil and could become rancid if kept at room temperature for more than 3 months.

Spaghetti Squash Tamal

 **SERVES 12 TO 18**

1 large spaghetti squash
½ teaspoon salt
¼ teaspoon pepper
2 tablespoons butter
2½ cups minced sweet onions, like Vidalia

½ cup grated Romano cheese
1 (6-ounce) package Martha White cornbread mix
⅔ cup skim milk
½ cup shredded cheddar cheese

1. **Up to 3 hours ahead:** Preheat oven to 350°F Cut spaghetti squash in half lengthwise and remove seeds. Cover a baking sheet with aluminum foil and coat it with vegetable cooking spray. Place squash pieces, cut side down, on the foil. Bake 1½ hours or until squash shreds when pierced with a fork. Shred squash into a large bowl and season with salt and pepper.

2. Meanwhile, melt butter in large skillet over medium heat. Add onions and cook until translucent, about 10 minutes. Add onions and butter to spaghetti squash and mix well. Stir in Romano cheese. Adjust salt and pepper seasoning to taste. Place squash mixture in an 11-inch round or an 11 x 7-inch baking dish that has been coated with cooking spray.

3. About 30 minutes before serving, preheat oven to 450°F. Combine cornbread mix, milk, and cheese in a medium mixing bowl. Stir until well blended. Spoon batter over squash mixture. Bake for 18 to 20 minutes, uncovered, or until cornbread is golden.

CHEF NOTE: The larger the spaghetti squash, the thicker the strands will be and the more flavorful the taste. If you are watching your carbs, try substituting spaghetti squash for pasta and top with your favorite marinara sauce.

Spaghetti squash, an oval-shaped winter squash about 9 inches long and weighing 2 to 3 pounds, is called "the fun squash." Unlike other members of its family, which includes cucumber, watermelon, pumpkin and all the other squashes, spaghetti squash, when cooked, separates into crisp, tender, spaghetti-like strands. With a mild, sweet flavor that lends itself to many innovative preparations, spaghetti squash is a dieters dream—only 37 calories for a 4-ounce serving.

Stuffed Plum Tomatoes

On January 20, 1923, the *Miami Metropolis* noted: "Two weeks ago shipping [tomatoes from the truck farms of the Keys] began to northern and eastern markets, with a total of 5,000 crates at an estimated average net profit of $4 per crate. The quality of the vegetable is far above expectation." After the demise of the pineapple and key lime industries in the upper Keys, tomatoes became a cash crop for a time, with more than 50,000 crates shipped to the north each year at the peak of the crop's popularity near the end of the 1920s.

12 plum tomatoes
6 tablespoons minced yellow onions
½ teaspoon salt
¾ teaspoon freshly ground black pepper

2 tablespoons brown sugar
2 cups soft breadcrumbs
4 tablespoons Parmesan cheese

1. Cut tomatoes in half lengthwise. Scoop out pulp, leaving shell intact. Invert tomatoes on paper toweling to drain. Chop pulp and reserve.

2. Coat a nonstick skillet with vegetable cooking spray. Place skillet over medium-high heat. Add onions and cook until tender, about 3 minutes. Add chopped tomato pulp, salt, pepper, and brown sugar and stir to combine. Add breadcrumbs and mix thoroughly. Remove from heat.

3. Spoon breadcrumb mixture into tomato shells. Top with Parmesan cheese. Place tomatoes in an 11 x 9-inch baking dish, cover with plastic wrap, and refrigerate until ready to bake.

4. Preheat oven to 350°F. Remove plastic wrap from tomatoes. Bake for 15 minutes uncovered.

CHEF NOTE: Recycle your slightly stale bread for this and other recipes. Process it into crumbs in a food processor. Transfer the crumbs to a plastic zipper bag and freeze them. Then, when you need soft breadcrumbs for a recipe, you can simply measure out the frozen crumbs and add them to your preparation.

Sugar Snap Peas with Almond-Balsamic Vinaigrette

2 slices bacon

2 tablespoons minced red onions

2 tablespoons chopped almonds

1½ tablespoons dark brown sugar

2½ tablespoons balsamic vinegar

1 pound sugar snap peas

freshly ground black pepper

1. **Up to 1 day ahead:** Place bacon between two pieces of paper toweling on a microwave-proof plate. Microwave bacon on high for 2 minutes. Crumble bacon and set aside.

2. Place small nonstick skillet coated with cooking spray over medium heat. Add onions and sauté for 1 minute. Stir almonds into onions and sauté for 1 minute. Reduce heat to low. Add brown sugar and stir to coat almonds and onions. Add vinegar and heat, stirring constantly, until sugar is dissolved, less than 1 minute. Remove from heat and add crumbled bacon. Stir well. Place in a covered container and refrigerate until needed.

3. About 15 minutes before serving, place a large saucepan with steamer rack and 2 inches of water over medium-high heat. Add peas to steamer and steam for 3 to 5 minutes or until crisp-tender. Drain peas, rinse with cold water, and drain again.

4. Meanwhile, microwave vinaigrette for 1 minute or until heated through. Place beans back in pot and toss with vinaigrette. Place dressed beans on a platter and serve warm or cover platter with cling wrap until needed (up to 30 minutes) and serve at room temperature.

CHEF NOTE: You don't need to buy the crème de la crème of balsamic vinegar for this recipe ($30 to $40/bottle)—save that for a tomato, basil, and mozzarella salad. But expect to pay about $15 for a decent bottle of real balsamic vinegar.

Balsamic vinegar, as most of us know it, is an American marketing phenomenon that has almost nothing in common with real balsamic vinegar. Ninety-five percent of such vinegar found in our supermarkets is red wine vinegar with caramel coloring. Real balsamic vinegar has been produced for scores of centuries in Modena and Reggio-Emilia, Italy, and aged in wooden barrels, like wine, for a minimum of 12 years. The very best is as precious and expensive as a rare wine and is used, drop-by-drop, as a condiment or seasoning. Fausto's Food Palace in Key West (522 Fleming Street) has a good selection of quality, mid-priced balsamic vinegars.

Vegetable Rolls with Yogurt-Mint Sauce

Culinary traditions from nearby Caribbean countries have long influenced the cuisine of the Florida Keys. Now, in the twenty-first century, new inspirations from far-flung countries around the globe are translating ho-hum ingredients into new taste sensations. These vegetable rolls marry common root vegetables, dries fruits, and traditional Middle Eastern seasonings, evoking the essence of Persian empire.

1 tablespoon sesame oil

4 small yellow onions, chopped

2 cups grated carrots

10 garlic cloves, minced, plus 2 cloves garlic, crushed

½ cup raisins

½ cup diced dried apricots

½ teaspoon cumin seeds

¼ teaspoon ground cinnamon

⅛ teaspoon cayenne pepper

2 tablespoons fresh lemon juice

2 tablespoons honey

3 teaspoons salt, divided

freshly ground black pepper

½ cup pine nuts, dry-toasted

16 ounces plain yogurt

1 English cucumber or 2 small cucumbers, peeled, seeded, and grated

3 tablespoons finely chopped fresh mint

½ pound goat cheese

1 package (20 count) Azuma® egg-roll wrappers (about 6 inches square)

1 tablespoon butter or margarine, melted

1. Place oil in a large, nonstick skillet over medium-high heat. When oil is hot, add onions, carrots, and minced garlic. Cook for 10 minutes, stirring frequently. Transfer vegetables to a large mixing bowl. Add raisins, apricots, cumin seeds, cinnamon, and cayenne pepper. Toss together then add lemon juice, honey, 2 teaspoons salt, 1 teaspoon freshly ground black pepper, and pine nuts. Mix together well and allow mixture to cool for about 20 minutes. (Mixture can be placed in an airtight container and refrigerated for up to 2 days.)

2. Meanwhile, prepare the yogurt-mint sauce: Mash crushed garlic cloves and 1 teaspoon salt together in a medium bowl. Stir in yogurt, cucumber, and mint. Season further with salt and pepper to taste. Cover and place in the refrigerator to chill. (Sauce can be refrigerated up to 1 week; it does not freeze well.)

3. Preheat oven to 400°F. Divide goat cheese into 15 equal-size pieces. Working with 1 wrapper at a time, on a clean, dry, flat surface, place the wrapper with point facing toward you. Brush top point with a little melted butter. Place about 2 teaspoons vegetable filling in the center of the wrapper, shaping the filling into a log. Top filling with a piece of cheese.

4. Fold the wrapper envelope style: First fold in the left and right points, then fold the point nearest you over the filling, and roll wrapper to completely enclose the filling, sealing roll with the buttered point. Repeat process with the remaining 14 wrappers. Place vegetable rolls, seam side down, on a foil-lined baking sheet. Bake 5 minutes and turn rolls. Bake 5 minutes more or until rolls are golden and crispy.

5. Serve vegetable rolls topped with a yogurt-mint sauce.

CHEF NOTE: The traditional wrap for these rolls is a cross between phyllo dough and a spring roll wrapper. Azuma Large Egg Roll Wrappers (20 to a package) are a great New World substitute and can be found in most supermarkets. You can prepare and bake the vegetable rolls up to 2 days ahead and refrigerate them. Simply reheat rolls at 300°F for about 5 minutes before serving. Serve as an appetizer, a vegetarian entrée, or a vegetable course alongside a grilled steak or chop.

Rice, Beans, Tubers, and Pasta

4

Side dishes on an early Keys dinner table usually consisted of only those vegetables that could be successfully grown in the dooryard garden, such as plantains, eggplants, and okra. Other dietary staples—black beans, black-eyed peas, rice, flour, sweet and white potatoes, grits, and dried garbanzos and navy beans—were ordered in bulk and delivered to the islands only sporadically by ship from the mainland or from Cuba.

Rice was the most popular side dish, followed closely by grits—which some considered "the staff of Key West life"—and black beans. The first major Cuban immigration in the 1860s introduced different fresh starches to the island—boniatos, malanga, yucca, calabaza, breadfruit, and chayote—all of which, imported from Cuba, have become staples in most Keys Cuban communities.

Pasta was first brought to the Keys with the advent of the railroad and the influx of "strangers" but didn't really take hold here until the latter part of the twentieth century when all of America began its love affair with noodles. Virtually all the cultures influencing today's Conchfusion cuisine use some form of noodles in their cooking—Japanese, Chinese, Italian, German, Indonesian, even the Arab countries of the Middle East. These imported dietary staples of today's cuisine are increasingly available in Florida Keys supermarkets.

LEFT: *Twenty-first century Keys resorts are a far cry from pioneer homesteads.*
Credit: Little Palm Island Resort & Spa.

Bowties Dressed with No-cook Sun-dried Tomato Sauce

In the days before modern canning methods, Italians dried sliced summer tomatoes on their tile roofs for use in winter months. Dehydrated by the sun, the tomatoes became sweet, chewy, and flavorful. Early Keys pioneers undoubtedly did the same. Today, most tomatoes labeled "sun-dried" are commercially dried in ovens and dehydrators and then either dry-packed or packed in oil. Dry-packed sun-dried tomatoes should be rehydrated before using.

2 (14.5-ounce) cans chopped tomatoes, drained

10 sun-dried tomatoes, rehydrated in water 5 minutes, drained and chopped

2 tablespoons capers, rinsed and drained

½ cup pine nuts, dry-toasted

1 tablespoon minced garlic

¼ cup grated Parmesan cheese

½ cup snipped fresh basil leaves, cut in thin strips

1 pound dried bowtie pasta

salt and freshly ground black pepper

1. **Up to 1 day ahead:** Combine all ingredients except pasta, salt, and pepper in a large bowl. Place in a covered container and refrigerate overnight.

2. **Before serving:** Place sauce in a large bowl and bring to room temperature. Cook pasta in a large pot to al dente following package instructions, about 12 minutes. Drain pasta and add it to the tomato mixture. Toss well to combine. Season with salt and pepper to taste. Serve with additional Parmesan cheese on the side.

CHEF NOTE: This quick and easy lunch or light supper can be made with penne, ziti, or orecchiette if desired.

Citrus Orzo with Tomato-Basil Feta

½ cup fresh orange juice
½ cup plus 1 tablespoon olive oil
1 tablespoon fresh lemon juice
4 teaspoons grated fresh orange peel
2 teaspoons grated fresh lemon peel
½ teaspoon ground cinnamon
1 cup grape tomatoes, quartered

2 cups thinly sliced and julienned English cucumbers
1 cup chopped scallions
½ cup chopped fresh mint
8 ounces tomato-basil feta cheese
1 pound orzo pasta
salt and freshly ground black pepper

1. **Early in the day or 1 day ahead:** Whisk together orange juice, ½ cup olive oil, lemon juice, citrus peels, and cinnamon in a small bowl. Transfer to a covered container and refrigerate.

2. Combine tomatoes, cucumbers, scallions, mint, and feta cheese in a medium bowl. Toss to mix well. Transfer to a covered container and refrigerate.

3. **Before serving:** Bring orange juice and tomato mixtures to room temperature. Cook orzo in a large pot of water over high heat to al dente according to package directions. Drain pasta. Place orzo in a large bowl and toss with 1 tablespoon olive oil. Add tomato and orange juice mixtures to orzo and toss well to combine. Season with salt and freshly ground black pepper to taste. Serve immediately or cover and refrigerate for up to 24 hours. Bring to room temperature before serving.

CHEF NOTE: Orzo is one of the most underutilized of all forms of pasta. Resembling kernels of rice or melon seeds, orzo exudes the mouthfeel of risotto-style rice. Orzo means "barley" in Italian.

Citrus trees have long graced dooryard gardens in the Florida Keys, providing an essential component of Keys cuisine for centuries. Today, however, due to a raging outbreak on the mainland of citrus canker (a bacterial disease that causes leaf and fruit drop), Keys residents are restricted from planting non-indigenous citrus trees. If a citrus tree develops the canker, it must be cut down immediately.

Originally grown in China, grape tomatoes were introduced to this country by Andrew Chu, a vegetable grower in Wimauma, Florida, in the late 1990s. Their popularity was meteoric. Grape tomatoes have a higher sugar content than most cherry tomatoes and reportedly have a shelf life of up to 45 days. These kid-friendly tomatoes can be eaten in one squirtless bite.

Feta-Bleu Orecchiette with Roasted Tomatoes and Baby Spinach

1 pound grape tomatoes cut into quarters or 1 pound plum tomatoes cut into eighths
1½ tablespoons olive oil
salt and freshly ground black pepper

1 pound dried orecchiette
2 ounces crumbled blue cheese
3 ounces crumbled feta cheese
4 ounces baby spinach, washed and spun dry

1. Preheat oven to 350°F. Place tomatoes and olive oil in a small bowl. Season with salt and pepper to taste. Transfer tomatoes to a nonstick baking sheet. Spread tomatoes into an even layer. Roast for 10 minutes or until softened and the skin starts to pull away.

2. Meanwhile, cook orecchiette to al dente according to package directions. Drain and set aside.

3. Mix together the blue and feta cheeses in a small bowl. Place half the crumbled cheeses in a large bowl. Add the roasted tomatoes and gently toss until cheese melts. Add the spinach and warm pasta and toss gently. When mixture has cooled slightly, add remaining cheese and toss once again. Season with salt and freshly ground black pepper to taste. Serve warm or at room temperature.

CHEF NOTE: Orecchiette look like little ears or discs of pasta. Spinach should be placed under warm pasta so that it wilts.

Four-Cheese Macaroni Alfredo

1 pound elbow macaroni
4 tablespoons (½ stick) butter
3 tablespoons flour
2 cups chicken broth
¼ cup sherry
1 cup heavy cream
1 cup shredded Fontina cheese

½ cup shredded Gruyère cheese
½ cup shredded Emmenthaler cheese
½ teaspoon thyme
⅛ teaspoon nutmeg
salt and freshly ground black pepper
⅓ cup fresh breadcrumbs
¼ cup grated Parmesan cheese

1. Cook macaroni in a large pot over medium-high heat to al dente according to package directions, about 9 minutes. Drain, return to pot, and set aside.

2. Melt butter in a large nonstick skillet over medium heat. Sprinkle in flour and cook 1 minute, stirring constantly. Gradually add chicken broth, stirring constantly. Bring mixture to a boil and cook 1 to 2 minutes, stirring constantly. Gradually stir in sherry and cream and bring just to a boil. Remove from heat and add Fontina, Gruyère, and Emmenthaler, stirring until the cheeses melt. Add thyme, nutmeg, and salt and pepper to taste. Add cheese sauce to macaroni in pot and mix well.

3. Coat a 13 x 9-inch baking pan with vegetable cooking spray. Place macaroni and cheese mixture into baking pan. Mix breadcrumbs and Parmesan cheese in a small bowl. Sprinkle atop macaroni mixture. Bake uncovered at 375°F for 30 minutes.

CHEF NOTE: This adult version of the kids' favorite, mac'-and-cheese, is fit for a dinner party. Decadently rich, this crowd pleaser can be prepared in advance (up to the baking stage) and frozen until needed. Bring to room temperature before baking.

One-pot meals have long been a dinner staple in the Florida Keys, originating with the English influences of the original Bahamian settlers. Over time, "strangers" brought their own classics south with them, including the ubiquitous macaroni and cheese. Updated to take advantage of the wonderful imported cheeses available in the Keys today—Fontina, Emmenthaler, Gruyère, and Parmigiano Reggiano—this recipe is reminiscent of a fine dish of fettuccine Alfredo.

Pasta with Fresh Spinach, Tomatoes, Mushrooms, and Chick Peas

Says Eliott Barton, chef of Mangia Mangia Restaurant in Key West, who developed this recipe, "The colors on this dish are brilliant due to the quick cooking. The tomatoes are bright red, the spinach a deep green, and the pure white of the feta cheese result in the tri-color so popular in the Italian culture."

½ pound short pasta, such as penne

⅓ cup olive oil

1 cup quartered baby portobello mushrooms

2 teaspoons minced garlic

1 tablespoon diced shallots

⅓ cup canned chick peas, drained

2 tablespoons snipped fresh basil

2 generous pinches oregano

2 shakes crushed red pepper (to taste)

1 large tomato, seeded and cut into 1-inch dice

10-ounces baby spinach, washed and spun dry

salt and freshly ground black pepper

4 ounces feta cheese

1. Cook pasta in a large pot of water to al dente according to package directions. Drain pasta and return it to the pot.

2. While pasta is cooking, place oil in a large nonstick skillet over medium heat. When oil is hot add mushrooms, garlic, shallots, and chick peas. Sauté until mushrooms are almost tender, shallots are translucent, and garlic has lost its raw flavor, 3 to 4 minutes. Add basil, oregano, and crushed red pepper and continue cooking for 30 seconds. Add tomatoes and mix into other ingredients. When tomatoes are heated through, add spinach, cover, and steam until spinach wilts, about 2 minutes. Toss all ingredients so that they are coated with oil. Season to taste with salt and freshly ground black pepper.

3. Divide the pasta between 2 individual serving dishes. Top pasta with half the spinach mixture. Crumble half the feta cheese atop each dish of pasta.

CHEF NOTE: This dish comes together in the time it takes to cook the pasta, so be sure to have all ingredients cleaned, chopped, and ready to go. You can use any short pasta in this recipe. Chef Barton recommends radiatore or miniature lasagna noodles if you can find them.

Spicy Tahini Noodles

1 tablespoon sesame oil

8 scallions, minced, white and green parts separated

6 large cloves garlic, minced

1½ tablespoons minced fresh gingerroot

¾ teaspoon red pepper flakes

1 (14.5-ounce) can vegetable broth

3½ tablespoons sugar

3 tablespoons rice wine vinegar

3 tablespoons soy sauce

2 tablespoons tahini (ground sesame paste)

½ cup white wine vinegar

1 tablespoon Old Bay or Old Savannah seafood seasoning

¾ pound large shrimp (21/25 count)

1 pound dried linguine

1 tablespoon canola oil

1 seedless English cucumber, cut in thin slices, then halved

2 teaspoons sesame seeds, dry toasted

1. **Up to 2 days ahead:** Place sesame oil in a large nonstick skillet over medium heat. When oil is hot, add scallion whites, garlic, gingerroot, and red pepper flakes. Sauté 2 to 3 minutes or until garlic is softened but not browned. Add vegetable broth, sugar, rice wine vinegar, soy sauce, and tahini. Bring to a boil and cook 8 minutes, stirring constantly, or until the tahini has dissolved and mixture has reduced by one-third. Cool to room temperature, transfer to a covered storage container, and refrigerate until just before serving.

2. **Up to 1 day ahead:** Place 2 cups water, white wine vinegar, and seafood seasoning in a large pot over high heat. Bring to a boil. Add shrimp and boil 1 minute or just until shrimp turn pink. Remove from heat and drain in a colander. Rinse with cold water. Transfer to refrigerator until cool enough to handle. Peel and devein shrimp, leaving tails intact. Transfer shrimp to a plastic zipper bag and refrigerate until serving.

3. **One hour before serving:** Place tahini sauce in a small saucepan over low heat. Bring to a simmer until sauce is heated through. Meanwhile, cook linguine in a large pot of water to al dente according to package directions. Drain pasta and return it to the pot. Toss with canola oil. Add tahini sauce and toss to coat.

4. **To serve:** Mound linguine in center of a large serving platter. Border pasta with cucumber slices. Sprinkle scallion greens over cucumber slices. Arrange shrimp over scallion greens and cucumber slices. Sprinkle sesame seeds over tahini noodles and shrimp and serve.

The Middle East and the middle Keys collide in this Conchfusion creation that combines the spicy, peanutty taste of tahini noodles with Florida Keys shrimp. Tahini is a smooth, rich paste made of hulled and ground sesame seeds. Sometimes called "the butter of the Middle East," tahini has a creamy consistency and a strong, nutty flavor.

CHEF NOTE: The cucumber slices and shrimp cool the fire of these noodles. You can find tahini at most supermarkets. (You can make this dish up to 2 hours ahead, cover with plastic wrap, and refrigerate until serving. Bring to room temperature before serving.)

Pasticcio di Spaghetti

The simple definition of pasticcio is "a miscellaneous mixture or a hodgepodge," something Keys cooks have been fashioning for generations. This dish is a mix of cooked pasta, sauce, cheese, and a variety of extras, all baked in a large skillet and upended to form a spaghetti cake. Cuban cooks would have created their hodgepodge with rice, vegetables, and chicken, and Conchs most likely baked theirs with fish and the bounty of their dooryard gardens.

1¼ pounds hot turkey sausage, removed from casing and crumbled

1 (14.5-ounce) can whole tomatoes, drained

15 kalamata olives, pitted

¼ cup snipped fresh basil leaves, cut in thin strips

2 tablespoons capers, rinsed and drained

2 tablespoons olive oil, divided

1 sweet onion, like Vidalia, halved and thinly sliced

1 large clove garlic, minced

¼ teaspoon crushed red pepper flakes

¾ pound thin spaghetti

2 eggs, beaten

¾ cup grated Parmesan or Romano cheese

1. Place crumbled sausage in a large nonstick skillet over medium-high heat. Cook, stirring frequently, until sausage is cooked through, about 5 minutes. Remove sausage with a slotted spoon and drain on paper toweling.

2. Place tomatoes, olives, basil, and capers in a food processor. Pulse until chopped coarsely. Remove tomato mixture to a plate and set aside. Place drained sausage in food processor and pulse until uniformly chopped.

3. Place 1 tablespoon olive oil in a large skillet over medium-high heat. When oil is hot, add onions and sauté, stirring frequently, for 5 minutes or under onions are tender. Add garlic and red pepper flakes and cook 1 minute more. Add tomato mixture and bring to a simmer. Add sausage and stir to mix well. Remove mixture from heat, transfer to a large bowl, and set aside.

4. Add spaghetti to a large pot of boiling water and cook to al dente according to package instructions, about 9 minutes. Drain spaghetti and return to the pot. Add sausage mixture to spaghetti and mix well. Add beaten eggs and toss to evenly coat pasta mixture with egg. Add grated cheese and toss to mix. (Mixture can be refrigerated in a covered container for up to 2 days.)

5. Preheat oven to 400°F. Place 1 tablespoon olive oil in an ovenproof 10-inch skillet. With a basting brush, coat all inner surfaces of skillet with oil. Place skillet over medium-high heat until oil is hot. Place spaghetti mixture in skillet, pressing with the back of a large spoon to form a compact layer. Cook spaghetti mixture, without stirring, for 5 minutes.

6. Remove skillet from stove and place in oven. Bake for 30 minutes or until top is golden brown. Remove from oven. Loosen edges with a knife and invert onto a large serving platter. Cut into wedges and serve.

CHEF NOTE: You can also make this dish in a springform pan if you wish. Simply place it on a round platter and remove the side ring before serving.

Plantains

Introduced to the Florida Keys by Cuban immigrants, plantains quickly became a staple of Conch cooking. Trading schooners from Cuba brought plantains to the Key West market in the early settlement days, but Key West Conchs and Cubans alike soon learned that the plant thrived in their dooryard gardens. Actually a member of the banana family and, therefore, a fruit not a vegetable, plantains could be called the rogue of the clan. At each stage of ripeness, the plantain morphs into an entirely different foodstuff.

A good source of potassium, fiber, and vitamin C, plantains are used in three different stages of maturity—unripe, semi-ripe, and very ripe. They are rarely eaten raw, instead treated as a starchy vegetable and baked, fried, or boiled. Unripe plantains are green and very hard. Most often green plantains are sliced and fried in oil or twice-fried to create *tostones*. Semi-ripe plantains become yellow and are dotted with black spots. These are good for boiling and mashing, or sliced thin and deep-fried as *marquitas*, or plantain chips. When plantains look like overripe bananas, their skins totally brown-black in color and their flesh somewhat mushy, they are fully ripe. At this point, the plantain's starches have turned to sugar and they are ready to bake.

...

Actually a member of the banana family and, therefore, a fruit not a vegetable, plantains could be called the rogue of the clan.

...

Semi-ripe and ripe plantains are easy to peel, but the peel of a green plantain is more difficult to remove. To peel a green plantain, first trim off the ends. Then, with a sharp paring knife, cut four lengthwise slits along the ridges of the skin, being careful not to cut into the flesh. Pull off the strips of skin, one at a time. Use the knife to separate the skin from the flesh if necessary.

Tostones

Serves 4 as a side dish

If you don't have a deep-fat fryer to make these twice-fried green plantains, use a large skillet, fill it three-quarters full with oil, and fry plantains over medium-high heat.

3 green plantains
1 gallon canola oil
salt

1. Make 4 vertical cuts in the skin of each plantain and peel it off. Cut plantain on the diagonal, crosswise, into 1-inch chunks. Meanwhile heat oil to manufacturer's recommended level in a deep-fat fryer to 375°F.

2. Place plantain chunks in fryer's wire basket and submerge into hot oil. Fry for 3 minutes, or until they barely become golden brown. Remove plantains from oil and drain on several pieces of paper toweling.

3. Place several more toweling pieces atop once-fried plantains. With the heel of your hand, flatten the plantain chunks. Place flattened plantains in wire basket and return it to hot oil. Fry until golden brown, about 3 more minutes. Remove tostones and drain on paper toweling. Sprinkle with salt to taste. Serve warm.

Marquitas

Serves 4 for a snack

These fried plantain chips are the Conch answer to potato chips. Serve them with a Cuban press sandwich (see Index).

3 semi-ripe plantains
1 gallon canola oil
salt and pepper

1. Peel plantain. (If skin doesn't come away easily, follow directions for green plantains on previous page.) Cut the plantain, crosswise and on the diagonal, into paper-thin slices using a mandolin or sharp knife. Meanwhile heat oil to manufacturer's recommended level in a deep-fat fryer to 375°F.

2. Place plantain slices in fryer's wire basket and submerge into hot oil. Fry for 3 to 4 minutes, or until golden brown. Remove plantain chips and drain on paper toweling. Sprinkle with salt and pepper to taste. Allow chips to cool.

Baked Sweet Plantains

Serves 4 to 6

Don't let the brown sugar in this recipe fool you into thinking this is dessert fare. Serve it as a starchy side dish to accompany your main entrée.

4 tablespoons butter, divided
4 ripe plantains, peeled and cut on the diagonal into ½-inch-wide slices
¼ cup dark brown sugar
½ cup light rum
¼ cup fresh pineapple juice

1. Preheat oven to 350°F. Place 2 tablespoons butter in an 11 x 7-inch baking dish and microwave for 1 minute to melt butter. Place plantain slices in a single or slightly overlapping layer atop the butter. Sprinkle brown sugar over plantains. Combine rum and pineapple juice in a measuring cup and drizzle over plantains. Cut remaining 2 tablespoons butter in half, then cut each half into tiny pieces (about 20). Sprinkle butter over plantains. Bake, uncovered, for 40 minutes. Remove from oven and turn over each plantain slice in the baking dish. Allow plantains to cool for 10 minutes.

Spinach-Ricotta Pennoni

Nearly every ethnic cuisine on earth has an ongoing love affair with the noodle. The Florida Keys is no exception. Conchfusion cooks benefit from a wide range of gourmet pastas on the market today, such as pennoni. Pennoni is a dried tubular pasta whose ends are cut on a sharp diagonal. Available smooth or with a ridged surface, pennoni is about the same length as penne but much chunkier and wider.

3 tablespoons olive oil

1 cup chopped sweet onions, like Vidalia

2 cloves garlic, minced

10 ounces fresh baby spinach, washed and spun dry

15 ounces ricotta cheese

1 extra-large egg, slightly beaten

½ cup snipped fresh curly parsley

3½ ounces prosciutto, thinly sliced then diced

½ teaspoon salt, divided

½ teaspoon freshly ground black pepper, divided

1 cup Parmesan cheese, divided

1½ tablespoons butter

1½ tablespoons flour

2 cups whole milk

dash of nutmeg

1 pound dried pennoni or other short tubular pasta

1. Place olive oil in a 5-quart pot over medium-high heat. When oil is hot, add onions and garlic. Sauté, stirring frequently, until onions are soft and garlic is fragrant, about 3 minutes. Add spinach and sauté, stirring constantly, until spinach is just wilted, about 1½ minutes. Remove from heat. Transfer spinach mixture to a colander to cool and drain.

2. Place ricotta, beaten egg, parsley, prosciutto, ¼ teaspoon salt, ¼ teaspoon pepper, and ⅓ cup Parmesan cheese in a large bowl. Mix well with a spoon to combine. Set aside.

3. Melt butter in a large saucepan over medium-low heat. Add flour and whisk for 2 minutes to form a roux. Increase heat to high. Add milk in a slow stream, whisking constantly, and bring mixture to a boil. Reduce heat to low and whisk in ¼ teaspoon salt, ¼ teaspoon pepper, and dash of nutmeg. Remove from heat and whisk in ⅓ cup Parmesan cheese. Place cover on pan.

4. Chop drained spinach mixture and add it to ricotta mixture. Stir to combine well.

5. Meanwhile, bring a large pot of water to boil over high heat. Add pennoni, reduce heat to medium-high, and bring it back to boil. Cook, stirring occasionally so that pasta doesn't stick, for 10 minutes or until pennoni is al dente and still maintains a tubular shape. Drain in a colander and rinse well with cold water. Drain again.

6. **To assemble:** Coat a 13 x 9-inch baking dish with vegetable cooking spray. Spread 1 cup cheese sauce in bottom of baking dish. With a small spoon, stuff each pasta tube with spinach mixture (make about 22 tubes). Place stuffed pasta close together in the cheese sauce in a single layer. Pour remaining 1 cup cheese sauce evenly over stuffed pasta. Sprinkle remaining 1/3 cup Parmesan cheese over sauce. (Cover baking dish with aluminum foil and refrigerate until needed, up to 24 hours. Bring to room temperature before baking.)

7. **To cook:** Preheat oven to 425°F. Bake pennoni for 20 minutes, covered, until it is bubbly. Remove foil. Turn on broiler. Broil pasta 5 minutes or until top is lightly browned.

CHEF NOTE: If you can't find pennoni or other short, wide tubular pasta, you can substitute the longer dried cannelloni in this recipe.

Coconut Basmati Rice Pilaf

The coconut's origins have never been fully agreed upon, but coconuts were noted in sixth-century Egypt, and Marco Polo found them in India and elsewhere in the Far East on his travels. The buoyant, waterproof coconut shell allowed coconuts to travel by sea as far as the tropics, where they washed ashore, sprouted, and multiplied. All parts of the coconut tree were used by the indigenous peoples of these tropical islands: wood from tree trunks for building houses and furniture; leaves to weave thatch roofs and fences; shells for kitchenware and utensils; oil pressed from the dry nut; and, of course, the flavorful coconut milk and flesh, which became the basis for most tropical cuisines.

2 cups basmati rice
1 (14-ounce) can coconut milk
1½ teaspoons salt
¼ cup butter

½ cup diced sweet onions, like Vidalia
½ cup golden raisins
½ cup roughly chopped cashews
salt and freshly ground black pepper

1. Place rice in a large, nonstick pot. Cover rice with water and, with your hands, agitate the rice, releasing the starch. Pour off the cloudy water and repeat this process until the water is clear. Pour off the water a final time and drain rice in a colander. Place drained rice, 2 cups water, coconut milk, and salt in a large pot. Stir to combine. Bring to a fast boil over high heat. Reduce heat to low. Cover pot and simmer rice until just tender and liquid is absorbed, about 25 to 30 minutes.

2. Meanwhile, melt butter in a large nonstick skillet. Add onions, raisins, and cashews. Sauté, stirring occasionally, for 3 minutes.

3. When liquid has been absorbed and rice is tender, fluff rice with a fork. Add onion mixture to rice and toss with a fork. Season with salt and pepper to taste. Transfer to serving bowl. (Rice can be chilled and refrigerated overnight. Microwave for 3 minutes or until heated through before serving.)

CHEF NOTE: Substitute dried cranberries or dried cherries for the raisins for a different flavor boost. Rehydrate them in ¼-cup warm water and then drain them before using in this recipe.

Cuban Black Beans

1 (14-ounce) package dried black beans
1½ teaspoons salt, divided
2 tablespoons olive oil
1 large yellow onion, chopped
1 large green pepper, chopped
4 large cloves garlic, minced

1 teaspoon dried oregano
¼ teaspoon freshly ground black
 pepper
2 bay leaves
1 teaspoon sugar (optional)
½ teaspoon vinegar (optional)

1. **One day ahead:** Sort through beans, discarding broken ones. Rinse and drain beans. Place beans in a large soup pot and cover with 8 cups water. Cover pot and allow beans to soak at room temperature overnight.

2. When beans have soaked for 24 hours, place pot (with beans and soaking water) over high heat. Add 1 teaspoon salt. Cover pot and bring to a boil. Reduce heat to medium-low and cook for 2 hours or until beans are tender. (Test tenderness by pinching a bean between your thumb and index finger. If the bean feels soft and it splits when pinched, it is done.) If water evaporates completely while cooking beans, add a little more so that the beans will be suspended in liquid and not burn.

3. Meanwhile, place olive oil in a large nonstick skillet over medium heat. When oil is hot add onions, green peppers, garlic, oregano, ½ teaspoon salt, and black pepper. Sauté, stirring frequently, for 5 minutes or until onions have softened and mixture is fragrant. Remove from heat and set aside until needed.

4. When beans are tender add onion mixture and bay leaves. Stir well to combine. Reduce heat to low. Cook beans uncovered, stirring occasionally, for 30 minutes more, or until liquid reduces to form black bean gravy that is thick and creamy. Add sugar or vinegar if desired, stirring well to blend flavors. Remove bay leaves before serving.

Frijoles negros, or black beans, are a staple of Cuban cuisine. Cuban black beans are often served topped with a cupful of hot yellow rice. Dried black beans must be picked through carefully to remove small stones and discolored or misshapen beans, and then rinsed thoroughly. The beans should be soaked for at least 10 hours to rehydrate before they are cooked.

CHEF NOTE: Cubans generally do not put vinegar in their black beans, usually preferring the addition of a little sugar for a slightly sweet taste instead. If you prefer your beans a bit tarter, delete the sugar and add an equal amount of vinegar instead. Or, you can opt for neither.

Pineapple-Currant Couscous

1 cup currants
½ cup pineapple juice
⅓ cup minced sweet onions, like Vidalia
1 tablespoon apple cider vinegar

2 cups water
1 tablespoon butter
1 (7-ounce) package Casbah couscous with roasted garlic and olive oil

The instant-cooked grain marketed as couscous today is actually made from semolina flour and could technically be considered pasta. Millet couscous, long a staple in the cuisine of North Africa, was relegated to use as bird or poultry feed in Western cultures until recently. Millet couscous has been steamed and cracked, much like bulgur wheat and requires a longer cooking time than instant couscous.

1. Place currants, pineapple juice, onions, and vinegar in a small bowl. Mix with a spoon to combine. Set aside to allow currants to plump in the juices.

2. Place water and butter in a 2-quart saucepan over medium-high heat and bring to a boil. Add couscous. Bring again to a boil. Remove saucepan from heat, and cover pan. Allow couscous to rest 5 minutes, then fluff with a fork. Add currant mixture and toss with a fork to combine with couscous. Cover pan and allow couscous to cool to room temperature before serving.

CHEF NOTE: You can substitute mango or apricot nectar or orange juice for the pineapple juice if you like. The seasoned couscous is essential to this recipe, but you can substitute another brand if you can't find Casbah brand. Simply follow directions on the box to prepare.

Tomato, Basil, and Mozzarella Risotto

2 cups seeded and diced tomatoes

¼ cup snipped fresh basil

1 tablespoon plus 2 teaspoons olive oil

½ teaspoon salt

1 large clove garlic, minced

5¼ cups (42 ounces) low-fat chicken broth

½ cup finely chopped sweet onions, like Vidalia

1½ cups uncooked Arborio rice

⅓ cup chardonnay or dry white wine

½ cup shredded part-skim mozzarella cheese

¼ teaspoon freshly ground black pepper

1. Combine tomatoes, basil, 1 tablespoon olive oil, salt, and garlic in a small bowl. Stir to combine. Set aside.

2. Bring chicken broth to a simmer in a medium saucepan over medium-low heat (do not boil). Reduce heat to low and keep broth warm.

3. Place 2 teaspoons olive oil in a large nonstick skillet over medium-high heat. Add onions and sauté until softened, about 2 minutes. Add rice and cook for 1 minute, stirring constantly. Add wine and cook 1 minute or until liquid is almost absorbed, stirring constantly. Add ½ cup warm broth and stir constantly, until broth is absorbed. Continue adding broth, ½ cup at a time and stirring until all broth is absorbed, about 20 minutes.

4. Add tomato mixture and cook 2 minutes, stirring constantly. Remove risotto from heat. Stir in cheese and pepper. Serve immediately.

CHEF NOTE: More difficult to find than Arborio, Superfino Carnaroli rice is considered the finest of the risotto rices. Look for it in gourmet specialty stores.

Rice has long been a food staple in the Florida Keys, routinely arriving by ship in the early days of the Keys. Arborio rice, traditionally used in risotto, is a more recent introduction to the islands. This rice has short, chunky grains that release starches when cooked. The kernels swell as the risotto liquid is absorbed and stick together slightly, giving the resulting dish a creamy consistency.

Rice Pilaf Timbales

Pine nuts, also known as pignolia or pinon, are actually the seeds of stone pine trees that grow along Italy's Mediterranean coast. The kernels are hand-harvested from the pine's cones, where they grow encased in hard husks between the scales of the cone. High in protein, pine nuts become rancid quickly, so they should be stored in the freezer and dry-toasted before using.

2 cups uncooked basmati rice
10 threads saffron
2 tablespoons pine nuts
8 ounces small shrimp, cooked, peeled and chopped in food processor
1 teaspoon olive oil
1 (10-ounce) package fresh spinach
6 tablespoons butter, divided

1 cup chopped yellow onions
1 clove garlic, minced
¼ teaspoon salt
⅛ teaspoon freshly ground black pepper
ground nutmeg
6-cup heatproof mold
parsley sprigs

1. Place rice in a large, nonstick pot. Cover rice with water and, with your hands, agitate the rice, releasing the starch. Pour off the cloudy water and repeat this process until the water is clear. Pour off the water a final time and drain rice in a colander. Return rice to pot and add 3 cups water. Bring to a boil, uncovered, over medium heat. Reduce heat to low, cover with a tight-fitting lid and cook for 12 minutes or until water is absorbed and rice is tender. Remove from heat and fluff rice with a fork.

2. Place 2½ cups cooked rice in each of two medium bowls. Grind saffron threads with a mortar and pestle until finely powdered. Add saffron to rice in one bowl and toss to combine. Place pine nuts in a small, nonstick skillet over medium heat. Toss until toasted, about 2 to 3 minutes. Add toasted pine nuts to saffron rice and mix well. Mix chopped shrimp with the white rice in the second bowl. Set both bowls of rice aside.

3. Place olive oil in a large pot over medium-high heat. Add spinach and sauté, stirring constantly, until just wilted, about 3 minutes. Drain spinach in a strainer, pushing spinach against strainer with the back of a spoon to release as much water as possible. Coarsely chop spinach, then drain and press again. Set aside.

4. Place 3 tablespoons butter in a medium skillet over medium heat. When butter is melted, add onions and sauté for 4 minutes or until golden. Add garlic and sauté for 1 minute. Add chopped spinach and sauté for 1 minute more. Add salt, pepper, and a sprinkling of nutmeg to taste. Set aside.

5. **To assemble**: Butter the mold. Place the pine nut-saffron rice in the mold and press firmly with the back of a spoon to form a tight layer. Repeat this process with the spinach mixture and finally the shrimp rice, each time pressing the mixtures firmly into the mold with the back of a spoon. Divide the remaining butter into 20 small pieces and sprinkle evenly across top of rice mold. Press each butter piece into the rice.

6. Preheat oven to 375°F. Bake rice mold, uncovered, for 30 minutes, or until rice is heated through. Invert mold on a serving platter. Tap bottom of mold several times, then carefully remove mold. Garnish rice mold with sprigs of parsley.

CHEF NOTE: This colorful timbale of rice, spinach, and shrimp can be assembled ahead of time and refrigerated for up to 12 hours. (Bring to room temperature before baking.) You can use previously cooked rice if you like.

Saffron Basmati Rice

Introduced on Duck Key by one of my dearest longtime friends—an Iranian-born avid angler and parttime resident—this dish follows the traditional Persian method for cooking rice. The rice is slowly steamed, then inverted like an upside-down-cake onto a platter. In a Persian household, the golden-brown, crunchy *tadik* that tops the rice "cake" is the most coveted part of the meal.

CHEF NOTE: This aromatic rice is a little tricky to make at first, but worth every bit of effort. It is most successful when made in a large quantity. The rice freezes wonderfully. Divide leftover rice into meal-size portions and freeze in airtight containers. Simply microwave to reheat.

3 cups basmati rice
2 teaspoons salt
3 tablespoons olive oil

3 tablespoons butter
10 threads saffron, ground

1. Place rice in a large, nonstick pot. Cover rice with water and, with your hands, agitate the rice, releasing the starch. Pour off the cloudy water and repeat this process until the water is clear. Pour off the water a final time, then add cold water to 3 inches above the rice, about 12 cups. Add salt to water.

2. Cover pot and place over high heat. Bring rice and water to a rolling boil (keep an eye on this as it can boil over quickly). Reduce heat to medium-high, remove cover, and boil rice, stirring occasionally, until it softens, starts to puff, and tastes al dente, about 5 to 7 minutes.

3. Remove pot from heat and drain rice in a colander. Thoroughly rinse drained rice with cold water and drain again. Set rice in colander aside. Wipe out the pot with paper toweling to remove any starch residue and return it to the burner over high heat. Add olive oil and butter. When butter is melted and mixture is blended, remove 2 tablespoons of mixture to a small cup and set aside. In a small bowl, dissolve ground saffron with about 1/3 cup boiling water. Add to oil-butter mixture in the pot and stir to mix.

4. Add drained rice to the pot. With a wooden spoon, press rice around the edges, creating a small space between rice and edge of pot around the circumference. With the handle of the spoon, poke 6 holes in the rice to the bottom of the pan. Drizzle reserved 2 tablespoons oil-butter mixture into the holes. Cook on high heat so that liquid under rice boils. When steam rises in the space between rice and edges of pot and from the holes poked in the rice, place 3 pieces of paper toweling atop pot, making sure all edges are covered. Replace lid and press down so that pot is sealed completely. Reduce heat to low and steam rice for at least 1 hour or up to 1 1/2 hours, without removing lid.

5. **To serve:** Remove lid and paper toweling. Place a large platter over pot. Gripping both pot handles and platter, upend contents of pot onto platter. Rice will be held together as if in a large cake by the crispy covering of *tadik*. (If *tadik* should stick to the pan, remove it with a spatula and place atop rice on platter.)

Yellow Rice

1 tablespoon olive oil

1 cup chopped sweet onions, like Vidalia

1 cup chopped green bell peppers

2 large plum tomatoes, chopped

1½ cups water

¼ teaspoon ground annatto or ⅛ teaspoon ground saffron

½ teaspoon salt

¼ teaspoon freshly ground black pepper

1 cup long-grained rice, washed and drained

1. Place olive oil in a 4-quart saucepan over medium-high heat. Add onions and peppers and sauté, stirring frequently until onions become translucent, about 2 minutes. Add tomatoes, water, ground annatto, salt, and pepper. Stir mixture and bring it to a boil. Add rice gradually, stirring constantly, and bring to a boil again. Reduce heat to low, cover, and simmer for 25 to 30 minutes or until all liquid has been absorbed. Fluff rice with a fork before transferring to a serving dish.

CHEF NOTE: Ground annatto seed, slightly sweet and spicy, is commonly added to Cuban rice as a coloring, instead of the more expensive saffron. The whole seeds are known as *achiote* seeds in Mexican and Latin markets. This rice recipe, updated from an early 1900s recipe, is rather bland, which is the way Conchs preferred it. If you want to add a kick to the dish, add ¼ teaspoon crushed red pepper flakes.

Yellow rice was a virtual staple of every meal for early Key Westers—Conchs and Cubans alike. They believed properly cooked rice must have light, fluffy grains that do not stick together. Such rice was referred to as "one-one" because each grain was separate.

Apple-Bacon Roasted Golds

Even with our copious tropical bounty, apples remain one of the coveted fruits that can't be grown in a dooryard garden. Gala apples appear in the late summer—a whirl of red-orange with yellowish stripes. Crunchy, juicy, and full of flavor, they were developed in New Zealand in 1934 as a cross between Kidds Orange Red and Golden Delicious apples.

1½ pounds Yukon Gold potatoes, peeled

2 tablespoons olive oil

salt and freshly ground black pepper

4 regular slices bacon, cut into ½-inch pieces

½ cup diced sweet onions, like Vidalia

⅓ cup apple-cider vinegar

1 Gala or other sweet-tart apple, peeled, cored, and diced

1 tablespoon snipped fresh parsley

1 teaspoon snipped fresh chives

1. Preheat oven to 400°F. Cut potatoes in half lengthwise, then slice them into ½-inch-thick pieces. Place potatoes in a medium bowl and add olive oil. Toss to combine. Season with salt and pepper to taste and toss again. Coat a baking sheet with vegetable cooking spray. Spread the potatoes in a single layer on sheet and roast until slightly browned and easily pierced with a fork, 18 to 20 minutes. Remove from oven and set aside.

2. Meanwhile, place bacon in a large nonstick skillet over medium-high heat and cook, stirring frequently, until crispy, about 10 minutes. Using a slotted spoon, transfer bacon to paper toweling to drain. Add onions to the skillet and cook, stirring occasionally, until the onions have softened, about 3 minutes. Reduce heat to low. Add vinegar, stirring to mix well. Add the roasted potatoes, diced apples, and bacon and gently fold everything together until evenly coated. (Can remove from heat and hold at this point for up to 30 minutes. Reheat on low for 2 minutes or serve at room temperature.) Add parsley and chives just before serving. Adjust salt and pepper to taste. Gently toss to combine.

CHEF NOTE: Instead of chives, try adding fresh rosemary, tarragon, or dill for a change of pace.

Grandma's Potato Salad

 SERVES 8

6 large Yukon Gold potatoes, boiled, skinned, and diced

1 medium sweet onion, like Vidalia, diced

1 cup diced celery

4 hard-boiled eggs, peeled and chopped

1 cup Miracle Whip or mayonnaise

1 teaspoon yellow mustard

2 teaspoons sugar

2 tablespoons milk

salt and freshly ground black pepper

1. Mix together potatoes, onions, celery, and eggs in a large bowl. In a separate medium bowl, mix together Miracle Whip, mustard, sugar and then add milk, one tablespoon at a time, to thin. Toss dressing with potato mixture, coating ingredients thoroughly. Season with salt and freshly ground black pepper to taste. Cover potato salad and refrigerate for at least 2 hours or overnight to chill thoroughly.

CHEF NOTE: My family wouldn't consider buying deli potato salad. This recipe originated with my German grandmother and now my grown children serve it as well. We think using Miracle Whip is essential, but you can use mayonnaise for an equally tasty dish; just add a little more sugar.

It is said that during the Alaskan gold rush of 1897, potatoes were practically worth their weight in gold. They were so valued for their vitamin C content that miners actually traded gold for potatoes. Perhaps that is why Canadian botanists who cross-bred a North American white potato with a wild South American yellow-fleshed variety named their discovery Yukon Gold, now wildly popular. Florida, too, is poised to hit potato gold. In early 2006 growers will begin marketing a yellow-fleshed baking potato that has 25 percent fewer calories and 30 percent fewer carbohydrates than the other gold potatoes.

Garlic-Onion Mashed Potatoes with Make-ahead Herb Gravy

Thanksgiving and Christmas holiday meals in the Florida Keys mirror those up north, with turkey, mashed potatoes, and gravy starring center-stage. With temperatures in the 70s or 80s, however, preparing such a feast without the cook wilting in the kitchen requires some advance planning and maneuvering.

POTATOES

4 pounds Yukon Gold potatoes, peeled and cut into 1-inch chunks

1 tablespoon salt

4 tablespoons butter

3 cloves garlic, peeled and finely minced

$\frac{1}{2}$ cup minced sweet onions, like Vidalia

$1\frac{1}{2}$ cup hot milk

1 teaspoon salt

$\frac{1}{2}$ teaspoon black pepper

1. **Early in the day:** Place potatoes and salt in a large pot with water to cover. Bring to boil on high, reduce heat to medium, and cook about 12 minutes or until tender. Meanwhile, sauté butter, garlic, and minced onions in a small skillet for 3 minutes or until onions are translucent. Remove from heat. Drain potatoes.

2. Place a food mill over a large bowl and rice potatoes. When last of potatoes is placed in food mill, add butter, garlic, and onion mixture and process it through food mill. (Bits of onion and garlic will remain in the food mill.) Then pour milk, $\frac{1}{2}$ cup at a time, through the food mill. Mix potatoes with a large spoon after each addition of milk. Add salt and pepper and stir potatoes until smooth. Place potato mixture in a 2-quart ovenproof dish that has been coated with vegetable cooking spray. Cool, cover with plastic wrap, then aluminum foil, and refrigerate until needed.

3. **To serve:** Preheat oven to 325°F. Remove plastic wrap from potatoes and re-cover tightly with aluminum foil. Place in oven for 30 minutes or until potatoes are heated through.

GRAVY

½ cup minced sweet onions, like Vidalia

1 medium clove garlic, minced

2 cups canned chicken broth

3 tablespoons flour

¼ cup apple juice

1 tablespoon lemon juice

½ cup evaporated skim milk

1 teaspoon Gravy Master or Kitchen Bouquet

1 teaspoon finely minced fresh rosemary

¼ teaspoon dried thyme, crushed

⅛ teaspoon salt

¼ teaspoon freshly ground black pepper

3 tablespoons turkey drippings (optional)

1. **Up to 2 days ahead:** Sauté onions and garlic in 3 tablespoons chicken broth in a medium saucepan over medium heat for 4 minutes. Add flour and stir 1 minute. Slowly add the rest of the broth, stirring constantly. Add apple juice, lemon juice, evaporated milk, Gravy Master, rosemary, thyme, salt, and pepper. Bring to a boil, reduce heat to low and simmer for 10 minutes, until thickened slightly. Remove from heat and place in a blender. Pulse on liquefy for 30 seconds. Place in a covered container and refrigerate until needed.

2. **To serve:** Thirty minutes before serving, place gravy in a saucepan over low heat. Simmer on low, stirring occasionally, until ready to serve. (If you are serving mashed potatoes and gravy with roast turkey, whisk in 3 tablespoons turkey drippings.) Makes 2 cups.

CHEF NOTE: I rice these potatoes through a food mill. Though it is more work, the result is rich, creamy, and lump-free. Best of all the potatoes can be reheated and still taste like freshly mashed with none of the last-minute hassle. This gravy recipe is quick, easy, tasty, and can be prepared several days in advance. I think using fresh rosemary is the key to this finely seasoned gravy, but ½ teaspoon dried rosemary will do in a pinch.

Malanga Pancakes

Malanga, a large clublike tuber, takes the place of the white potato in Cuba. Native to the American tropics, malanga has a nutty, walnut-like flavor. Once peeled it has a waxy, slippery texture. Because malanga discolors quickly when peeled, it should be placed in cold water until needed.

3 cups grated raw malanga (peeled)
1 1/2 cups grated onion, liquid drained in a sieve
3 eggs, well beaten

1 1/2 teaspoons salt
3 tablespoons flour
3 tablespoons butter or margarine

1. Place grated malanga and grated onion in a large bowl. Stir to mix. Add eggs and salt. Stir to mix. Sprinkle mixture with flour and stir to combine.

2. Preheat oven to 250°F. Melt 1 tablespoon butter in a large skillet over medium-high heat. Working in 3 batches, place four 1/2-cup measures of malanga mixture in skillet and flatten with back of a large spoon. Cook until underside of each is golden brown, then flip and brown other side. Remove malanga pancakes to an ovenproof platter and place in oven to keep warm. Repeat process with rest of the butter and the malanga mixture. Serve pancakes with a dollop of butter, sour cream, or applesauce.

CHEF NOTE: Malanga is available in Latin markets. Test freshness by piercing the skin with your fingernail. It should be crisp like a water chestnut. You can substitute white potatoes in this recipe.

Mustard-Dill New-Potato Salad

2 pounds small new potatoes,
  quartered

1 teaspoon salt

2 dill pickles, halved lengthwise and cut
  into thin strips, crosswise (½ cup)

1½ cups thinly sliced celery

1 cup chopped red onions

2 tablespoons Dijon mustard

⅓ cup mayonnaise

⅓ cup sour cream

freshly ground black pepper

2 tablespoons plus 1 teaspoon snipped
  fresh dill weed

2 tablespoons plus 1 teaspoon snipped
  fresh chives

1. Place potatoes, salt, and enough water to cover by 2 inches in a large pan over medium-high heat. Bring to a boil and cook for 15 minutes or just until potatoes are tender. Drain in a colander. Refresh with cold water and drain again. Allow to cool.

2. Place pickle strips, celery, and onions in a large bowl. Add cooled potatoes. Toss to mix. Set aside.

3. Place mustard, mayonnaise, sour cream, pepper, 2 tablespoons each snipped dill and chives in a small bowl. Mix well to combine. Pour mixture over potato and vegetable mixture and toss lightly to coat. Transfer to a covered container and refrigerate until needed, up to 2 days.

4. **To serve:** Place salad in a serving bowl. Sprinkle with 1 teaspoon fresh dill and 1 teaspoon fresh chives.

CHEF NOTE: If you buy the Stackables brand dill pickles, which come sliced lengthwise, use as many as necessary to get ½ cup of thinly sliced pickle pieces.

Dill, which grows like, well, a weed in Florida Keys dooryard gardens, is actually an annual herb (*anethum graveolens*) and a member of the parsley family. While this recipe calls for dill weed (the featherly leaves of the plant), the seeds have traditionally been used to pickle everything from vegetables to fish and seafood.

Salt of the Sea

In the early Keys settlements of the 1800s, food preservation presented a daunting challenge. With little ice and no refrigeration, no chemical preservatives or home-canning, fresh food had to be preserved by smoking, pickling, drying,

packing in sugar syrup, or salting. Although salt was crucial in the preservation of turtles, finfish, and shellfish—the basis of lucrative trade with Cuba—salt was a scarce commodity, brought to the island grocers only occasionally by cargo vessels and levied with a stiff duty tax.

Settlers discovered that when seawater in shallow areas cut off from tidal circulation evaporated, a coarse salt remained. At first the salt was harvested from salt ponds on Duck Key and

Raking Salt, Turks Islands, B. W. I.

Key West for local use. In 1830, however, Richard Fitzpatrick made an attempt at a commercial saltworks. Leasing 100 acres of land in the southeastern end of Key West, which usually flooded at high tide, he divided the area into compartments—100 feet long and 50 feet wide—called "pans." Two-foot-high coral rock walls fitted with small, wooden floodgates separated the pans.

Once the pans were filled with saltwater, the floodgates were closed. After much of the water had evaporated, the floodgates were opened slightly to allow more water to flow into the pans. This process continued until just before the start of the rainy season, at which time all the water was allowed to evaporate from the pans. The coarse sea salt that remained was raked into piles, loaded into wheelbarrows, and made ready for export.

...

An early rainy season ruined Fitzpatrick's 1832 salt harvest and by 1834 he had abandoned his endeavor altogether.

...

This primitive method of salt production was carried out by slaves. They endured high temperatures and humidity and had to stand in salty brine most of the day, often developing painful boils. The relentless Keys sun reflected off the salt crystals and seawater, sometimes causing partial blindness.

An early rainy season ruined Fitzpatrick's 1832 salt harvest and by 1834 he had abandoned his endeavor altogether. Other attempts at the Key West salt industry were made in ensuing years, with production peaking just before the Civil War. Production ceased during the war, then resumed again in 1865. Owners of the salt ponds changed repeatedly, but all came to the conclusion that without slave labor, salt production by solar evaporation was not profitable enough to continue. In 1906 the land was sold to a reality company, which subsequently divided it into residential plots.

LEFT: *Working the salt pond manufacturing salt.*
Credit: Turks and Caicos National Museum.

Twice Baked Sweet Potatoes in Orange Cups

4 juice oranges	¾ teaspoon cinnamon
1½ cups mashed baked sweet potatoes	⅛ teaspoon nutmeg
3 tablespoons light brown sugar	⅛ teaspoon allspice
3 tablespoons golden raisins	3 tablespoons heavy cream
3 tablespoons butter, melted	1 egg, yolk and white separated

1. Cut 3 oranges in half. Juice each half orange with an electric juicer. Reserve juice. With a small spoon, pull inner membranes from orange peel, creating a smooth orange cup. Set aside. Grate the peel of the last orange. Reserve. Cut orange in half and juice it. Combine orange juices and set aside.

2. Place mashed sweet potatoes, 3 tablespoons of the fresh-squeezed orange juice, grated orange peel, brown sugar, raisins, butter, cinnamon, nutmeg, allspice, cream, and egg yolk in a large bowl. Stir with a large spoon to mix well.

3. Place egg white in a medium bowl. Beat with an electric mixer until stiff. Fold beaten egg whites into potato mixture.

4. Divide sweet potato mixture among the 6 orange cups. Transfer to a covered container and refrigerate until needed, up to 2 hours.

5. Preheat oven to 300°F. Place each orange cup in a muffin tin to stabilize it upright. Bake for 25 minutes or until heated through and puffy.

CHEF NOTE: You will have much more freshly squeezed orange juice than you will need for this recipe. Place extra juice in an ice cube tray and freeze. Remove frozen cubes and place in a zipper bag. Return cubes to the freezer until you need freshly squeezed orange juice for another recipe.

Sweet potatoes were a staple of the early Conch diet. Conchs usually served them simply—boiled in salted water, then peeled, sliced, and buttered. In the 1850s, Jonathon Thompson, aka Happy Jack, had a plantation on Sugarloaf Key. (Sugarloaf Key was named after the sugarloaf pineapple that was cultivated there for a time.) Happy Jack raised tropical fruits and vegetables and was particularly noted for his superior sweet potatoes. He accidentally killed himself in 1858 when he inadvertently tripped a spring gun as he attempted to kill a deer.

Yuca with Garlicky Sour Orange Sauce

Yuca, pronounced *yoo-ka* and also known as cassava, is a staple in Cuban cuisine and that of Central and South America and the Caribbean islands. It was the basis of the diet of the Taino Indians of Cuba and then Spanish settlers and African slaves. Yuca's flavor and its odor while cooking are very distinctive, making it a food one either loves or hates. This starchy tuber has tough skin that resembles bark and a fibrous cord running through its center, both of which must be removed before cooking. Fresh yuca spoils very quickly so using frozen or canned yuca has gained popularity in the Keys in recent years.

2 pounds frozen yuca

4 teaspoons salt, divided

2 teaspoons key lime juice

1 head garlic, cloves separated and peeled

1 large sweet onion, like Vidalia

½ cup olive oil

1 cup sour orange juice

1. Place yuca in a 4-quart nonstick saucepan and add water to cover by 2 inches. Add 2 teaspoons salt and key lime juice. Place pan over high heat. When water comes to a boil, reduce heat to medium-low and simmer uncovered until tender, about 30 minutes. Drain yuca and cut it into 2-inch chunks, removing fibrous cord that runs through it. Return yuca to pan.

2. Meanwhile, crush garlic cloves by firmly pressing them with the flat blade of a chopping knife. Transfer garlic to a mortar and pestle, a few crushed cloves at a time, and pound until mashed. Add 2 teaspoons salt and pound salt into mashed garlic. Set aside.

3. Cut onion in half and then thinly slice each half so that you have about 3 cups of onion half-rings. Set aside.

4. Place olive oil in a large nonstick skillet over medium heat. Add garlic and onions and sauté 5 minutes or until onions are translucent. Add sour orange juice and cook, stirring constantly, until mixture bubbles. Remove from heat and pour over yuca.

5. Return yuca to burner and increase heat to medium-high. Cook yuca in garlic sauce, stirring frequently, until sauce reduces to a glaze and totally coats yuca, about 3 minutes. Remove from heat and serve.

CHEF NOTE: If you can't find sour orange juice in your supermarket, you can substitute a mixture of 2 parts orange juice to 1 part lemon juice. In this recipe you'd need ⅔ cup orange juice and ⅓ cup lemon juice.

Rosemary Roasted Boniato Fries

6 boniatos, peeled and cut into eighths

2 tablespoons olive oil

3 tablespoons snipped fresh rosemary

2 teaspoons kosher salt

2 teaspoons freshly ground black pepper

1. Preheat oven to 350°F. Place all ingredients in a large bowl and toss well to combine. Coat a large, nonstick baking sheet with vegetable cooking spray. Spread potatoes onto sheet in one layer. Roast for 45 minutes, turning about every 15 minutes, until browned and cooked through.

CHEF NOTE: White potatoes and American sweet potatoes are equally as tasty prepared this way. Substitute an equal amount. Boniato or potato fries are a great accompaniment to Herb-roasted Lamb Dijon (see Index).

Cuban sweet potatoes are called *boniatos*. They look similar to the American sweet potato only on the outside. The flesh, however, is white instead of yellow and their flavor is quite different. Less sweet than the orange sweet potato, boniatos have a nutty flavor and a subtle, spicy sweetness that is easily overwhelmed by heavy seasoning. Because the white flesh discolors quickly, boniatos should be peeled under running water.

Guacamole Tortilla Stack

Two horticultural types of avocados are widely marketed in the United States. The West Indian avocado, commonly called the Florida avocado because it is widely cultivated in the Sunshine State, is a large fruit with a smooth, green skin and a low fat content (7 percent). It prefers a tropical climate. The Hass avocado, much smaller than the West Indian type, has bumpy black skin, a much higher fat content, and is grown in California.

1 ripe Florida avocado (or 2 Hass avocadoes), peeled and mashed

3 large plum tomatoes, seeded and diced

¾ cup finely diced red onions

1 clove garlic, minced (or ⅛ teaspoon garlic powder)

½ teaspoon salt

¼ teaspoon freshly ground black pepper

2 tablespoons key lime juice

1 large jalapeno pepper, seeded and minced

2 tablespoons snipped fresh cilantro

1 (16-ounce) can fat-free refried beans

1 (10-ounce) can enchilada sauce

1 package of 10 (6-inch) corn tortillas

1½ cups shredded jalapeno-cheddar cheese

½ cup sour cream

1. **To make guacamole:** Combine avocado, tomatoes, onions, garlic, salt, pepper, key lime juice, jalapeno pepper, and cilantro in a large bowl. Stir to mix well. Transfer to a covered container and refrigerate at least 1 hour to marry flavors.

2. Preheat oven to 425°F. Lightly coat a 9-inch pie plate with vegetable cooking spray. Combine refried beans and 1½ cups guacamole in a medium bowl. Spread 2 tablespoons enchilada sauce over bottom of prepared pan. Place 1 tortilla over sauce. Spread ¼-cup guacamole-bean mixture over tortilla. Sprinkle with ¼ cup shredded cheese. Continue layering sauce, tortilla, bean mixture, and cheese, ending up with a tortilla. Spread top with remaining sauce and sprinkle with remaining cheese.

3. Coat a sheet of aluminum foil with vegetable cooking spray. Place foil, oiled-side down, over tortilla stack. Bake for 20 to 25 minutes or until tortillas are heated through. Cut into 4 wedges and top each with a dollop of sour cream.

CHEF NOTE: Guacamole was more often served at winter cocktail parties of "strangers" in early Key West than as a part of a Conch family dinner. When avocados were in season, early Conchs simply would slice and serve them plain, as an accompaniment to meat or fish. Serve this dish alongside grilled chicken for dinner or serve alone as a light lunch or supper.

Cheese Ravioli with Pink Sauce

1 tablespoon finely chopped shallots
1 tablespoon dry sherry
1 tablespoon butter or margarine
1 tablespoon flour
1 cup skim milk
½ cup tomato puree

⅛ teaspoon salt
⅛ teaspoon white pepper
2 teaspoons snipped fresh marjoram or
    1 teaspoon dried marjoram
9 ounces fresh cheese-filled ravioli
freshly grated Parmesan cheese

1. Place shallots and sherry in a deep nonstick sauté pan over medium heat and sauté for 1 to 2 minutes or until translucent. Add butter. When butter is melted, sprinkle with flour. Stir flour into butter and chopped shallots to form a roux. Slowly add milk, stirring constantly to a smooth consistency. Add tomato puree and stir until blended. Add salt, pepper, and marjoram and continue to cook for 5 more minutes, stirring occasionally.

2. Meanwhile, cook ravioli in a large pot of water to al dente according to package instructions.

3. **To serve:** Divide ravioli among individual pasta bowls. Spoon pink sauce over pasta. Sprinkle with Parmesan cheese.

CHEF NOTE: This sauce is light and flavorful. If you'd rather opt for a richer version, substitute heavy cream for the milk in this recipe.

Even if cooks in early Key West created homemade raviolis, they would have been hard-pressed to make this sauce with anything but canned evaporated milk. Fresh milk was illusive in the days before refrigeration. A single man led his lone cow down Duval Street, going house to house, where he milked his cow on the spot. Families paid five or ten cents for the milk—usually half foam—but it couldn't be fresher!

Fish and Seafood  5

Surrounded by the waters of the Atlantic Ocean and the Gulf of Mexico and fed by Gulf Stream currents, the Florida Keys has always enjoyed rich piscatory resources. From the days of Native American maritime hunter-gatherers to the Conchs, Cubans, and "strangers" living in the Keys today, fish and seafood has remained the primary focus of the islands' cuisine.

Nearly 200 years ago, Cubans regularly fished these waters, bringing their piscine prizes back to their island country a scant 90 miles away. Bahamians also discovered the vast aquatic pantry of the Keys, which induced them to pack up their families and immigrate to the islands. The Conchs, as the Bahamians were self-named, were considered "nearly amphibious," for it seemed they could fish, turtle, sponge, and handle a boat shortly after they learned to walk. Eventually the Florida Keys became the adoptive home of both cultures, a merger that proved fortuitous for all.

The handwritten *Key West Cookbook* (Key West Woman's Club, 1949) nostalgically describes fishing in the 1940s: ". . . and there are always the bridges, where one many sit drowsily for nothing, hand-line in hopeful hand, until a venturesome grunt, snapper or grouper brings one up wide awake."

LEFT: *Clawless and spiny, the Florida lobster has a strong tail muscle, ca. 1962.* **Credit: State Archives of Florida.**

Baked Dolphinfish in Thai Red Curry Sauce

Any Florida Keys angler who has ever seen a rainbow of schooling dolphin (*Coryphaena hippurus*) will tell you the fish's identity crisis is unfounded—this is not Flipper! At the dining table, Conchs, Cubans, "strangers," and visitors alike feast on the moist, sweet, white-fleshed fillets, which on our islands are always, always called dolphin or dolphinfish. Elsewhere in the country, to eliminate any confusion with the bottlenose dolphin, which is a mammal, the fish are marketed as mahi mahi.

2 tablespoons prepared red curry paste, such as Taste of Thai
1 cup coconut milk, divided
2 tablespoons fish sauce
1 tablespoon sugar
½ teaspoon salt
1 egg, beaten
1 cup snipped fresh basil
1½ pounds dolphinfish (mahi mahi) fillets

1. Place red curry paste, ½ cup coconut milk, fish sauce, sugar, and salt in a small bowl. Stir to mix well. Stir in beaten egg and then snipped basil.

2. Place fish fillets in a shallow glass or plastic dish. Pour curry mixture over fillets. Turn fillets so that they are well coated. Cover and refrigerate for 1 hour to marinate.

3. Preheat oven to 375°F. Coat an 11 x 7-inch baking dish with vegetable cooking spray. Remove fillets from marinade and place in a single layer in baking dish. Add remaining coconut milk to marinade and stir to mix well. Pour mixture over fillets.

4. Cover dish with aluminum foil and bake for 30 minutes, or until fish flakes when tested with a fork. Serve with Saffron Basmati Rice (see Index) or Coconut Basmati Rice Pilaf (see Index).

CHEF NOTE: Banana leaves add an aromatic flavor to foods cooked in them. If you have access to banana leaves, either from your dooryard garden or from an Asian market, you have several options to use them in this recipe. Cut banana leaves into 12-inch square pieces (remove center spine of leaf). Place them in a large bowl and cover with boiling water for 5 minutes so they won't crack when you work with them. Drain leaves before using. You can cover the baking dish with a layer of banana leaves instead of using aluminum foil. Or, if you have a large steamer, wrap the fish in banana leaves and then steam the packets: Place a fillet atop a square of banana leaf. Top with about 2 to 3 tablespoons curry sauce. Fold in short sides of banana leaf, then the two long sides, envelope style. Tie the packets securely with kitchen twine. Steam for 20 minutes or until fish flakes when tested with a fork (open 1 packet to test for doneness after 15 minutes).

Black Grouper in Island Spices with Pineapple Salsa

 SERVES 4

½ teaspoon madras curry powder

½ teaspoon allspice

½ teaspoon cardamom

½ teaspoon coriander

1 teaspoon cinnamon

½ teaspoon ground fennel

1 teaspoon Chinese 5 spice powder

½ teaspoon crushed red pepper

salt

½ teaspoon white pepper

¼ teaspoon ground ginger

⅛ teaspoon nutmeg

¼ teaspoon ground cloves

2 cups diced fresh pineapple

1 large tomato, seeded and chopped

¼ cup snipped fresh cilantro, or flat leaf parsley

3 tablespoons minced red onions

2 teaspoons minced, seeded jalapeno peppers

½ tablespoon sugar or more to taste

1 teaspoon ground cumin

freshly ground black pepper

2 pounds black grouper or other firm white fish fillets

¼ cup olive oil, divided

The firm-fleshed, mild-flavored grouper, member of the sea bass family, lives on the rocky sea bottom in deep water offshore. Black groupers are known to grow as large as 50 pounds and 3 feet in length.

CHEF NOTE: Bagatelle restaurant in Key West serves this island-spiced fish dish with a coconut-date sauce: Place 12 pitted dates and 1½ cups dark rum in a medium saucepan over high heat. Cook for 3 minutes, then flambé rum until all alcohol is burned off. Remove from heat and place in a blender with 10 ounces coconut milk and 1 tablespoon butter. Blend until smooth. Place one-quarter of the sauce on each plate and top with a grouper fillet.

1. **Up to 1 month ahead:** Place curry powder, allspice, cardamom, coriander, cinnamon, fennel, 5 spice powder, crushed red pepper, ½ teaspoon salt, white pepper, ginger, nutmeg, and cloves in a small bowl. Stir to mix well. Transfer to a covered container and set spice mix aside until needed.

2. **At least 3 hours and up to 1 day ahead:** Place pineapple, tomatoes, cilantro, red onions, jalapenos, sugar, and cumin in a small bowl. Season with salt and pepper to taste. Cover bowl with plastic wrap and refrigerate until needed.

3. Place spice mix on a large plate. Press each fillet into spice mix, presentation side down. Place 2 tablespoons olive oil in each of 2 large nonstick skillets over medium-high heat. Place fillets, spice side down, in skillet and sauté for 2 to 3 minutes. Carefully turn fillets over with a spatula and cook for 2 to 3 more minutes, or until fish flakes when tested with a fork. Transfer fillets to individual plates and top with about ½ cup salsa.

On the reef, yellowtail can be identified by a prominent yellow stripe that begins at the mouth and runs mid-laterally to its deeply forked, brilliantly yellow tail. At the table, however, there is no mistaking yellowtail's sweet, delicate flavor, which makes it probably the most requested snapper in Keys seafood restaurants.

Basil-Crusted Yellowtail Snapper with Fresh Herb-Tomato Sauce

10 tablespoons butter or margarine
½ cup Japanese breadcrumbs (Panko)
¼ cup snipped fresh basil
2 eggs
2 tablespoons 2% or whole milk
¼ cup flour
1 pound yellowtail snapper fillets
1 large shallot, minced
3 cloves garlic, minced

1 tablespoon snipped fresh chives
1 tablespoon snipped fresh oregano
1 tablespoon snipped fresh cilantro plus 2 sprigs
2 ounces dry white wine
1 ounce fresh lemon juice
2 tomatoes, peeled, seeded, and chopped
salt and freshly ground black pepper

1. Place butter in a small glass bowl. Cover with plastic wrap and microwave at 15-second intervals until melted. Set aside. Skim off any foam and fat that rises to the top. Place breadcrumbs and basil in a large shallow dish. Mix well and set aside. Place eggs and milk in another large shallow dish and whisk until well blended. Set aside.

2. Preheat oven to 350°F. Place flour in a small strainer and dust both sides of each fillet. Dip both sides of fillets in egg mixture, then coat each side evenly with breadcrumb mixture. (You can prepare fillets to this point, place them on a baking sheet, and refrigerate up to 1 hour.)

3. Place half the melted butter in a large sauté pan over medium heat and add fillets. Cook fillets over medium heat about 3 to 4 minutes or until undercoating is golden brown. Turn fillets and continue cooking 3 minutes or until flip side is golden brown and fish flakes when tested with a fork.

4. Remove fillets to a baking sheet with a spatula and place them in oven while preparing sauce. Return sauté pan to burner over medium heat. Place shallots, garlic, and snipped chives, oregano, and cilantro in pan. Add wine and lemon juice and deglaze pan for 1 minute, stirring constantly. Add tomatoes and stir to combine. Season with salt and freshly ground black pepper to taste. Slowly add remaining butter, stirring constantly. Remove sauce from heat.

5. **To serve:** Place half the fresh herbed tomato sauce on each of two dinner plates. Place half the yellowtail fillets atop the sauce on each plate. Garnish each with a sprig of cilantro.

CHEF NOTE: You can substitute any firm, white fish fillets for the yellowtail in this recipe. If fillets are thicker than yellowtail, adjust cooking time accordingly.

This is probably the most requested dish on the menu of the Fish House restaurant in Key Largo, and for good reason. The Mediterranean-inspired ingredients cavort in perfect balance, and the fish couldn't be fresher. The Fish House maintains a small, fresh seafood market right on premises.

Fish Matecumbe a la Fish House

1 cup chopped sweet onions, like Vidalia

1 (3.5-ounce) jar capers, drained and rinsed

2/3 cup chopped shallots (4 to 5 shallots)

3 cups chopped fresh tomatoes with juices (about 5 medium or 8 plum tomatoes)

1/4 cup snipped fresh basil

salt and freshly ground black pepper

1/3 cup fresh lemon juice

1 cup olive oil

2 1/2 pounds fish fillets, such as snapper or grouper

1. **At least 1 hour ahead or earlier in the day:** Place onions, capers, shallots, tomatoes, basil, 1 1/2 teaspoons salt, 3/4 teaspoon pepper, lemon juice, and olive oil in a medium nonmetal bowl. Stir to combine. Cover bowl and refrigerate mixture until needed.

2. Preheat broiler. Place oven rack at least 4 inches but no more than 6 inches from broiler. Coat a high-rimmed baking sheet with vegetable cooking spray. Place fish fillets in a single layer on the bottom of the pan. Season fillets with salt and pepper. Spoon tomato mixture atop fillets, dividing evenly (about 1/4 cup per fillet). Pour mixture's remaining liquid over the fillets.

3. Broil fish fillets for 5 (snapper) to 10 (grouper) minutes or until fish flakes when tested with a fork. Watch cooking process closely. Fish will cook quickly; do not overcook. Remove fillets to a serving platter. Spoon all remaining tomato mixture and juices over fillets.

CHEF NOTE: I shouldn't play favorites, but hands down, this is my favorite fish preparation in all of the Florida Keys. Equally as tasty prepared with snapper or grouper, it is melt-in-your-mouth lovely.

Fish Tacos

½ cup plain yogurt

½ cup mayonnaise

1 tablespoon Old Sour (see Index) or 1 tablespoon lime juice and ½ minced jalapeno

1 teaspoon minced capers

½ teaspoon oregano

½ teaspoon ground cumin

1 tablespoon snipped fresh dill or ½ teaspoon dried dill weed

¼ teaspoon cayenne pepper

1 pound yellowtail snapper fillets

salt and freshly ground black pepper

2 tablespoons butter or margarine

1 avocado, peeled, seeded, and cut in large dice

2 cups shredded cabbage

1 package (12) taco shells or flour tortillas, heated

1. Place yogurt, mayonnaise, Old Sour, capers, oregano, cumin, dill, and cayenne pepper in a small bowl. Stir to combine. Cover and refrigerate until needed.

2. Cut snapper fillets into 2-inch-wide strips. Sprinkle both sides of fillets generously with salt and pepper. Melt butter in a large nonstick skillet over medium-high heat. Add fillets to skillet and sauté, about 1 minute per side, until fish is opaque and flakes when tested with a fork. With fork break fish into bite-size pieces. Place in a serving dish.

3. **To serve:** Place fish, white sauce, avocado, cabbage, and taco shells or tortillas in serving dishes. Assemble a taco by first placing a layer of fish in taco shell. Add a dollop of sauce and top with avocado and shredded cabbage. If desired, accent with more Old Sour.

CHEF NOTE: Traditional fish tacos call for batter-fried fish, but so as not to mask the exquisite flavor of the fresh yellowtail, I've lightened this recipe. I prefer crispy corn tortillas or soft flour tortillas, but it is a personal choice. Use warm corn tortillas if you like.

Fish tacos probably were first eaten thousands of years ago when North American natives wrapped their offshore catch in corn tortillas. Ralph Rubio is credited with popularizing the fish taco in the United States, when, after tasting them in Baja, Mexico, in 1983, he opened a San Diego restaurant dedicated to their preparation that spawned a fast-food craze. Not yet reaching signature dish status here, the fish taco, nevertheless, is a natural union of indigenous ingredients of the Florida Keys.

The Enduring Legacy of the Sea

What is there about the surrounding seas that attract more than 1,000 species of fish to the Florida Keys? First and foremost is the Gulf Stream, or Florida Current, which moves through the Florida Straits between Cuba and Key West, and flows northward along the coast of Florida. Much like a warm tropical river—25 to 40 miles wide—the Gulf Stream hosts the northern migration of myriad species from the Caribbean, constantly restocking Keys waters.

Mother Nature also has gifted the Florida Keys with the continental shelf. This shallow area extends into the backcountry mangrove-spotted waters of the Gulf of Mexico and also stretches from the oceanside shoreline of the islands for many miles before plunging into the bluewater. Covered with dense turtlegrass, coral sand, or muddy muck, these areas—called the flats—are the nursery and feeding grounds for many marine families.

Creatures of the sea have been the dominant force for all who have encountered the Florida Keys since Native Americans first inhabited the islands in A.D. 800. Archaeologists, who have discovered kitchen middens, or mounds, of fish and sea-turtle bones and conch shells here, believe the Tequestas, Calusas, Matecumbes, and other Carib tribes were seafarers by necessity. The bountiful piscatory harvest—conch, shrimp, lobster, stone crabs, green turtles, snappers, groupers, dolphinfish, redfish, snook, spotted sea trout, cobia, wahoo, kingfish, mackerel and more—has played a starring role in the cuisine and daily life of the Florida Keys ever since.

Once considered Havana's pantry, the prolific waters surrounding the Florida Keys have always been a fisherman's nirvana. Experienced seamen from the Bahamas began harvesting Keys waters, then under Spanish control, in the early 1700s, trading green-turtle meat, conch, finfish, and crawfish with Cuba, 90 miles to the south. In return, they obtained such coveted staples as spices, knives, rope, and, of course, rum.

Fishing was the principal industry in Key West from its inception. By 1822, the port was second only to New York, attracting clipper ships from many foreign shores. Fishermen came from Cuba, the Bahamas, St. Augustine, and as far away

LEFT: *Commercial fishermen fishing from smackees, ca. 1850.*
Credit: State Archives of Florida.

as Connecticut, to fish the Keys waters eight months a year. Their presence so stimulated the economy of the young seaport that Key West became the largest city in Florida.

Early commercial fishermen fished by hand line for reef fish—snapper, grouper, grunt, triggerfish, dolphinfish—using Bahamian-style live-well sloops called smacks or smackees. Ice was at a real premium in the Keys, available only in limited quantities of winter block ice shipped by schooner from the northeast. So the live-well, a water-filled box built into the hull of the boat with holes drilled throughout to allow for the circulation of saltwater, kept the catch alive until it could be transferred to floating pens in Key West harbor or marketed in Cuba. Each smack carried 5,000 to 7,000 pounds of fish to Havana per trip. By 1885, ice plants were operating in Pensacola, and large 60- to 100-foot-long sailing schooners, with 10-man crews and 20-ton ice capacity, began fishing Keys waters, staying at sea up to a month at a time.

By 1912, Flagler's East Coast Railroad Extension from the mainland to Key West opened up new means of getting fish to market and Keys fisheries boomed. Powerboats began to replace the sailing smacks, but most reef fish were still taken with baited hand lines. Marathon developed as another major fishing port. In 1927 William Parrish opened a commercial fish house in Marathon, shipping 3 million pounds of Spanish and king mackerel to Miami in its first year of operation alone.

By 1949, fish markets at the north end of Elizabeth Street lined the waterfront. "Fish cars," or saltwater pens, containing live fish were tied to the docks. A buyer selected his fish; then it was taken out of the car with a dip net, killed, and dressed immediately. Walter H. Norman recalls in his book *Nicknames and Conch Tales*: "At the foot of Front Street there used to be a fish market...The fish house was run by Peter Roberts and his son...Mother used to send me down to Peters and say: 'Now junior, bring home about three or four nice yellowtails and have Peter cut the backbone out.' Well, I'd get on my bike and head for Peter's place. At the dock he had several fish 'cars' in the water in which he kept fish. One could go over and look at the fish and pick out the one he wanted. Peter would come over with a net and scoop him up, take him over to clean him, and with his agility, clean him in less time than it took you to read this. The fish were so fresh that when I got home with them and mother put salt on them in preparation for cooking, they would quiver."

The fishing fleet usually came into port about 4 P.M. and tied up at the dock. A person could buy fresh fish from the crew, who sold their catch directly from their boat's wells. Or as Norman remembers, sometimes it was sold door to door: "There used to be an old Cuban man who sold fresh fish at your front door. He had a wheelbarrow that had a wooden box built on it and iced fresh fish inside. His cry was, 'Langusta fresca.' Sometimes he would cry, 'Grits and grunts, five cents a bunch.' There was another Cuban fellow who sold conchs by the bunch. He had an old broomstick with notches cut into it. To this stick he would attach six raw conchs and tie a bunch at each notch. He would then put the broomstick over his shoulder and off he would go, selling all he could. Crawfish were also sold in this manner. Both crawfish and conches were sold six for a quarter."

The industry has evolved over the ensuing decades—perhaps not as colorfully—but fishing still remains one of the most important livelihoods in the Florida Keys.

Fish Vera Cruz

This preparation is one of the most enduringly popular dishes served at Key Largo's Fish House Restaurant, which is renowned for its fresh fish. Fishermen literally bring their daily catch to the restaurant's back door, so it is often only minutes from line to linen.

2 whole tomatoes, peeled, seeded, and chopped
1 jalapeno or habanero pepper, seeded and chopped
1 large clove garlic, minced
¼ sweet onion, like Vidalia, chopped (about ½ cup)

2 scallions, chopped
¼ bunch fresh cilantro, snipped (about ½ cup)
¼ cup olive oil, divided
2 pounds firm, white fish fillets
salt and freshly ground black pepper

1. Place tomatoes, jalapenos, and garlic in a medium saucepan over medium heat. Cook for 8 minutes or until tomatoes have cooked down to a liquid. Remove from heat and set aside to cool slightly. Transfer tomato mixture to a blender and pulse until smooth. Return tomato mixture to saucepan. Add onions, scallions, and cilantro. Stir to combine. Cover, reduce heat to low, and cook until sauce is heated through. Keep sauce warm until serving.

2. Place 2 large nonstick skillets over medium-high heat. Add 2 tablespoons olive oil to each skillet and heat until a sprinkle of water sizzles in the oil. Season fish fillets with salt and freshly ground black pepper to taste. Place fillets, presentation side down, in skillet. Sauté for 2 to 3 minutes, until undersides of fillets are opaque. Carefully turn fillets with a spatula and sauté another 2 minutes, or until fish flakes when tested with a fork.

3. Place a pool of sauce on each of 4 dinner plates. Divide fillets into 4 portions and place atop sauce.

CHEF NOTE: This recipe calls for a jalapeno pepper, but substitute a habanero if you like your food extra spicy. Fish House owner C. J. Berwick advises: "Cooking time will vary based on the thickness of the fish fillets and the type of fish, but it should take no more than 3 to 5 minutes on each side."

Ginger-Horseradish Grilled Dolphinfish

 SERVES 4

½ cup peeled, grated fresh horseradish root

½ cup peeled, chopped fresh gingerroot

¼ cup soy sauce

2 teaspoons minced fresh garlic

6 tablespoons honey

1 cup mayonnaise

2 pounds dolphinfish fillets

4 tablespoons melted butter

1. **Early in the day:** Place grated horseradish, chopped gingerroot, soy sauce, garlic, and honey in a blender. Pulse until mixture is fully chopped and blended. Add mayonnaise. Pulse until smooth. Place in a covered container and refrigerate until needed.

2. Preheat both gas grill and broiler. Brush both sides of fish fillets generously with melted butter. Place fillets on a nonstick fish grilling rack that has been coated with vegetable cooking spray. Grill fillets, basting with excess butter, for 5 minutes or until fillets are almost opaque. Do not overcook. Transfer fillets to a baking sheet. Top each fillet with a generous portion of ginger-horseradish sauce. Place fillets under broiler until sauce bubbles and fish flakes when tested with a fork, about 5 minutes. Remove from heat and serve immediately.

CHEF NOTE: Fresh horseradish root and gingerroot yield maximum flavor in this recipe.

Jackie, Johnny, and George Eigner, chef/owners of Fish Tales Fish Market and Eatery (MM 53, Marathon) called this dish Wasabi Dolphin when they served it at their former restaurant, the popular Grassy Key Dairy Bar. The recipe doesn't actually use the green root of the Asian herb (*Eutrema wasabi*), however, which is a member of the mustard family. The Eigners' recipe uses wasabi's traditional white horseradish-root cousin *Amoracia lapathifolia*.

Grilled Indo Snapper

Tamarind is a sticky brown pulp harvested from inside the bean-shaped pods of the tamarind tree, which is commonly found in dooryard gardens in the Keys. Tamarind syrup is made from juices extracted from this pulp and can be used to add a fruity tart flavor to curries, soups, stews, salad dressings, and dipping sauces. Look for tamarind syrup at Asian or international markets. Lemon or lime juice sweetened with a little brown sugar makes for an acceptable—although not authentic—alternative.

1 cup Coco Lopez cream of coconut
1/2 cup pineapple juice
1/4 cup tamarind syrup
1/4 cup sweet Thai chili sauce
2 tablespoons Thai chili garlic paste
1/4 cup teriyaki sauce
2 tablespoons rice wine vinegar

2 tablespoons soy sauce
3 to 4 tablespoons honey
3 dashes cayenne pepper (optional)
1/4 teaspoon red pepper flakes (optional)
2 heaping tablespoons peanut butter
2 pounds snapper fillets

1. **Up to 2 weeks ahead: To make Indo marinade/dressing:** Place cream of coconut in a blender. Add pineapple juice, tamarind syrup, and sweet chili sauce. Pulse until smooth. Add chili garlic paste, teriyaki sauce, vinegar, soy sauce, and honey. Pulse until smooth. Taste dressing. Add cayenne and red pepper flakes if you'd like the dressing spicier. Add peanut butter and pulse until smooth. Transfer to a covered container and refrigerate until needed. Makes about 2 1/2 cups.

2. **Early in the day:** Place snapper fillets in a 13 x 9-inch baking dish. Pour marinade over fillets and turn them with a fork until well coated. Cover dish with plastic wrap and refrigerate for at least 2 hours, turning in marinade occasionally.

3. Preheat gas or charcoal grill. Coat a nonstick fish grilling rack with vegetable cooking spray. Remove fillets from marinade and grill for 6 minutes or until fish flakes when tested with a fork. Place marinade in a small pitcher and microwave for 1 minute or until hot. Place grilled fillets on a serving platter and drizzle with Indo sauce. Serve with remaining sauce on the side.

CHEF NOTE: This spicy, peanutty marinade also makes a great salad dressing, tossed with such firm greens as romaine and iceberg. You also can drizzle it on steamed vegetables.

Grilled Yellowfin Tuna with Wasabi Drizzle

 SERVES 4

¼ cup wasabi powder

3 tablespoons cold water

½ cup mayonnaise

½ tablespoon brown sugar

4 (8-ounce) sushi-grade yellowfin tuna steaks

4 ounces butter, melted

Durkee Grill Creations seafood seasoning salt or other fish seasoning of choice

2 tablespoons sesame seeds, toasted

1. Place wasabi powder in a small bowl. Slowly stir in water to make a loose paste. Add mayonnaise and brown sugar. Stir to mix well. Transfer to a plastic squirt bottle. Refrigerate until needed.

2. Scrape grill until it is very clean. Heat grill until very hot. Brush butter on one side of tuna steaks. Place steaks on grill, butter side down. Grill 1½ minutes. Brush top side of steaks with butter. Flip steaks over and grill an additional 1½ minutes. Remove tuna from grill. Season with seafood seasoning to taste.

3. Cut each tuna steak across the grain into ½-inch-thick slices with a sharp knife. Place slices in a fan on each dinner plate. Drizzle slices with wasabi and sprinkle with sesame seeds. Serves 4.

CHEF NOTE: Chef Lance Hill suggests that an electric knife works particularly well in slicing the tuna steaks. You can find plastic squirt bottles (much like those used for ketchup and mustard in 1950s diners) in most stores selling kitchen supplies.

Yellowfin tuna (*Thunnus albacares*) inhabit the warm waters of the Atlantic, Pacific, and Indian Oceans. Growing as large as 400 pounds, the yellowfin tuna distinguishes itself from other members of its family by its bright yellow dorsal and anal fins. The fish's firm flesh varies from pink in smaller fish to deep red in larger specimens. Barracuda Grill in Marathon created this wildly popular yet simple preparation for grilled yellowfin, which chefs Lance and Jan Hill recommend be quickly cooked and served rare.

Hogfish Marsala

Although also known as hog snapper, hogfish is actually a member of the wrasse family. This strange looking fish has a wide, reddish body and a long flat snout, its porcine resemblance no doubt responsible for its name. Hogfish primarily feed during the day on mollusks, crabs, and sea urchins, and in a year can consume nearly five times their body weight. A high quality food fish regarded by many as the best tasting of all reef fish, hogfish is at risk of becoming endangered due to intense fishing.

3 tablespoons butter, divided

8 ounces baby portobello mushrooms, thinly sliced

2 tablespoons chopped shallots

2 teaspoons flour

½ cup dry marsala

2 teaspoons coarse-grain mustard

2 tablespoons snipped plus 8 sprigs fresh parsley

¼ cup heavy cream

1 cup hazelnut flour or plain flour

2 pounds hogfish or any snapper

2 tablespoons olive oil, divided

salt and freshly ground black pepper to taste

1. Place 1 tablespoon butter in a large, nonstick skillet over medium heat. When butter has melted, add mushrooms and shallots and cook until tender, about 5 minutes. Sprinkle with flour and stir to coat mixture. Slowly add marsala, stirring constantly. Add mustard and snipped parsley and stir to combine. Slowly add heavy cream, stirring constantly until mixture is heated through and thickened slightly. Reduce heat to low and cover until needed.

2. Meanwhile, preheat oven to 200°F. Coat both sides of fish fillets with flour. Place 1 tablespoon butter and 1 tablespoon olive oil in a large, nonstick skillet over medium-high heat. When butter has melted, add half the fish fillets and sauté until undersides are golden, 2 to 3 minutes. Turn fillets with a spatula and continue cooking just until fish flakes when tested with a fork. Transfer fillets to an ovenproof platter and place fish in the oven to keep warm. Add remaining 1 tablespoon butter and 1 tablespoon oil to skillet and sauté remaining fillets according to directions above.

3. **To serve:** Divide snapper fillets evenly among each of 4 dinner plates. Salt and pepper to taste. Top with one-quarter of the marsala sauce. Garnish each serving with 2 sprigs fresh parsley.

CHEF NOTE: The hazelnut flour imparts a special flavor to this dish, but if you can't find it in your local market or if one of your family or guests has a nut allergy, you can substitute plain flour instead. Hogfish is a lucky catch in the Keys. You can substitute any type of snapper fillets or any other firm white fish. If you find the sauce thickens too much, add a small amount of water to thin it and heat it through before serving.

Macadamia Nut-Encrusted Snook with Banana-Rum Sauce

¼ cup flour

½ teaspoon salt

¼ teaspoon freshly ground black pepper

1 (6.5-ounce) can roasted macadamia nuts

2 pounds thick snook fillets, washed and dried

1 egg, beaten

2 tablespoons olive oil

¼ cup cream de cocoa

¼ cup coconut rum

1 ripe banana, mashed

¼ cup heavy cream

Found in the backcountry waters of the Keys, snook cannot by Florida law be caught and sold commercially. Many Keys resident anglers feel that catching a snook is akin to sighting a meteor shower—rare and phenomenal. Perhaps the best-tasting fish in the Florida Keys, snook for dinner is a privilege afforded only to locals.

1. Preheat oven to 400°F. Place flour, salt, and pepper in a small bowl and stir to mix. In a food processor, finely chop macadamia nuts. Place chopped nuts on a dinner plate. Place flour mixture in a small strainer and lightly dust fillets with flour mixture. Then brush fish with beaten egg wash. Firmly press fillets into nuts, coating all sides of the fish.

2. Place olive oil in a large, nonstick skillet over medium-high heat. When oil is hot, add fish fillets. Brown fillets, about 3 minutes per side. Transfer fillets to a baking dish and place in the oven. Bake fish about 10 minutes, or until it flakes in the thickest part when touched with a fork.

3. Meanwhile, place cream de cocoa, coconut rum, and mashed banana in the same skillet in which you browned the fillets. Stir to mix, then flame alcohol. Cook over medium heat, stirring frequently, until sauce reduces by two-thirds, about 5 minutes. Add heavy cream and continue stirring until sauce is smooth and has a silky consistency.

4. Place a large pool of banana-rum sauce on each of 4 dinner plates. Divide fillets into 4 servings and place atop sauce. Pass extra sauce.

CHEF NOTE: Because snook is a rare delicacy in the Keys, not available commercially or in restaurants, if your angler isn't fortunate enough to catch one, substitute grouper instead. And if you are a northerner, use any firm white fish that is about ¾ inch thick.

Nearly every Florida Keys restaurant worth its salt offers a rendition of fish almandine, so popular is this preparation. This recipe combines the best features from two of the best restaurant adaptations: Fish Tales in Marathon and Sundowner's in Key Largo.

Mangrove Snapper Amaretto-Almandine

1½ cups sliced almonds
3 eggs, beaten
2 tablespoons flour
4 large mangrove snapper fillets (about 2 pounds)

salt and freshly ground black pepper
8 tablespoons (1 stick) plus 3 tablespoons butter
¼ cup amaretto

1. Place almonds on a large dinner plate. Place beaten eggs in a medium bowl. Place flour in a small strainer. Dust fish fillets with flour. Season with salt and pepper to taste. Dip fillets in egg wash, coating all sides. Press each fillet into sliced almonds, completely coating one side with the nuts. Return each nut-coated fillet to a platter until needed.

2. Melt 3 tablespoons butter in a large nonstick skillet over medium heat. Place fillets, almond-coated side down, into the skillet. When underside is light brown, turn fillets over. Continue cooking until fish flakes when tested with a fork, 4 to 5 minutes.

3. Meanwhile, melt remaining 8 tablespoons butter in a small saucepan over medium-high heat. Add amaretto and cook, stirring rapidly with a wire whisk, until sauce is reduced by one-third.

4. Place each fillet, almond side up, on a dinner plate. Top with Amaretto sauce. Serves 4.

CHEF NOTE: You can use any firm fleshed white fish fillets for this recipe.

Mediterranean-style Fish Fillet Packets

 SERVES 6

3 large tomatoes, cut into 12 (¼-inch) slices

¼ cup finely chopped shallots

6 (6-ounce) snapper fillets, cut in half crosswise

½ cup pitted and chopped kalamata olives

2 tablespoons capers, rinsed and drained

salt and freshly ground black pepper

6 pinches dried thyme

¼ cup fresh lemon juice

1 tablespoon extra virgin olive oil

1 tablespoon snipped fresh basil

1 tablespoon snipped fresh dill

1. Preheat oven to 450°F or preheat grill. Cut twelve 12-inch squares of aluminum foil. Set a square on the work surface so that one corner points toward you. At the imaginary midline that divides the square into two triangles, place a slice of tomato and a small amount of shallot. Top with a piece of fish, a portion of the olives and capers, salt and pepper to taste, and a pinch of thyme.

2. Sprinkle with lemon juice, olive oil, basil, and dill. Bring the top and bottom triangle points together and roll foil to secure tightly. Then finish sealing the packages by firmly folding over each of the remaining side triangle edges three times, until airtight. Place the packet on a large baking sheet, seam side up. Repeat with the remaining foil squares and ingredients.

3. Bake for 15 minutes (rotating the pan in the oven after 10 minutes to ensure even cooking) or place packets on gas grill. Fish is done when opaque and flaky when touched with a fork. (Open one packet to test.)

4. Serve 2 packets per person, allowing each diner to open his or her own at the table.

CHEF NOTE: Parchment paper is a little more difficult to work with, but you can substitute it in this recipe for a little fancier presentation.

The fruit of the olive tree is botanically classed as a drupe, similar to the peach or plum. Most olives are grown in the countries surrounding the Mediterranean Sea. Considered one of the best Greek olives, the almond-shaped kalamata is eggplant in color with a rich, fruity flavor. The fruit is soaked in wine vinegar to cure it. Sometimes the olives are slit to the pit so the fruit can absorb more of the vinegar's flavor.

Ponzu Snapper in Rice Paper

Ponzu sauce, a Japanese dipping sauce, has as many interpretations as there are innovative chefs. The sauce, based on soy sauce and citrus juices, dances a delicate balance on the taste buds, bursting with sour, sweet, and spicy flavors simultaneously.

CHEF NOTE: You can use any firm white fish in this recipe. If fillets are thick, increase cooking time accordingly. Do not overcook. Garden Gourmet Ginger Spice Blend, an Australian product now sold in the produce section of most supermarkets, is an easy alternative to grating fresh ginger. You'll find Asian sweet chile sauce in the international aisle of your supermarket.

¼ cup fresh key lime juice
¼ cup fresh orange juice
¼ cup soy sauce
¼ cup brown sugar
¼ cup canola oil
1 teaspoon Asian sweet chile sauce
2 tablespoons grated gingerroot

2 large cloves garlic, chopped
½ cup snipped fresh basil
8 rice paper rounds (8 to 10 inches in diameter)
8 small snapper fillets (about 2 pounds)
salt and freshly ground black pepper
¼ cup olive oil, divided

1. **Up to 6 hours ahead:** Place key lime and orange juices, soy sauce, brown sugar, canola oil, chile sauce, grated gingerroot, and garlic in a blender. Pulse until smooth. Transfer to a glass or plastic container. Stir in basil. Cover ponzu sauce and refrigerate until needed.

2. Place warm water in a large (12-inch), round, shallow baking dish. Working one rice paper round at a time, immerse rice paper in water for a few seconds. Remove paper to counter work surface and allow to stand about 30 seconds, until it becomes pliable. Place a snapper fillet in the center of the rice paper. Season with salt and pepper to taste. Drizzle 2 teaspoons ponzu sauce over fillet. Fold rice paper over length of fillet. Then fold in the two short ends, envelope style. Finally, fold remaining side over packet and roll fillet over, so that it is completely enclosed and the seams are pressed tightly together. Set aside. Repeat with remaining 7 rice paper rounds and fish fillets.

3. Place 2 large nonstick skillets over medium-high heat. Add 2 tablespoons olive oil to each skillet and heat until a sprinkling of water sizzles when dropped in the oil. Add 4 rice-paper-wrapped fillets to each skillet, seam sides down, making sure they are not touching. Sauté until undersides are golden brown, about 2 minutes. Carefully turn packets and continue cooking for 1 to 2 minutes more, or until fish flakes when tested with a fork.

4. Meanwhile, microwave ponzu sauce for 1 minute or until warm. Transfer 2 fish packets to each of 4 dinner plates. Drizzle about ¼ cup ponzu sauce over each portion.

Potato-crusted Dolphinfish with Basil-Horseradish Sauce

SERVES 4

¾ cup light sour cream
¼ cup light mayonnaise
2 tablespoons prepared horseradish
2 tablespoons snipped fresh basil
1 tablespoon fresh lemon juice
1 teaspoon soy sauce
1 heaping teaspoon minced garlic
1 cup low-fat buttermilk

¼ teaspoon salt
¼ teaspoon freshly ground black pepper
1 (4-ounce) package Idahoan Southwest Mashed Potato Flakes
2 pounds dolphinfish fillets
6 tablespoons butter, divided

1. **Up to 1 day ahead:** Mix sour cream, mayonnaise, horseradish, basil, lemon juice, and soy sauce in a small bowl. Stir until smooth. Cover and refrigerate until serving.

2. Combine garlic, buttermilk, salt, and pepper in a wide, shallow bowl. Spread potato flakes in an even layer on a dinner plate.

3. Dip dolphinfish fillets into buttermilk mixture, then push into potato flakes, coating both sides. Place coated fillet on a clean dinner plate. Repeat process with remainder of fillets.

4. Place a large, nonstick skillet over medium-high heat. Melt 3 tablespoons butter in pan, swirling to evenly coat. Add dolphinfish fillets and cook 2 to 3 minutes or until undersides are golden brown. Carefully remove fillets to dinner plate. Melt remaining 3 tablespoons butter in skillet. Return fillets to skillet, turning them over so that the other side browns, 2 minutes more. Test fillets with a fork. If the fish flakes, it is done. Place fillets on a serving platter. Serve with basil-horseradish sauce.

CHEF NOTE: Dolphinfish fillets tend to be long and narrow. Cut them into 4- to 5-inch lengths before cooking. This recipe also works well with the small, narrow ends of the fillets, called dolphin fingers. Cook the fingers only briefly, until flaky, and serve on a bun with basil-horseradish sauce and lettuce.

Marketed as mahi mahi in the rest of the United States so as not to confuse consumers with the bottle-nosed mammal in marine parks, dolphinfish, as it is called in the Florida Keys, is popular and versatile. One of the most beautiful fish in tropical waters, live dolphinfish are an iridescent rainbow of blue, green, and yellow colors. The meat of the dolphinfish is large-flaked and sweetly moist.

High in vitamins A and C, tarragon leaves have long been an essential flavoring in French cooking. There are two types of tarragon, French and Russian. More savory, French tarragon is considered more desirable because of its light anise-like flavor. But actually both French and Russian tarragon originated in Russia.

CHEF NOTE: If you don't have a double boiler, place a stainless steel bowl over a saucepan that is partially filled with water. Make sure the water touches the bowl, but don't make water level too high or when the bowl is full of ingredients, the boiling water may slosh over the side into your butter sauce.

Sautéed Snapper with Champagne-Tarragon Butter Sauce

2 shallots, finely chopped
6 tablespoons Champagne vinegar
16 tablespoons (2 sticks) butter
1 tablespoon dried tarragon

1 tablespoon heavy cream
2 pounds snapper fillets, washed and patted dry
4 fresh tarragon sprigs

1. Place shallots and vinegar in a double boiler over medium heat. Cook, stirring frequently, until vinegar reduces to 2 tablespoons.

2. Meanwhile, cut butter into 16 tablespoons. When vinegar is reduced, turn heat to medium-low and add 12 tablespoons butter, one tablespoon at a time, stirring constantly until all butter has melted.

3. Remove from heat and turn off burner. Stir tarragon and heavy cream into butter mixture. Cover and set aside on turned-off burner.

4. Preheat oven to 200°F. Melt 2 tablespoons butter in a large nonstick skillet over medium heat. Add half the fish fillets, presentation side down. Sauté until fish is nearly opaque, 3 to 4 minutes. Turn fillets over and brown other side about 1 minute or until fish flakes when touched with a fork. Place fillets on an ovenproof platter and place them in the oven to keep warm. Add remaining 2 tablespoons butter to skillet. When butter has melted, repeat sauté process with remaining fillets and remove them to warm platter.

5. Divide fillets among individual plates. Spoon a generous portion of butter sauce atop fillets. Garnish each serving with a sprig of fresh tarragon.

Snapper Piccata

 SERVES 4

1 cup flour
2 pounds yellowtail or other snapper
  fillets
salt and freshly ground black pepper
¼ cup olive oil

1 cup chicken broth
¼ cup fresh lemon juice
¼ cup capers, rinsed and drained
4 tablespoons (½ stick) butter
¼ cup snipped fresh parsley

1. Preheat oven to 200°F. Place flour on a large dinner plate. Dredge snapper fillets in flour to coat. Season with salt and pepper to taste. Place oil in a large nonstick skillet over medium-high heat. When oil is hot, add snapper fillets and sauté for 2 minutes. Turn fillets and sauté 1 minute more or until fish flakes when tested with a fork. Place fillets on an ovenproof platter, cover with aluminum foil, and place them in the oven to keep warm.

2. Add chicken broth to the same skillet and stir with a wooden spoon to release any bits that may be stuck to the pan. Cook, stirring occasionally, until broth reduces by half, about 5 minutes. Add lemon juice and capers, and cook until heated through. Add butter and stir until melted. Remove fillets from warming oven. Adjust seasonings to taste. Pour lemon-caper sauce over fillets. Sprinkle with parsley.

CHEF NOTE: The lemon-caper sauce in this recipe is light, refreshing, and not artery-clogging. For a thicker, richer dish, sauté fillets in butter instead of olive oil and add more butter in the finish.

Found at the coral reef and in smaller patch reefs closer to shore, snappers travel in schools and like to feed at night. Sweeter and more tender than grouper, snapper is probably the most important fish family in the Florida Keys. The clan is a large one—mangrove or gray, mutton, lane, cubera, dog, and more—but the most famous cousin remains the yellowtail.

Pink Gold

Commercial fishermen working the waters near the Dry Tortugas, 70 miles west of Key West harbor, made a remarkable discovery in the late 1940s: The belly of a captured shark was full of large pink shrimp, a phenomenon they had not seen before. Thus stumbling upon a bountiful shrimping area, they hit a lucrative mine of pink gold, and the Key West shrimping industry began.

Commonly called Key West pinks, the shrimp are nocturnal, swimming at night and burying themselves in the sand all day. (They reportedly jump like grasshoppers in the dark, eyes sparking iridescent orange when flashed with a light.) This species, *Penaeus duorarum*, or pink shrimp, changes color to match its surroundings. So, pink shrimp found along the Atlantic seaboard are brown, like the rocky sea bottom. Those on the Gulf coast are lemon-yellow like the sand. In the Florida Keys, however, pink shrimp actually do turn a bright pink so they blend in with their coral habitat.

Fifty- to 100-foot-long boats harvest the shrimp by dragging one to four large nets along the sea bottom behind the vessel. First, a "try" net is thrown to determine how concentrated with shrimp the beds are. If deemed prolific with pinks, the expansive nets are lowered from trawling booms. The nets are cone-shaped, like wind socks, with large mesh at the mouth and a smaller mesh at the tail, which allows the smallest shrimp to fall through the mesh, netting only the larger, more marketable shrimp.

By 1950, 300 shrimp boats from many southern ports were harvesting the waters of the Tortugas. They unloaded their catch on the docks of "Fish House No. 4," a fish processing house and ice plant operated by the Singleton family at Key West Bight. Here, in what has been reborn as the main dining room of the Conch Republic Seafood Company Restaurant (Key West Historic Seaport area), hundreds of workers stood at long tables, beheading the shrimp, then icing the crustaceans and packing them in wooden crates for shipment.

For the next 30 years, the average catch of Key West pinks was 9.7 million pounds a year. In the 1960s and

1970s, during the shrimping season from November to July, more than 400 boats operated out of Key West harbor alone. Legend maintains that a person could walk from boat to boat for the entire length of the seawall and never touch the water. But following a record year in 1981, when shrimping accounted for nearly half the total value of the Key West fishing industry, harvests began to decline. By 1988, the shrimping industry moved to Stock Island, just outside Key West, reduced to a fleet of only 175 trawlers.

Theories abound as to why the Florida Keys shrimping industry has continued to decline. Some environmentalists believe the decreasing water flow across the Everglades into the Florida Bay shrimp nursery grounds and the subsequent sea grass die-off in the Bay was at least partially to blame. Others blame mosquito pesticides that until recently have been sprayed by plane over the islands and near-shore waters. Some fault government regulations: To minimize the inadvertent capture of sea turtles and non-targeted fish in the shrimp nets, turtle exclusion devices (TEDS) and by-catch reduction devices (BRDS) became mandatory in the 1980s. Shrimpers complain about

ABOVE: *Shrimping boomed in Key West until the late 1980s; shrimp fleet, ca. 1968.* **Credit: State Archives of Florida.**

the high cost of living in Key West, the increased fuel prices, the overfishing of shrimp beds by outsiders, and an increase in foreign-market imports. Also, with the continuing tourism boom, waterfront property has become much too valuable to allocate for shrimp boat docks.

The shrimp boom may be over in the Florida Keys, but shrimpers still work out of the Stock Island docks. Pink gold remains a coveted entrée on every

restaurant menu. And Key West pinks find markets as far north as the Carolinas. On the night of the March full moon, shrimpers hold the annual Blessing of the Shrimp Fleet ceremony. The shrimp boats, decorated with lights and ribbons, sail slowly past the docks like homecoming floats. Then they move into the Gulf and, one by one, extinguish their lights, moving into the darkness like the ghostly specters they may one day become.

A member of the sea bass family, the grouper lives in deep water amid rocky out-croppings, or at the coral reef, 4 miles offshore. More than 50 species live in Florida waters, but three—black, gag, and red grouper—stand out in the waters of the Keys. The lean fish has a tough skin, which must be removed before cooking. Its large, white-flaked flesh earns grouper a much-coveted spot—along with snapper and dolphinfish—in the reigning piscatory triumvi-rate of the Florida Keys.

Wasabi-Ginger Grilled Grouper

2 tablespoons wasabi powder
4 scallions, finely chopped
4 cloves garlic, minced
2 tablespoons peeled and minced fresh gingerroot

½ cup soy sauce
½ cup mirin
¼ cup brown sugar
2 teaspoons sesame oil
2 pounds grouper fillets

1. **For the marinade:** Combine wasabi powder and 1 tablespoon water in a small cup. Set mixture aside for 10 minutes to make a thick paste. Place scallions, garlic, and gingerroot in a medium bowl. Stir to mix. Whisk in soy sauce, mirin, brown sugar, and sesame oil. Add wasabi paste and stir to mix well. Makes 1 cup.

2. Place grouper fillets in a 13 x 9-inch baking dish or a freezer-weight zipper bag. Pour marinade over fillets. Refrigerate and marinate fillets for 1 hour, turning occasionally.

3. **To cook:** Remove fillets from marinade. Place marinade in a small saucepan. Heat to boiling. Remove and reserve for basting.

4. Coat a nonstick fish grilling rack with vegetable cooking spray. Place fillets on rack over a gas or charcoal grill. Baste fish with reserved marinade until cooked through, about 10 minutes per inch of thickness, or until fish is opaque and flakes with the touch of a fork.

CHEF NOTE: Mirin is a sweet, golden-colored cooking wine made from glutinous rice. Essential in Japanese-style recipes, it is available in the Asian section of most supermarkets. You can substitute rice wine in this recipe but the glaze will not be as sweet.

Chardonnay Shrimp

4 tomatoes, seeded and diced

8 scallions, green and white parts sliced

1 cup loosely packed snipped cilantro
 plus 4 sprigs

1 tablespoon key lime juice

1 tablespoon minced garlic

1 teaspoon salt

1 teaspoon cumin

hot sauce to taste

1 pound linguine

1 tablespoon olive oil

36 large shrimp (21-26), peeled and
 deveined

1 cup chardonnay

1. **Up to several hours ahead:** Combine tomatoes, scallions, snipped cilantro, key lime juice, garlic, salt, cumin, and hot sauce in a medium bowl. Cover and refrigerate until ready to use.

2. Place a large pot of water over medium-high heat. Add linguine and cook to al dente according to package directions. Drain pasta and return it to pot. Cover pot to keep linguine warm and set aside.

3. Heat olive oil in a large nonstick skillet over medium-high. Add shrimp to the pan and cook for 1 minute on each side, until they just become pink. Add tomato salsa mixture to shrimp and stir to mix well. Add chardonnay and stir. Cover and cook for 1 to 2 minutes longer, until shrimp are just cooked through and tomato mixture is hot. Remove from heat.

4. Place desired size serving of pasta in each of 4 large pasta bowls. Spoon shrimp and sauce over top of linguine. Garnish each with a sprig of cilantro.

CHEF NOTE: To seed a tomato, cut tomato in half crosswise. With your index finger, gently scoop out seeds. Turn tomato over and drain on paper toweling.

Imaginative preparation and presentation showcase the entrees at the Barracuda Grill, a small, bustling bistro in the heart of Marathon. Owner-chefs Jan and Lance Hill combined their considerable culinary talents to create this subtly flavored shrimp offering.

Because conch meat is so tough and rubbery, it must be tenderized before using it for culinary preparations. The large white muscle on the conch is cut down the middle and the two sides are then pounded repeatedly with a mallet until very, very thin. It takes several conchs to make a pound of meat. Conch is available pre-tenderized and frozen.

Coconut Cracked Conch with Horseradish-Ginger Sauce

½ cup ketchup
1 tablespoon prepared horseradish
1 tablespoon grated fresh gingerroot
1 cup unsweetened grated coconut
½ cup seasoned dried breadcrumbs

¼ teaspoon salt
⅛ teaspoon cayenne pepper
¼ cup honey
1 pound tenderized conch steaks

1. Preheat oven to 425°F. Line a baking sheet with aluminum foil and coat with vegetable cooking spray. Set aside

2. **To make horseradish-ginger sauce:** Place ketchup, horseradish, and gingerroot in a small bowl. Stir to mix well. Cover and refrigerate until needed.

3. Place coconut, breadcrumbs, salt, and pepper in a food processor and pulse until well mixed. Transfer coconut mixture to a large, shallow dish.

4. Place honey in a medium glass bowl and microwave it for 30 seconds or until heated through.

5. Dip a conch steak into honey, turning to completely coat both sides. Press conch steak into coconut mixture; turn steak over and press other side into coconut. Place conch steak on baking sheet. Repeat process with rest of conch steaks.

6. Bake conch for 9 minutes or until bottom crust is browned and conch is cooked through. Place baking sheet under the broiler and broil for 1 minute or until top crust is golden brown. (Watch carefully because coconut browns quickly.) Serve with horseradish-ginger sauce.

CHEF NOTE: Gourmet Garden makes a ginger spice blend that is a real effort saver when it comes to needing grated gingerroot for a recipe. Made in Australia and found in most U.S. supermarkets in the produce section, the ginger is packaged in an easy-to-use tube.

Herbed Feta Shrimp

1 cup chopped yellow onions

¼ cup white wine

2½ cups peeled, seeded, and chopped fresh tomatoes

2 tablespoons chopped fresh parsley

1 teaspoon dried oregano

1 teaspoon dried dill weed

½ teaspoon crushed red pepper flakes

¼ teaspoon salt

1½ pounds large shrimp (21-26), peeled and deveined

8 ounces feta cheese, crumbled

3 tablespoons snipped fresh basil

1. Place onions and wine in a large nonstick skillet over medium heat and sauté until translucent, about 5 minutes. Add tomatoes, parsley, oregano, dill weed, red pepper flakes, and salt. Reduce heat to medium-low and cook for 10 minutes.

2. Add shrimp and cook, stirring frequently, just until they turn pink, about 6 minutes. Reduce heat to low. Stir in feta cheese. When cheese is melted, sprinkle with fresh basil. Serve over Saffron Basmati Rice (see Index).

CHEF NOTE: You can substitute 3 (14.5-ounce) cans recipe-ready diced tomatoes (drained) for fresh as a time saver. Substitute scallops for shrimp and serve over cavatelli pasta instead of rice for an equally tasty dish.

Legends about fresh basil abound. Ancient Greeks and Romans screamed curses at the basil seeds as they were planted, believing this was the only way the herb would grow. They also believed that if left under a pot, a basil leaf would morph into a scorpion. Some even believed the distinctive odor of basil would cause scorpions to grow in one's brain. Given such superstitions, it is a wonder that this remarkable plant was ever given a culinary chance. But today, found in the cuisine of virtually every culture, basil ranks as the world's most popular herb. In the Keys, basil grows to shrublike proportions in dooryard gardens.

Florida Keys Paella

A popular dish in all cultures the Spanish colonized, paella was introduced to the Florida Keys by Cuban immigrants. The word *paella* is believed to have originated as part of the Egyptian-Arabic dialect (*baqiyah*), meaning "left-overs." Legend has it that when the Arabs ruled Spain, fishermen and servants who worked for the rulers were allowed to take away left-overs after a major feast. The workers mixed together the seafood, chicken, and rice for easier transport home. Eventually peasants made the dish from scratch. In Spain the rice was colored by saffron because it was plentiful, but Cubans in the Keys often use the less expensive ground annatto (achiote) commonly found in super-markets.

1 pound large shrimp
2 sticks celery, cut into quarters
1 medium yellow onion, quartered plus 1 cup chopped onions
1 large carrot, cut in thirds
2 cups cream sherry
1 (14.5-ounce) can diced tomatoes
½ teaspoon cayenne pepper
½ teaspoon white pepper
¾ cup olive oil, divided
4 large cloves garlic, minced
1 green pepper, cut into ¼-inch strips
2 peeled and seeded fresh tomatoes, chopped

2 dry chorizo sausages (3-ounces total), cut into ¼-inch slices
2 pounds skinless, boneless chicken thighs (about 6 thighs)
½ pound boneless pork loin, cut into 1-inch chunks
1 teaspoon salt
¼ teaspoon thyme
½ teaspoon ground saffron
2 cups Arborio rice
2 lobster tails, meat removed and cut into 1-inch chunks
1 pound littleneck clams, scrubbed

1. Peel and de-vein shrimp; reserve shells. Place shrimp in plastic zipper bag and refriger-ate until needed. Place shrimp shells in a 4-quart pot over high heat. Add celery, quar-tered onion, carrot, and sherry. Place tomatoes in a blender and puree. Add pureed tomatoes to pot. Season with cayenne and white peppers and stir to mix well. When mixture comes to a boil, reduce heat to low, cover and simmer for 1½ hours, stirring occasionally.

2. Meanwhile, make the sofrito: Place ¼ cup olive oil in a large skillet over medium heat. Add chopped onions, garlic, green pepper, chopped fresh tomatoes, and chorizo sausage. Sauté, stirring constantly until most of liquid has evaporated and mixture is thickened, about 10 minutes. Cover and set aside.

3. Place ¼ cup olive oil in a large skillet over medium-high heat. Season chicken thighs and pork loin chunks with salt and thyme. Place thighs, topside down, in skillet. Sauté until underside is brown, then turn thighs over and brown other side, about 7 minutes.

Remove chicken to a plate and cover with aluminum foil. Add pork. Sauté, stirring often, until pork is browned, about 4 minutes. Remove pork to plate with chicken. Set aside until needed.

4. Preheat oven to 400°F. Strain shrimp stock through cheesecloth, discarding shells and vegetables. Reserve 1½ cups stock for paella and freeze the rest for future use. Place reserved stock, 1½ cups water, and saffron in a large glass container, cover with plastic wrap, and microwave for 2 minutes or until mixture comes to a boil.

5. Meanwhile, place ¼ cup olive oil in a large skillet over medium heat. When oil is hot, add rice and sauté, stirring constantly, for 2 minutes. Add hot stock and stir to mix. Add sofrito mixture and stir to combine all ingredients. Transfer rice mixture to an 18-inch paella pan or two 12-inch round baking pans. Place chicken pieces and pork evenly in pan, pressing meat into rice mixture. Add shrimp and lobster, evenly distributing seafood and pressing into rice mixture.

6. Place paella in oven. Bake uncovered for 35 minutes (do not stir). Top paella with clams and cook 5 minutes more, until clams have opened. Remove paella from oven and place on heatproof pad. (Rice will continue to cook when removed from oven.) Cover with kitchen towel and allow it to rest for 5 minutes. Serve paella tableside.

CHEF NOTE: A traditional paella pan is a large, round, shallow pan called a *paellero*. You can also make paella in a similarly sized ovenproof skillet or two smaller baking dishes.

Lobstermania

The Cubans called them *langouste*; **Key Westers said they were crawfish. And, before World War I these plentiful crustaceans were considered nothing but fish bait. Lobsters! Not your mighty Maines, or American lobster, from up north. These are the tropical variety,** *Palinurus argus*, **known in much of the world as spiny or rock lobsters. Here they are known as Florida lobsters, now a much-coveted delicacy in Keys culinary circles.**

ABOVE: *Wooden lobster traps.* Credit: State Archives of Florida. **RIGHT:** *The Florida lobster, ca. 1962.* Credit: State Archives of Florida.

Unlike its Downeast cousin, the Florida lobster is clawless. But spineless it is not. Characterized by two large hooked horns over the eyes, spines all over its hard-shelled body, a pair of long, jointed antennae, and 10 spiderlike legs, the crustacean also has a powerful tail muscle—the source of almost all the lobster's meat—that propels it backward at warp speed at the first hint of danger.

In the first half of the twentieth century, Keys lobstermen worked from skiffs in shallow nearshore waters, where they harvested the crustaceans with primitive long-handled dip nets called bully nets (a circular frame attached at a right angle to the end of a pole and supporting a conical bag of webbing). They also used cast nets and "grains," a type of spear. Lobster "landings" averaged about 350,000 pounds per year until the 1940s. (In 1920 lobster was 4 cents a pound in Key West and was sold on the street.) Then demand from northern markets dramatically increased and harvesting methods began

evolving. By the 1970s, standard wooden traps, which are still used today, became common practice. The traps are placed at depths up to several hundred feet, and the lobsters are captured alive. Landings increased to 5.1 million pounds per year and have remained steady for decades, making lobstering one of Florida's most important industries.

The spiny lobsters harvested in Florida Keys waters may have had their beginnings as far away as South America. Mating of the spiny lobster takes place from March through July. (Lobsters cannot be harvested during this time.) A female carries clusters of fertilized eggs under her abdomen for about three weeks before they hatch. The hatchlings, which resemble flat, transparent larvae, drift in ocean currents that move in a northerly pattern from South America, through the Caribbean Sea, around the Gulf of Mexico, into the Florida Straits (between Cuba and the Florida Keys), and up the oceanside of the Keys. During this nine-month journey, the lobster larva passes through 11 stages of develop-

ment, until it resembles a transparent 1-inch-long lobster. Finally able to swim on its own and aided by counterclockwise currents, the organism, called a postlarva, moves shoreward, finally settling into the shallow Keys waters of Florida Bay, where it molts into a juvenile. In 3 years the juvenile reaches maturity, leaving its bayside nurseries and heading out to the coral reef, 4 miles offshore in the Atlantic.

The last consecutive Wednesday and Thursday in July is designated sport lobster season in the Florida Keys, when amateurs can take a crack at harvesting the crustaceans before the commercial season opens. The event takes on festival proportions in the Keys, with every hotel, motel, and campground filled to capacity. Divers are allowed to net six lobsters per person per day, from sunrise to sunset.

Spiny lobster is marketed—fresh or frozen, raw or cooked—as whole lobster, tails, split tails, or lobster meat. Frozen tails are usually marketed as rock lobster tails. Uncooked, a spiny lobster has mottled coloring of yellow, brown, orange, and blue all over its body. When cooked, it turns a bright red-orange like its northern cousin. A 1-pound whole Florida lobster yields about ⅓ pound cooked lobster meat.

Grilled Florida Lobster Tails

Serves 4

4 lobster tails
8 tablespoons (1 stick) melted butter, divided
salt and freshly ground black pepper

onion powder (optional)
garlic powder (optional)
1 key lime, quartered

1. Preheat gas grill. With a sharp knife or kitchen scissors, butterfly each tail by cutting through the outer shell and meat, but not through the underside shell. Spread the tails open and drizzle 2 tablespoons melted butter over lobster meat. Sprinkle with salt and pepper to taste. Sprinkle with onion and/or garlic powder if desired.

2. Place each tail on a double-thick piece of aluminum foil (12 x 8 inches) and fold the foil envelope style, sealing tightly. Grill for 15 to 20 minutes or until the shells are bright red and the meat, when tested with a knife, is no longer translucent. Divide remaining 6 tablespoons of melted butter among 4 small dishes. Squeeze a quartered key lime into each dish of butter. Serve butter with lobster tail.

Jumbo Shrimp with Rigatoni a la Mangia Mangia

Mangia Mangia, which means "eat, eat," in Italian, is Key West's definitive pasta restaurant. The chef makes all pasta and innovative sauces, like this one, fresh on the premises every day.

CHEF NOTE: Chef Eliot Barton of Key West's Mangia Mangia restaurant advises: "Prepare all ingredients in advance. If using fresh pasta, this dish can be cooked in the time the pasta takes to cook (barely 3 minutes). If using dried pasta, adjust timing by first starting the pasta, and when nearly done, sauté the shrimp."

2 cups arugula, well washed and spun dry

3 leaves radicchio, torn in small pieces

3 spears Belgian endive, cut lengthwise into thin julienne

1 tablespoon lemon juice

2 tablespoons extra-virgin olive oil

¼ cup olive oil

12 jumbo shrimp, peeled and deveined

1 heaping tablespoon finely chopped garlic

1 finely chopped shallot

2 ounces thinly sliced prosciutto, cut into julienne

salt and freshly ground black pepper

¼ teaspoon crushed red pepper flakes

8 large kalamata olives, pitted and chopped

1 large tomato, seeded and cut into 1-inch cubes

½ pound rigatoni pasta

freshly grated Romano cheese

4 lemon wedges for garnish

1. Toss arugula, radicchio, and endive together in a small bowl and set aside. Mix lemon juice and extra-virgin olive oil in another small bowl and set aside.

2. Heat ¼ cup olive oil in a 12-inch skillet over medium-high. Add shrimp, garlic, shallot, prosciutto, salt and pepper to taste, and crushed red pepper flakes. Moving the pan almost constantly to ensure even cooking of shrimp, sauté until shrimp appears no longer translucent and nearly cooked through, about 3 minutes. Add olives and tomatoes and toss them in the oil only long enough to heat tomatoes through, about 1 minute. (The dish is finished before the tomatoes appear soft.)

3. Meanwhile, cook pasta according to chef's note. Drain pasta well. Place a serving of rigatoni on each of 2 plates. Top each plate of pasta with half the shrimp mixture. Cover with a generous portion of grated Romano cheese. Top each plate with half the mixed greens. Drizzle lemon dressing over greens. Serve with lemon wedges to squeeze over entire dish.

Scallops Caribbean

2 pounds dry diver sea scallops
2 tablespoons olive oil
salt and freshly ground black pepper
¼ cup low-fat chicken broth
⅓ cup plus 1 tablespoon crushed
  pineapple, lightly drained

3 tablespoons Major Grey's mango
  chutney
2 tablespoons Myers's dark rum
2 tablespoons butter

1. Rinse scallops and pat dry on paper toweling. Place scallops and olive oil in a medium bowl. Toss gently to coat scallops with oil. Sprinkle with salt and pepper to your preferences and toss again. Cover bowl with plastic wrap and refrigerate scallops until needed.

2. Place chicken broth, pineapple with juices, and chutney in a medium saucepan over medium-high heat. Bring mixture to a boil, stirring frequently, and boil until liquid reduces by half. Reduce heat to low. Add rum and carefully flame it. Stir in butter, one tablespoon at a time. Cover saucepan and keep warm over low heat until needed.

3. Place a large nonstick skillet over high heat for 1 to 2 minutes or until skillet is hot and nearly smoking. Turn stove's exhaust fan on high. Add scallops and sear them for 2 minutes, stirring constantly, until they are browned and cooked through. Do not overcook.

4. Divide scallops among dinner plates. Spoon a portion of the sauce over scallops and serve immediately.

CHEF NOTE: You can usually get dry diver scallops from a reputable fishmonger.

Dry scallops are sea scallops that have not been treated with sodium tripolyphosphate solution (STP). They brown much better than wet scallops, those that have been subjected to this preservative. Diver scallops are harvested in the Atlantic Ocean by scuba divers, not caught in drag nets offshore. When scallops are labeled dry and/or diver, it guarantees that they are not actually cut-out circles of skate wings (a ray type fish), which is what many supermarkets sell as scallops today.

Shrimp and Chutney-Rice Lavash Wraps

Of all the ancient flatbreads so popular today for wrap sandwiches, Armenian lavash may be the oldest. History maintains early peoples pounded hard grain into flour, then mixed it with water forming a batter that they poured over a hot rock. When the batter had cooked through, they peeled the bread off the rock. By Biblical times, long sheets of dough were stretched and then baked in clay ovens, and the bread has been prepared the same way for thousands of years. Nomads across the Asian continent may have invented the original wrap sandwich centuries ago: They rolled lavash around a mixture of meat and vegetables, eliminating the need for containers or utensils.

2 teaspoons olive oil
2 tablespoons chopped red onions
2 tablespoons chopped Anaheim peppers
1 clove garlic, minced
12 ounces large shrimp (21-25 count), peeled, deveined, and cut in half lengthwise through the body
1/2 teaspoon grated fresh lime peel
1/2 teaspoon dried thyme
1/8 teaspoon freshly ground black pepper
1/8 teaspoon ground cinnamon
1 1/2 cups halved red seedless grapes
2 teaspoons fresh lime juice
1/8 teaspoon bottled hot sauce
2 cups cooked white rice
1/2 cup Major Grey's mango chutney
4 garlic-and-herb or other flavored lavash bread rounds (11-inch diameter)

1. Heat olive oil in a large nonstick skillet over medium heat. Add onions, peppers, and garlic. Sauté until the onion is tender, about 3 minutes. Add shrimp, lime peel, thyme, black pepper, and cinnamon. Sauté, stirring frequently, until shrimp is barely cooked and no longer translucent, about 4 to 5 minutes. Add grapes, lime juice, and hot sauce. Mix well and remove from heat.

2. Place cooked rice in a microwaveproof container and microwave on high for 1 1/2 minutes, or until rice is hot. Add chutney to rice and stir to mix well.

3. Place lavash bread rounds in a large plastic zipper bag. Seal and microwave on high for 30 seconds or until heated through. Remove lavash from bag and, working two at a time, place lavash on kitchen counter. Spread 1/2 cup rice and one-quarter of the shrimp/grape mixture on the lower half of each lavash round. Fold in the sides, then tightly roll up the lavash. Place the wraps seam-side down on a serving platter. Cut each wrap in half on the diagonal.

CHEF NOTE: I prefer Boghosian Valley Bread flavored lavash, which you can find in most any supermarket, but any lavash flatbread will work in this recipe.

Shrimp and Lobster Key Lime a la Fish House

8 tablespoons (1 stick) butter plus
    2 tablespoons

1 tablespoon Louisiana-style hot sauce

½ tablespoon key lime juice

½ tablespoon minced garlic

2 pounds medium shrimp (21-25
    count), peeled and deveined

1½ pounds spiny lobster tails (about 4
    small), removed from shells and
    coarsely chopped

1 pound fresh mushrooms, sliced

¼ cup chopped scallions

¼ cup white wine

6 cups hot cooked rice

1. **Early in the day:** Place 8 tablespoons butter in a small bowl and allow it to soften at room temperature. Add hot sauce and lime juice; stir to mix well. Cover bowl with plastic wrap and refrigerate this key lime butter until needed.

2. Melt 2 tablespoons plain butter in a large nonstick skillet over medium-high heat. Add shrimp and lobster and sauté, stirring frequently, until shrimp just turns pink, about 2 to 3 minutes. Do not overcook. Reduce heat to medium. Add mushrooms, scallions, and wine. Sauté, stirring frequently, until just tender, about 2 to 3 minutes. Remove from heat. Add key lime butter and stir until butter melts and is well blended with seafood. Serve with hot rice.

CHEF NOTE: You can substitute scallops for the lobster or shrimp in this dish or use a combination of all three. Serve this buttery entree with your favorite pasta instead of rice if you like.

The campy nautical décor at the Fish House restaurant in Key Largo belies the depths of culinary talents lurking in the kitchen, to which this buttery seafood dish will attest. Owners C. J. Berwick and Doug Prew offer this and other scintillating entrees at their upscale fine-dining establishment Encore, next door, as well.

Stone Crabs
Keys Renewable Resource

Unique to Florida waters, stone crabs have long been a culinary delicacy in the Keys. With small reddish-brown bodies covered with mottled black spots and mallet-sized claws, these non-swimming scavengers feed upon oysters, scallops, other mollusks, and sometimes even each other. The stone crab's two claws serve distinct purposes: The larger claw, the crusher, is used to fight off predators or hold food, while the smaller claw, the ripper, cuts the food like a scissors. Interestingly, a marking on the inside of the crusher claw resembles a thumbprint.

ABOVE: *Stone crab claws, a Keys delicacy, ca. 1963.* Credit: State Archives of Florida.

Since the 1960s, wooden slatted traps, weighted with slabs of concrete, have been used to commercially harvest the stone crabs. Before the beginning of the stone crab season, which runs from October 15 to May 15, fishermen assemble hundreds of traps and treat them for rot. With the start of the season, they transport the traps from storage to their boats, then out to open water. Here the traps are set in a straight line, and each is marked as the fishermen's domain by a numbered, color-coded buoy that is registered with the State. Every day the traps are baited with a fresh supply of smelly rotting grouper or snapper heads.

When attracted to the bait, the stone crab goes in a one-way door. Once trapped, the crab falls prey to one of its two most dangerous enemies, octopus or man. Of the two, the octopus is deadliest. Slipping through the trap's slats, the octopus slides its mantle atop the crab's body, wrapping itself around the crab, just out of reach of its claws. With its birdlike beak, the octopus eats a hole in the top of the crab's shell, partially consuming the body, and abandoning the carcass.

The crab fares slightly better if captured by man. Florida law forbids fishermen from harvesting whole stone crabs because the crabs have the unique ability to regenerate severed appendages. So instead of killing the crab, the fishermen sever the claws at the joints and place the crab back in the sea. "If you put pressure on the claw in the right way, the crab will release it for you. If you force it, the claw breaks down near the body, the wound won't heal, and the crab will likely die," states Randy Hochberg, a stone crab researcher in St. Petersburg.

Until the 1970s only one of the two crab claws could be harvested so the crab would have some means of defense and be able to kill its prey. But research showed clawless stone crabs were still able to feed and survive, so the law was changed. Today commercial fishermen are allowed to harvest both claws as long as each measures 2¾ inches or more. It takes approximately 18 months for the crab to grow a harvestable appendage, which can be regenerated three or four times in its lifetime. Time will tell whether the current law will cause Florida Keys' stone crab population to become depleted.

Attracted by a place to hide during the daylight hours, lobsters sometimes get caught in the stone crab traps and discover they cannot leave, an added bonanza for the fishermen. The lobster's only way out without capture is if a loggerhead turtle bashes in the trap while searching for mussels.

Stone Crab Claws

Seafood markets in the Florida Keys only sell stone crab claws fully cooked. Because icing or freezing raw stone crab claws causes the meat to stick to the inside of the shell, they are cooked immediately upon landing. A mild, sweet odor indicates freshness. Any hint of an ammonia smell means the crabs are old. Bright orange in color, with shiny black tips, the claw's heavy porcelain-like shell must be cracked before serving. If you plan to eat your stone crab claws within an hour or two of purchase, have the market crack them for you. Otherwise, crack the claws yourself, just before you eat them.

To properly crack a stone crab claw: With a wooden mallet (available at seafood markets) or a small hammer, make a firm, quick hit once on each side of the three segments—forearm, elbow, and claw. (Some people like to wrap the claw in a dish towel first, so that it cushions the blows and absorbs the leakage.) The shells also will crack like a crockery teacup if you hit one claw against the other. Separate the forearm and elbow segments. Then grasp the claw by the pincers, twist and pull. The entire lump of pincer muscle should come free with the pincer as a handle. (The meat should be sweet and firm textured. If it looks brownish or striated, or clings to the shell, the crab is old or has been frozen.)

To serve: Place cold cracked crab claws on a serving platter. Garnish with lime wedges and sprigs of parsley. Serve with mustard sauce. Pick the meat from the shells with a small cocktail fork.

Mustard Sauce

½ cup mayonnaise
½ cup sour cream
2 tablespoons Dijon mustard
1 tablespoon honey

1. Combine and stir all ingredients. Place in a covered container and refrigerate until needed.

Shrimp Pad Thai

Pad Thai, or fried noodles, is probably the most well known Thai dish in the world, so it is no surprise that it has traveled as far as the Florida Keys. The Thai secret to cooking is that each dish in the cuisine utilizes all five taste buds—spicy, sweet, salty, bitter, and sour—and this one is no exception. With as many versions as there are cooks, Pad Thai is the perfect showcase for Key West Pinks.

9 ounces fresh fettuccine noodles
2 tablespoons olive oil
3 tablespoons fish sauce
¼ cup ketchup
2 tablespoons sugar
3 tablespoons water
⅓ cup chopped lightly salted cocktail peanuts
¼ cup chopped scallions

¼ cup chopped fresh flat leaf parsley
½ teaspoon crushed red pepper
1 tablespoon canola oil, divided
1 pound large shrimp (21-25), peeled and deveined
5 large cloves garlic, minced
2 extra-large eggs, lightly beaten
2 cups bean sprouts
1 lime, cut into 6 wedges

1. Cook fettuccine noodles in a large pot of water to al dente, following package directions. Drain pasta and toss with olive oil. Set aside.

2. Combine fish sauce, ketchup, sugar, and 3 tablespoons water in a small bowl. Stir to combine. Set aside.

3. Place peanuts, scallions, parsley, and crushed red pepper in a small bowl. Stir to combine. Set aside.

4. Place 1 teaspoon canola oil in a large nonstick wok or stir-fry pan over medium-high heat. Add shrimp and stir-fry, stirring constantly for 3 minutes or until shrimp just turn pink. Remove shrimp from skillet and set aside.

5. Add 2 teaspoons canola oil to pan and heat. Add garlic. Stir-fry for 30 seconds. Add eggs and stir-fry for 30 seconds. Add fettuccine noodles and fish sauce and stir-fry for 1½ minutes. Return shrimp to pan and stir-fry for 30 seconds. Add bean sprouts and stir-fry for 15 seconds. Remove from heat and transfer to a large serving bowl. Sprinkle Pad Thai with peanut mixture and serve with lime wedges.

CHEF NOTE: I have Americanized this version of Pad Thai by substituting fettuccine noodles for traditional rice-stick noodles for a heartier meal.

Sizzled Shrimp Scampi with Ginger-Herb Butter Sauce

 SERVES 4

8 tablespoons (1 stick) butter, softened at room temperature

¼ cup snipped fresh cilantro

2 large cloves garlic, minced

2 tablespoons snipped fresh chives

1 tablespoon minced fresh gingerroot

2 teaspoons sesame oil

¼ teaspoon salt

¼ teaspoon white pepper

½ cup chopped shallots

¼ cup chopped red bell peppers

¼ cup chopped yellow bell peppers

3 cloves garlic, minced

¼ cup chopped red onions

2 pounds large shrimp (21-26 count), peeled and deveined

½ teaspoon bottled hot sauce

¼ cup white wine

2 tablespoons snipped fresh parsley

1 loaf French bread, cut into thin slices

1. **Up to one month ahead:** Place butter, cilantro, garlic, chives, gingerroot, sesame oil, salt, and pepper in a small bowl. Mix well with a spoon. Transfer this ginger-herb butter mixture to a 15-inch piece of plastic wrap. Fold plastic wrap over butter mixture and roll, forming a log, about 1½-inches in diameter. Twist ends and place underneath log. Wrap butter log in another piece of plastic wrap and freeze until needed.

2. **To prepare shrimp:** Cut two 1-inch slices from butter log. Bring butter to room temperature. (Reseal butter and return it to freezer.) Melt 1 piece of butter in a large nonstick skillet over medium-high heat. Add shallots, bell peppers, minced garlic, and onions. Sauté for 1½ minutes, stirring frequently. Add shrimp, hot sauce, and the other piece of butter and sauté, stirring constantly, until shrimp start to turn pink, about 1½ minutes. Add white wine and continue cooking until shrimp are pink and cooked through and wine has combined with butter mixture, 1 to 2 minutes more. Divide shrimp among 4 large, shallow soup or pasta bowls. Pour remaining butter sauce over shrimp. Sprinkle parsley over shrimp. Serve with crusty French bread to dip in the ginger-herb butter.

CHEF NOTE: If you like your scampi more on the hot and spicy side, add more hot sauce to taste or substitute Thai-style chili sauce for the hot sauce.

People tend to love or hate cilantro, and for some it is an acquired taste. Like so many commonly used herbs, cilantro had its beginnings in the lands bordering the Mediterranean Sea and was introduced to the Americas by the Spanish conquistadors. Cilantro, also called Chinese parsley, is the name of the plant's leaves only, however. The plant itself, as well as its seeds, is properly called coriander.

Credited over the centuries with everything from bleaching freckles to neutralizing poisons and curing the common cold, lemon juice is a staple in Conchfusion cuisine. Two types of lemons exist—acid and sweet. Acidic lemons, which are grown commercially, are the common supermarket offering. Home gardeners grow the sweet varieties. Nearly every dooryard garden in the Florida Keys has a lemon tree, which blooms continuously and can produce up to 500 or 600 lemons a year.

Ultimate Crab Cakes with Spring Greens and Lemon Sauce

¾ cup dry white wine
¾ cup chicken broth
¼ cup fresh lemon juice
2 teaspoons cornstarch
1½ teaspoons sugar
4 tablespoons (½ stick) butter, divided
1 pound Phillips® pasteurized blue crabmeat, rinsed and patted dry
⅓ cup mayonnaise
½ cup thinly sliced scallions

¼ cup minced red bell peppers
¼ cup thinly sliced celery
2 tablespoons Dijon mustard
1 clove garlic, minced
⅛ teaspoon cayenne pepper
2 large eggs, beaten
¼ cup fresh breadcrumbs
1 pound spring greens
1 lemon, quartered

1. **To make lemon sauce:** Place wine and broth in a 2-quart saucepan over medium-high heat. Bring to a boil and cook about 8 minutes, stirring frequently, until mixture reduces by half (about ¾ cup). Mix together lemon juice, cornstarch, and sugar in a small bowl and slowly stir it into broth mixture. Keep stirring until sauce boils again. Stir in 2 tablespoons butter. Reduce heat to low, cover saucepan, and keep sauce warm.

2. **To make crab cakes:** Place crabmeat, mayonnaise, scallions, red pepper, celery, mustard, garlic, and cayenne pepper in a large bowl. Stir to mix well. Mix beaten eggs thoroughly into crab mixture. Add breadcrumbs and stir to mix well.

3. **To cook crab cakes:** Melt 1 tablespoon butter in each of 2 (10-inch) non-stick skillets over medium heat. Place six mounds of crab mixture in each skillet using the serving spoon from your cutlery set as a measure. Flatten each mound into a cake with the

back of the spoon. Cook 4 minutes. Carefully turn each cake over. (The cakes hold together tenuously because only a scant amount of breadcrumbs are used in this recipe.) Cook cakes an additional 2 minutes or until the underside is nicely browned.

4. **To serve:** Place 3 crab cakes on each dinner plate. Mix greens with 1/3 cup lemon sauce. Divide greens among plates. Spoon remaining sauce around crab cakes. Garnish with lemon wedges.

CHEF NOTE: Use backfin or lump grade blue crab for these crab cakes. If your pocketbook is flush and you can find it, substitute Dungeness or even stone crab. You can prepare the crabmeat mixture a couple of hours ahead of time and refrigerate it until you are ready to cook the cakes.

Tomato-Coconut-Curry Shrimp

Canned coconut milk is made when one part water and one part shredded raw coconut are simmered until frothy, then squeezed and strained through cheesecloth. It differs from two other coconut products on the market, unsweetened coconut cream and sweetened cream of coconut. Unsweetened coconut cream, also sold in cans, is one part water to four parts coconut and is therefore richer than coconut milk. Sweetened cream of coconut has the same proportions as unsweetened coconut cream but has been commercially sweetened for use in desserts and beverages.

2 tablespoons olive oil

1 medium sweet onion, like Vidalia, halved and thinly sliced

1 clove garlic, minced

½ tablespoon minced fresh gingerroot

1 jalapeno pepper, seeded and minced

1½ tablespoons Madras curry powder

3 cups peeled, seeded, chopped tomatoes

1 (14-ounce) can unsweetened coconut milk

1 teaspoon sugar

½ teaspoon salt

½ teaspoon crushed red pepper flakes

1 tablespoon fresh lemon juice

2 pounds large shrimp (21-25), peeled and deveined

¼ cup snipped fresh basil

3 tablespoons flaked, sweetened coconut

1. Place olive oil in a large skillet over medium heat. When oil is hot, add onions, garlic, gingerroot, and jalapenos. Cook, stirring constantly, until onion is softened, about 2 minutes. Add curry powder and stir into onion mixture. Cook 1 minute more. Add tomatoes, coconut milk, sugar, salt, crushed red pepper flakes, and lemon juice. Cook, stirring frequently, for 2 minutes, until slightly thickened.

2. Add shrimp and basil and cook, stirring constantly, for 2 minutes or until shrimp just turn pink and curl slightly, indicating they are cooked through. (Do not overcook.)

3. Remove from heat. Divide among 6 dinner plates. Sprinkle each portion with coconut. Serve curry with Coconut Basmati Rice Pilaf (see Index).

CHEF NOTE: Be sure to have all your ingredients chopped and ready to go before you begin this dish. It is quick and easy.

Old Sour

Old Sour has spiced up Florida Keys cuisine for more than three centuries, but it is probably safe to say, many twenty-first-century Conchs, "strangers," or visitors to the islands never heard of it. The Bahamian fishermen, or Conchs, who immigrated to the Keys in the early eighteenth century, always took a bottle of Old Sour with them on their boats, and virtually all Key Westers kept a bottle of the homemade seasoning at hand.

Old Sour is a mixture of fresh key lime juice, salt, and hot bird peppers. Usage of Old Sour differed between the Conch and Cuban cultures in Key West.

Cubans used Old Sour during cooking, but not after the dish left the stove. Conchs, on the other hand, kept a bottle on the table at all times, seasoning their food according to personal preference. Either way, Key West folks never ate fish or seafood without a few drops of this spicy liquid gold.

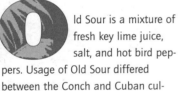

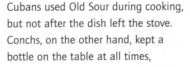

LEFT: *Two men grill at a fishing shack on tidal flats, ca. 1965.*
Credit: State Archives of Florida.

Old Sour

Early Key Westers were divided as to the proper containers for Old Sour. Some felt the bottles should be made of brown or green glass; others said it made no difference. My guess is that in the days before refrigeration, the dark glass might have impeded spoilage, a problem not encountered today.

2 cups fresh key lime juice, strained
1 tablespoon coarse or kosher salt
3 whole bird peppers

1. Place lime juice and salt in a glass jar. Seal and shake to combine. Place 3 bird peppers in a tall-necked glass bottle. Using a funnel, pour lime juice mixture into bottle and seal tightly. Allow mixture to rest at room temperature in a dark place for 2 weeks, then refrigerate for up to 4 months. Makes 1 pint.

Chef Note: A bird pepper is a tiny Thai chile, about 1-inch long and ½-inch wide. It is very, very hot. You can substitute twice as many serrano chiles if you can't find bird peppers.

Meat and Poultry  6

Until the completion of Flagler's Overseas Railroad Extension to Key West in 1912, fresh meat and poultry were rare dinner treats for some and a distant memory for many. Brought to the Keys by ship from the U.S. mainland or from Cuba, beef and pork, and to a lesser degree chickens, were special-occasion entrees. Veal and lamb were rarely encountered.

In spite of a Key West ordinance forbidding it in the early 1900s, residents kept chickens in their backyards throughout the city. Conchs raised Plymouth Rocks and Rhode Island Reds; Cubans preferred gamecocks. Occasionally settlers would shoot a deer and at least one dining account relates roast heron served at Christmas. But turtles, fish, and seafood remained dietary staples well into the twentieth century.

Members of the Key West Woman's Club recall in the *Key West Cookbook*, handwritten in 1949: "Living among Spanish speaking people as we do on the island, many of our meat recipes take a Spanish turn, which implies plenty of seasoning, plenty of onion and garlic, red pepper and green, thyme and tarragon, and one especially native—oregano."

LEFT: *Butcher by display at meat market, ca. 1910.* **Credit: State Archives of Florida.**

Asian Flank Steak

Most popular and well known of the mint family is peppermint, believed to be a hybrid of spearmint and watermint. Native to the Mediterranean and western Asia, peppermint has been valued for centuries as a treatment for digestive ailments. Combined with gingerroot, it is an effective treatment for motion sickness.

2¼ pounds flank steak
¼ cup fresh lime juice
¼ cup snipped fresh peppermint
¼ cup soy sauce
1½ tablespoons minced peeled gingerroot

1 tablespoon minced, seeded jalapeno peppers
2 cloves garlic, minced
8 sprigs of fresh mint

1. **At least 8 hours ahead:** Lightly score flank steak crisscross on the diagonal. Place in a 2-quart freezer-weight plastic zipper bag.

2. Combine lime juice, mint, soy sauce, gingerroot, jalapeno peppers, and garlic in a medium bowl. Pour over steak in zipper bag, seal, and refrigerate. Marinate for 8 to 12 hours, turning the bag occasionally.

3. Preheat gas grill. Remove steak from marinade. Place marinade in a small bowl and microwave it on high for 1 minute or until it boils. Reserve marinade for basting. Place steak on grill and cook for about 6 minutes per side, basting constantly with marinade, or until steak, when scored on the diagonal, is seared on the outside and still rare within. (Steak will continue cooking after it is removed from the grill, so be careful not to overcook it.)

4. Remove steak from grill and slice diagonally across the grain into thin slices. Place on a platter and garnish with sprigs of fresh mint.

CHEF NOTE: Peppermint is so easy to grow in your dooryard garden that it may take over all your other herbs. Because mint sends out proprietary runners, plant your mint, pot and all, into the ground to contain its growth.

Flank Steak Hare and Hound

1 cup brown sugar
⅓ cup yellow mustard
3 pounds flank steak

1. **Up to 2 hours ahead:** Place brown sugar and mustard in a small bowl and mix with a spoon to form a smooth, thick paste.

2. Place knife at an angle and thinly slice flank steak 1½-inches wide, across the grain. Separate slices into piles by size. Then divide sliced steak into 6 portions (about 7 ounces each), largest slices first, working to smallest slices. (You will have 6 piles of steak slices with shortest on top.)

3. Place a large piece of wax paper on kitchen counter. Beginning with the smallest slice of steak from one portion, brush slice generously with brown sugar/mustard mixture. Roll up slice around itself. Brush next slice with brown sugar mixture and roll it around previous slice. Continue slice by slice, until a pinwheel is formed. Secure with toothpicks. Repeat with other 5 portions of steak slices. Brush top and bottom of pinwheel steak logs with mustard-sugar mixture, making sure the top is well covered. Refrigerate, covered with aluminum foil, until needed.

4. Preheat gas grill. Grill flank steak pinwheels to medium rare, about 7 minutes per side, basting frequently with any remaining sugar mixture. (Steak will continue cooking when removed from grill so be careful not to overcook.)

CHEF NOTE: Flank is the only steak in the beef carcass containing an entire large muscle. Flank steak fibers run the entire length of the steak, so it should be cut on a diagonal across the grain for maximum chewability. When properly cooked, this lean, flat cut is fairly tender and extremely flavorful.

When one of my Duck Key friends lived in England for a while, he and his wife loved a rolled flank steak dish served regularly at the Hare and Hound Pub. This recipe, which he has been making for almost twenty years, is his best interpretation of the original. It is legendary on the island.

Ropa Vieja

The literal translation of this classic Cuban dish is "old clothes" or "old rags." It is so named because the meat, which is simmered for hours, is so finely shredded it resembles old tattered cloth. Ropa vieja is actually steak hash in a sofrito, or tomato-based sauce with onions, bell peppers, and garlic.

1½ pounds flank steak
2 large sweet onions, like Vidalia
6 cloves garlic
1 stalk celery, cut into thirds
½ cup white vinegar, divided
salt and freshly ground black pepper

2 tablespoons olive oil
1 green bell pepper, seeded and cut into thin strips
1 orange, yellow, or red bell pepper, seeded and cut into thin strips
1 (8-ounce) can tomato sauce

1. Place flank steak in a 4-quart saucepan. Peel 1 onion and cut it into quarters. Peel 3 cloves garlic and crush them with the back of a knife. Place onions, garlic, celery, ¼ cup vinegar, 1 teaspoon salt, and 1 teaspoon pepper in pan with flank steak. Add water to cover by 2 inches. Place saucepan over high heat and bring to a boil. Skim off foam with a kitchen spoon. Reduce heat to low, cover pan, and simmer for 1½ to 2½ hours or until meat is tender. Remove meat to a platter and allow it to cool. Reserve 1 cup meat broth. When meat is cool, shred it into strings and set aside.

2. **To make the sofrito:** Peel remaining onion, cut it in half, and then thinly slice it. Peel 3 cloves garlic and mince. Place olive oil in a large nonstick skillet over medium heat. When oil is hot, add sliced onions and minced garlic and sauté until tender, about 3 minutes. Add bell peppers and sauté 2 minutes. Add ¼ cup vinegar and 1 cup reserved broth. Cook over medium heat until most of the liquid has been absorbed, stirring frequently, about 10 minutes. Reduce heat to low and add tomato sauce and shredded beef. Stir to combine. Add salt and freshly ground black pepper to taste. Simmer mixture for 10 to 15 minutes, until sauce is heated through and mixture is bubbly.

CHEF NOTE: Traditionally, this mild dish is served with fresh Cuban bread and rice and beans. For a new twist with more kick, serve *ropa vieja* wrapped in flour tortillas. Top meat with several dashes of your favorite bottled hot sauce and sprinkle with shredded cheese.

Boliche

4 to 5 pounds eye of round roast
1 (12-ounce) bottle mojo sauce
6 links raw chorizo sausage (about
    1 pound)
1 large sweet onion, like Vidalia,
chopped

1 green pepper, chopped
3 tablespoons olive oil
1 (14.5-ounce) can diced tomatoes
    with juices

1. **One to 2 days ahead:** With a long, sharp knife, cut a pocket lengthwise in the roast, about 2 x 4 inches, to create a stuffing cavity. (Do not let the knife cut through the sides of the roast.) Place roast and cut-out piece of meat in a freezer-weight zipper bag. Pour mojo sauce over roast and seal zipper. Refrigerate overnight or up to 2 days.

2. Preheat oven to 350°F. Remove casings from chorizo sausage. Crumble sausage in a medium bowl. Place onions and bell peppers in a separate small bowl. Toss to mix. Add 1 cup vegetable mixture to bowl with sausage. Toss to mix.

3. Remove roast from marinade, reserving liquid. Place olive oil in a large covered pot or Dutch oven over medium-high heat. When oil is hot add roast and sear all sides, about 5 minutes. Remove pot from burner. Remove roast from pot, placing it on a side plate. Stuff cavity firmly with sausage mixture.

4. Add onion and bell pepper mixture to the pot, along with diced tomatoes with juice, and any remaining sausage mixture. Chop marinated cut-out piece of meat into ¾-inch dice and add to the pot. Stir to mix well.

5. Place reserved mojo marinade in a heatproof container and microwave for 1 minute or until boiling. Return roast to pot, placing it atop the vegetable mixture. Pour heated mojo marinade over roast. Cover pot and bake for 2½ to 3 hours or until meat is fork tender. Turn roast about every 30 minutes and baste with sauce.

6. **To serve:** Remove roast from pan and carve into ¾-inch slices. Stir mojo sauce in pot. Place slices on a platter and cover with sauce. Place sauce in a medium-size pitcher and serve alongside the meat. Serve boliche with yellow rice (see Index) and drizzle each serving of rice with mojo sauce.

A traditional Key West Cuban dinner, boliche is actually a stuffed pot roast made from beef round. Before roasting, a pocket is cut into the eye and stuffed with a variety of ingredients. Early recipes called for stuffing the cavity alternately with chopped ham and hard-boiled eggs. Cloves of garlic were inserted at intervals in the meat. Today, boliche is often stuffed with spicy chorizo sausage instead.

CHEF NOTE: My interpretation of boliche differs somewhat from the Cuban preparation, but the liberal use of mojo sauce is essential. If you can't find mojo (pronounced *mo-ho*) sauce in your grocery store or Spanish market, you can make your own: In a blender, place 2 cups orange juice, 2 cups lime juice, 1 cup olive oil, 6 cloves garlic, ¼ cup chopped onion, 2 tablespoons sherry, 2 teaspoons salt, 2 teaspoons oregano, 1 teaspoon cumin. Place in a jar with a tight-fitting lid. Make marinade at least 24 hours before using. It will keep in the refrigerator for 2 weeks.

Cultivated in tropical regions throughout the world, ginger-root has long been held in high regard. Today it is believed that gingerroot can lower cholesterol and reduce high blood pressure, and gingerroot tea is purported to cure a hangover and reduce morning sickness. In culinary circles, gingerroot shines. Its fiery, spicy flavor and pleasing aroma, long used in Asian cuisine, has become a staple in American kitchens.

Sesame-Gingered Sirloin with Arugula

½ cup soy sauce

½ cup sugar

¼ cup water

1 tablespoon finely snipped cilantro

1 tablespoon teriyaki sauce

¼ cup plus 2 teaspoons honey

3 tablespoons Persian lime juice

¾ teaspoon Kitchen Bouquet

2 teaspoons chopped garlic

1 teaspoon grated fresh gingerroot

3 teaspoons sesame oil

1 cup canola oil

1½ teaspoons sesame seeds

1½ teaspoons black sesame seeds

6 pounds boneless sirloin steak, 1¼-inch thick

10 ounces arugula, washed and spun dry

1. **To make the marinade:** Place soy sauce, sugar, and water in a blender. Process until sugar is dissolved. Add cilantro, teriyaki sauce, honey, lime juice, Kitchen Bouquet, garlic, and gingerroot and process to mix well. With blender on lowest speed, slowly add sesame and canola oils to emulsify the marinade. Transfer to a bowl and mix in sesame seeds with a wire whisk. Place in a covered container and refrigerate until needed. (Can be made up to 1 week in advance.) Makes about 2½ cups.

2. **One day ahead:** Place steak in a single layer in a large covered container. Pour 1½ cups sesame-ginger marinade over beef. (Refrigerate remaining ¾ cup marinade for serving.) Turn beef so that all surfaces are coated. Cover and refrigerate beef until several hours before serving. Turn beef in marinade occasionally.

3. **Three hours before serving:** Heat burners of a gas barbecue grill on high. Remove beef from marinade. Reserve marinade for basting. Grill beef, basting with reserved marinade, 7½ minutes per side, or until beef is just rare but not still bloody. Remove from grill to carving board and allow to rest at room temperature for 5 minutes (beef will continue to cook). Carve beef into ⅓-inch-thick slices.

4. **To serve:** On the center of a large serving tray, place beef slices in overlapping rows. Arrange arugula around this well of beef. Remove reserved sesame-ginger marinade from refrigerator. Drizzle about ¼ cup over beef and arugula. Cover beef platter with plastic wrap and refrigerate until serving. Bring to room temperature before serving. Serve with remaining ¾ cup marinade as a sauce on the side.

CHEF NOTE: Don't be scared off by the plethora of ingredients for this marinade. It comes together quickly in a blender and tastes so fantastic you'll lick the spoon. It also makes a great salad dressing.

Island Beef Stroganoff

The seeds of the papaya have long been used in the Florida Keys as a spice and a tenderizer. Resembling large black or gray caviar, papaya seeds are mildly pungent and have a piquant taste something like cress. The seeds contain papain, a milky substance that is commonly used in the production of commercial tenderizing powders.

½ cup plus 3 tablespoons olive oil, divided

2 tablespoons red wine vinegar

2 tablespoons key lime juice

½ teaspoon garlic powder

1 teaspoon McCormick Montreal Steak Seasoning

¼ cup fresh papaya seeds

2 pounds top sirloin, thinly sliced into ½-inch-wide by 2-inch-long strips

4 tablespoons (½ stick) butter, divided

8 ounces portobello mushrooms, thinly sliced

8 ounces white mushrooms, thinly sliced

1 medium sweet onion, like Vidalia, halved and thinly sliced (about 3 cups)

2 tablespoons flour

1 (14-ounce) can beef broth

1 tablespoon Dijon mustard

½ teaspoon Worcestershire sauce

1 pound egg noodles

1 cup sour cream

¼ cup snipped fresh parsley

1. **One day ahead:** Mix ½ cup olive oil, vinegar, lime juice, garlic powder, steak seasoning, and papaya seeds in a blender. Place beef in a freezer-weight zipper bag. Pour marinade over beef and mix well to coat all surfaces. Close bag and refrigerate overnight.

2. Place 1 tablespoon olive oil and 1 tablespoon butter in a large nonstick skillet over medium heat. When oil is hot and butter is melted, add mushrooms and sauté, stirring frequently, until mushrooms have softened and released most of their liquid. Drain mushrooms in a colander and place them in a large bowl.

3. Remove beef strips from marinade, shaking off excess marinade, and place strips on a plate. Place 2 tablespoons olive oil in a large nonstick skillet over medium-high heat. When oil is hot, add one-third of the beef strips and sauté, stirring constantly, just until beef is browned on all surfaces, about 1 to 2 minutes (do not overcook). With a slotted spoon, remove beef from skillet and place in bowl with mushrooms. Repeat this process twice, with remaining beef strips.

4. Rinse and dry skillet and return it to medium-high heat. Melt 3 tablespoons butter in skillet and add onions. Sauté, stirring frequently, for 4 minutes, or just until onions begin to soften and brown. Sprinkle onions with flour and mix well to combine. Slowly add beef broth, stirring constantly. Add mustard and Worcestershire sauce and cook for 1 to 2 minutes or until onion broth is thickened slightly.

5. Meanwhile, cook egg noodles in a large pot to al dente according to package directions. Drain and set aside.

6. Reduce skillet heat to low. Add beef strips, mushrooms, and any accumulated juices to onion broth mixture and stir well to combine. Stir in sour cream and continue cooking until mixture is just heated through, about 1 to 2 minutes longer.

7. Serve stroganoff over egg noodles. Sprinkle with parsley.

CHEF NOTE: Squeeze orange or lime juice over fresh papaya for a tropical breakfast treat. But first harvest the papaya seeds. You can place the seeds in a covered container and freeze them for up to three months. Most supermarkets stock green papayas in their produce sections. Wait until the papaya ripens to a soft orange color and begins to get a few dark spots before cutting into it.

Picadillo

Picadillo, or Cuban beef hash, ranks as one of Key West's most popular Cuban dishes. Everyone has a variation on the basic recipe, a complex concoction of ground beef, capers, onions, raisins, olives, green peppers, and tomato sauce. Some prefer it chunky, others like it finely mixed. Picadillo can be made days in advance; its flavor improves and mellows as it waits. Traditionally picadillo is served by itself, over rice with a garnish of chopped hard-boiled egg and fried plantains on the side.

2 tablespoons olive oil
3 cloves garlic, minced
1 cup chopped sweet onions, like Vidalia
2 pounds lean ground beef
½ teaspoon cumin
½ cup port wine
1 (6-ounce) can tomato paste

½ cup golden raisins
½ cup pimento-stuffed green olives, sliced
1 tablespoon olive juice
½ teaspoon salt
¼ teaspoon pepper
2 tablespoons capers, rinsed and drained
1 cup chopped green peppers

1. Place olive oil in a large skillet over medium heat. When oil is hot add garlic, onions, and ground beef and sauté for 5 minutes, stirring often, until meat is brown and cooked through. Drain meat mixture in a colander and return it to skillet. Add cumin, wine, tomato paste, raisins, olives, olive juice, salt, pepper, and capers. Reduce heat to low, cover skillet, and cook meat mixture for 20 minutes, stirring occasionally. Add green peppers and cook for 10 more minutes, stirring occasionally. (If you plan to refrigerate the picadillo and reheat, do not cook the green pepper until you reheat meat. Reheat on medium-low for 10 minutes in a large skillet before serving.)

CHEF NOTE: In old Key West, Cubans made sandwiches called *moyettes* with picadillo and small, hamburger-style buns. (Everywhere but in Key West this word is spelled mollettes, but since in Spanish the double "l"s are pronounced as "y," the Conchs corrupted the spelling over the years.) The edge of each bun would be broken off and all the breadcrumbs scooped out. Then the insides were filled with picadillo, and the broken edge of the buns fastened back on with toothpicks. The buns were dipped into eggwash, then rolled in cracker crumbs and deep-fried until golden brown. Here are new ways to enjoy classic picadillo: atop Gilda-brand scooped crackers; wrapped in a flour tortilla; as filling for tacos; in a hamburger bun as Sloppy Joes; stuffed in a mini pita. To make a more heart-healthy *moyette*, eliminate the deep-frying step.

Mexican Burrito Bake

2 pounds lean ground beef

2 cups chopped yellow onions

1 yellow bell pepper, seeded and finely chopped

2 large cloves garlic, minced

1 (1.5-ounce) package burrito seasoning mix

2 (8-ounce) cans roasted garlic tomato sauce

1 pound frozen baby gold and white corn, defrosted

2 (2.25-ounce) cans sliced black olives with jalapeno

1 (4-ounce) can green chiles, drained

1 package corn tortillas (12)

8 ounces white sharp cheddar cheese, shredded

2 cups crumbled white corn tortilla chips

8 ounces sour cream

8 ounces fresh salsa

1. Coat a large nonstick skillet with vegetable cooking spray and place it over medium heat. Add ground beef and sauté, stirring frequently, until browned, about 10 minutes. Drain beef in a colander, then return it to skillet. Add onions, bell pepper, and garlic and cook until onion is soft, about 10 minutes more. Reduce heat to low. Add seasoning mix and stir until beef mixture is well coated. Add tomato sauce and stir to combine. Cover and simmer beef mixture 10 minutes, stirring occasionally.

2. Meanwhile, mix together corn, olives, and chiles in a medium bowl. Set aside.

3. Coat a 13 x 9-inch baking dish with vegetable cooking spray. Cut 3 tortillas in half. Place tortilla halves in the bottom of the baking dish, cut sides abutting the edges of the dish. Place a whole tortilla in the space in the center of the dish, so that tortillas cover the entire bottom of the pan.

4. Place half the meat mixture atop the tortilla layer. Then place half the corn mixture atop the meat and half the cheese atop the corn mixture. Repeat the four layers: tortillas, meat, corn, cheese. (Cover with aluminum foil and refrigerate for up to two days, or cover tightly with plastic wrap, then aluminum foil, and freeze for up to 1 month.)

5. **To bake and serve:** Preheat oven to 375°F. Top burrito pie with crumbled tortilla chips. Bake uncovered for 30 minutes. Remove from oven and allow pie to rest for 5 minutes. Serve accompanied by sour cream and salsa.

With the Keys proximity to the Mexican Yucatan peninsula, it's natural that the corn tortilla became part of the Conchfusion cuisine. Traditionally, corn kernels were cooked with lime to remove the husk and then ground on a rock slab with a grinding stone. The ground corn was formed into small round balls by hand, and then flattened between two hands or on a banana leaf to form thin, round, corn cakes called tortillas. Today, corn tortillas are made with a simple metal or wooden press called a *tortilladora*.

CHEF NOTE: This recipe calls for ingredients you can keep on hand and is a breeze to prepare and serve, so it is a great choice when unexpected guests roll in, as they so often do in the Florida Keys. You can substitute taco mix for the burrito seasoning mix if you like.

Bourbon-Barbecued Baby Backs

Pork, introduced by the Spanish and a staple of Cuban cuisine, was produced in abundance on the island nation. Baby back ribs, today a gourmet delicacy, are cut from the loin section of the pig. Shorter and smaller than spareribs, baby backs are also leaner and meatier than spareribs, and have a much sweeter flavor.

4-5 pounds baby back ribs
¾ cup soy sauce
½ cup Marker's Mark bourbon
¼ cup Worcestershire sauce
¼ cup water
¼ cup canola oil

4 cloves garlic, minced
3 tablespoons brown sugar
2 tablespoons freshly ground black pepper
½ teaspoon ground ginger
1 teaspoon salt

1. **One day ahead:** Cut rib slabs into individual ribs. Place ribs in a freezer-weight zipper bag. Place remaining ingredients in a medium bowl. Stir to mix well. Pour marinade over ribs. Seal zipper bag. Place bag in another zipper bag. Seal and refrigerate overnight, turning occasionally.

2. Preheat one side of gas grill to medium-high. Place a shallow pan of water on the heated side of grill. (Heat should be hot enough to emit steam from pan but not so hot that it boils over.) Microwave marinade for 1 minute. Place ribs on unheated side of grill, close lid, and then cook ribs for 1¼ hours, turning and basting with marinade every 20 minutes, until ribs are tender and cooked through.

CHEF NOTE: Because baby back ribs are so lean, they can be easily overcooked. This steam/grill method guarantees a peppery outer crust and moist succulent meat around the bone. If you aren't a black pepper fan, reduce the amount of pepper in the marinade.

Lemon-Bourbon Pork Loin Roast

 SERVES 8

4½-pound boneless pork loin
2 tablespoons Dijon mustard
freshly ground black pepper
½ cup fresh lemon juice
1 cup Jim Beam bourbon whiskey

1 teaspoon salt
¾ cup light brown sugar
2 lemons, thinly sliced
½ cup water

1. With a long-tined fork, pierce all sides of pork loin deeply, so that marinade can penetrate. Rub all sides of roast with mustard. Place in a 13 x 9-inch baking dish. Cover top of roast liberally with freshly ground pepper.

2. Mix lemon juice, bourbon, and salt in a small bowl. Pour marinade over pork. Cover with plastic wrap and refrigerate overnight. Turn pork occasionally in marinade.

3. Preheat oven to 350°F. Remove roast from marinade. Reserve marinade. Press brown sugar onto all sides of roast. Place pork in a roasting pan. Roast uncovered for 1½ hours, basting occasionally with pan juices, or until an instant-read thermometer registers 175°F.

4. Transfer meat to a cutting board and cover with aluminum foil. Place reserved marinade, pan juices and drippings, lemon slices, and water in a small saucepan. Bring to a boil over medium heat. Boil for 2 minutes, stirring constantly, until mixture is reduced slightly and lemons are tender.

5. Carve meat into half-inch slices. Place on a serving platter. Top with lemon slices and a drizzle of sauce. Serve remaining sauce on the side.

CHEF NOTE: Fresh lemons are essential in this recipe. You can substitute any brand of bourbon whiskey for the Jim Beam.

Dijon, in eastern France, ranks as the capital of the mustard world. Making mustard there since the thirteenth century, the French have passed strict laws regulating what can be called Dijon mustard. In 1777 Monsieur Grey developed a strongly flavored mustard made with brown or black mustard seeds, white wine, and spices. Monsieur Poupon provided the financial backing for Grey's fledging manufacturing company, and Grey Poupon mustard was born. It remains the standard by which all Dijon mustards are judged to this day.

Cuban Press

One of the most popular Cuban dishes to take root in the Florida Keys is the Cuban press, a grilled, layered sandwich reminiscent of the classic American sub. A Cuban press consists of dill pickles, thinly sliced roast pork, thinly sliced ham, and Swiss cheese, layered in that order on a sliced loaf of Cuban bread, which is crusty on the outside and soft inside. Unlike the submarine sandwich, a press contains no lettuce, tomatoes, onions, mayonnaise, or bell peppers. Butter and mustard are optional.

The secret to a great Cuban press is in the grilling: The layered loaf of Cuban bread is cut into 6-inch-long pieces, each of which is coated on both sides with vegetable cooking spray and then placed in a sandwich press, called a *planca*. The press grills and compresses the sandwich until the meat has warmed in its own steam, the cheese has melted, and the bread is crispy and flattened to one-third its original size.

The origin of the Cuban sandwich is vague, but it was popular with workers in the Cuban sugar mills and cigar factories in the 1800s. Cubans immigrated to the Keys in large numbers after the Cuban Revolution in 1868, when Vicente Martinez Ybor moved his cigar-making factory from Havana to Key West. More than likely, the Cuban sandwich, which utilizes leftover Cuban roast pork, came with them.

Cuban roast pork is a loin roast that has been marinated for several hours in a mixture of sour orange juice, olive oil, garlic, onions, and oregano, then slow-roasted until tender (see Index). Cuban sandwich aficionados maintain this pork is a mandatory ingredient in an authentic press. The type of ham and cheese used in this sandwich is also important, say Cuban-Americans, who prefer a mild, sweet, cured ham and baby Swiss cheese so that their flavors don't overpower the other ingredients.

Though Cuban restaurants and delicatessens in the Florida Keys have

ABOVE: *Sign at Cuban café showing dishes offered.* **Credit: State Archives of Florida.**

...

A variation on the Cuban press is a *medianoche*, or midnight sandwich, which was traditionally eaten as a midnight snack upon returning home after a night on the town.

...

plancas in which to press the sandwiches, home cooks often have to improvise. A waffle iron, panini grill, George Forman grill, or bacon press will work. People have been known to cook the sandwich in a skillet and press it with a heated cast-iron frying pan or even a heated brick wrapped in aluminum foil.

A variation on the Cuban press is *medianoche*, or midnight sandwich, which was traditionally eaten as a midnight snack upon returning home after a night on the town. *Medianoche* contains the same filling ingredients as the press, but the sandwiches are made with egg bread, which is smaller and sweeter.

Señor Ybor, E. H. Gado, and other Key West manufacturers moved the entire cigar-making industry from Key West to Tampa, Florida—which offered them lower taxes—at the end of the nineteenth century. Once again, the Cuban press sandwich emigrated. Tampa already had a large population of Italian immigrants at that time, so it was probably inevitable that the Cuban press would be caught in a culture clash: A Cuban press sandwich made in Tampa always has a layer of salami. But in the Florida Keys, as in Cuba, the sandwich remains true to tradition.

Cuban Press

Serves 4

1 loaf Cuban or French bread, sliced in half lengthwise
1 jar hamburger dills or Sandwich Stacker dill pickle slices
1 pound thinly sliced Cuban roast pork
1 pound thinly sliced sweet cured ham
1 pound sliced baby Swiss cheese
3 tablespoons soft butter (optional)

1. Preheat sandwich press. Cut bread loaf into 6-inch-long pieces. Spread cut sides of bread with butter if desired. On the bottom slices of bread, layer sandwiches with generous portions of pickles, pork, ham, and cheese, in that order. Place top bread slices on sandwiches and coat both top and bottom bread slices with vegetable cooking spray.

2. Grill the sandwich for 4 to 5 minutes (2 to 3 minutes per side if using skillet and an iron pan for a weight), or until bread is golden brown, cheese is melted, and sandwich is flattened. Cut each sandwich on the diagonal and serve with plantain chips (see Index).

Mama Louise's Jerked Pork Chops

Jerking is the process of spicing, marinating, and grilling meats, a cooking method said to have begun with pre-colonial Arawak Indians in the Caribbean, who used allspice, also known as Jamaican pimento, to season and cook wild pigs. The many cultures that settled the islands—Spanish, British, Dutch, French, West African, East Indian, Portuguese—contributed a variety of herbs and spices from both the old and new worlds to the mix. Allspice, hot chile peppers, and salt are key ingredients in all jerk recipes, but the rest of seasonings—often closely guarded secrets—sometimes contain up to 30 herbs and spices.

1 tablespoon sugar
2 tablespoons salt
1 tablespoon thyme
1 tablespoon allspice
2 tablespoons garlic powder
3/4 teaspoon cinnamon
3/4 teaspoon nutmeg
1 1/2 teaspoons sage
1 1/2 teaspoons freshly ground black pepper
1 1/2 teaspoons cayenne pepper

3 tablespoons key lime juice
1/4 cup orange juice
1/4 cup soy sauce
3/4 cup white vinegar
1/4 cup olive oil
1 cup minced sweet onions, like Vidalia
3 scallions, minced
1 scotch bonnet pepper or 2 serrano peppers, seeded and minced
4 (12-ounce) bone-in pork chops, cut about 1 1/2 inches thick

1. **Several hours ahead:** Place sugar, salt, thyme, allspice, garlic powder, cinnamon, nutmeg, sage, black pepper, and cayenne pepper in a medium bowl. Stir well to combine. Add key lime and orange juices, soy sauce, vinegar, and olive oil, whisking to mix well with spices. Stir in onions, scallions, and hot peppers. Pour half marinade in a glass or plastic container. Add pork chops and top them with remaining marinade. Cover container and refrigerate for 3 to 4 hours.

2. Preheat gas grill. Grill chops, basting frequently with marinade, for 8 minutes per side, or until chops are a pale pink and nearly cooked through (the chops will continue cooking once removed from grill). Transfer any remaining marinade to a microwave-safe pitcher and heat for 1 minute, or until boiling. Serve chops accompanied with sauce.

CHEF NOTE: My neighbor Louise, who likes her jerk hot, hot, hot, believes the scotch bonnet pepper (heat 9 to 10) is essential in this recipe. But if you can't find it or you prefer that your jerk pack less of a wallop, like I do, the 2 serrano peppers (heat 7) are a good substitute.

Pulled Pork Barbecue

6 pounds boneless pork top loin

2 tablespoons butter or margarine

1 medium yellow onion, chopped

28 ounces Open Pit barbecue sauce

2 tablespoons Worcestershire sauce

1 tablespoon dry mustard

2 tablespoons brown sugar

½ cup ketchup

2 tablespoons white vinegar

garlic salt

lemon pepper

1. **To make pork:** Preheat oven to 325°F. Coat a large, disposable aluminum-foil roasting pan with vegetable cooking spray. Place pork in pan, fatty side up. Cover with aluminum foil and cook pork 4 to 6 hours or until it shreds with a fork. Remove pork from oven and transfer to a cutting board. Shred pork with a fork and set aside.

2. **To make sauce:** Meanwhile, melt butter in a large saucepan. Add onions and cook until soft but not brown. Add barbecue sauce, Worcestershire sauce, dry mustard, brown sugar, ketchup, vinegar, and garlic salt and lemon pepper to taste. Cover and simmer on low heat for 1 hour, stirring occasionally.

3. **To assemble:** Place barbecue sauce mixture and shredded pork in a large bowl and mix together with a spoon, making sure pork is thoroughly coated with sauce. Shredded pork can be served immediately or placed in a covered container and refrigerated for up to 3 days or frozen for up to 1 month. (To reheat: place pork in an ovenproof baking dish, cover with aluminum foil, and place in a 325°F oven for 15 to 20 minutes or until heated through.)

CHEF NOTE: Make Pulled Pork Barbecue Baskets for a handy way to serve leftovers for lunch: Preheat oven to 400°F. Using 1 (12-ounce) can Pillsbury Grands Biscuits, separate dough for each biscuit into 2 discs. Press each disc on the counter with your palm and fingers so that its diameter increases by about half, forms a circle, and is about ¼-inch thick. Place each circle in the cup of a muffin tin coated with vegetable cooking spray, and with your fingers press dough into bottom and up the sides to the top of each cup. Place 2 tablespoons hot pulled pork into each muffin cup. Top pork in each cup with 1 tablespoon shredded cheddar cheese. Bake for 8 to 10 minutes or until biscuit sides are golden brown. Makes 16.

When the Spanish discovered the Americas, they also found the Taino Indians of the West Indies cooking pork over a pit of coals. They called this cooking process *barbacoa*. The Spanish introduced the hog to Florida around 1540, knowing that pigs can live in the tropics under conditions in which cattle would perish. Jamestown settlers in Virginia brought hogs with them in 1607, and a territorial tradition of barbecue evolved in the south. Often called "pulled pork" because the meat is cooked until all the fat has melted away and the tough connective tissue has broken, the pork can literally be pulled apart by hand. Today, "strangers" from the U.S. southern states, now residing in the Keys, still argue about which recipe is authentic.

The Spanish introduced
the hog to both Cuba and
mainland Florida in the
sixteenth century, where
the animals thrived. Pigs
could withstand the high
temperatures and high
humidity of the subtropical
climate much better than
could cattle. Pork is a
staple of Cuban cuisine
to this day.

Sesame-Grilled Pork Tenderloin

¼ cup soy sauce

¼ cup orange juice

½ teaspoon dried orange peel

1 tablespoon peeled and minced fresh gingerroot

2 tablespoons honey

1 clove garlic, minced

1½ pounds pork tenderloin

¼ cup sesame seeds

1. **One day ahead:** Combine soy sauce, orange juice, orange peel, gingerroot, honey, and garlic in a small bowl. Place pork tenderloin in a freezer-weight plastic zipper bag. Cover with marinade and zip securely shut. Refrigerate 24 hours, turning occasionally.

2. Before grilling, remove meat from marinade. Place marinade in a small bowl and microwave 1 minute, or until boiling. Reserve marinade for basting. Roll pork in sesame seeds.

3. Preheat gas grill. Grill pork to medium rare, 10 to 12 minutes. Turn 3 times, so that all surfaces touch grill, basting with marinade constantly.

4. **To serve:** Slice tenderloin into medallions and place on a serving platter.

CHEF NOTE: Serve this pork tenderloin with Saffron Basmati Rice (see Index) or atop "The" Salad (see Index). The succulent meat is equally tasty either way.

Souse

On a typical Saturday night in old Key West, Conchs enjoyed a dish called souse. This culinary creation has not endured the test of time, however, for reasons that will soon become apparent. Souse was, in essence, pickled pork, made from the parts of the hog that most of today's cooks would not even consider touching, much less eating—heads, tails, feet, tongues, as well as tripe and chitlins.

Souse was to Key West and the Caribbean what Boston baked beans and brown bread were to New England—plain old comfort food. The hog parts were well washed, then placed in a pot with water and boiled a couple of hours, until tender. When cool, the tongues were skinned and cut into lengthwise slices, the feet—or trotters—were cut in half, meat was sliced from the head, and the tails, tripe, and chitlins were chopped.

A brine was prepared from key lime juice, water, salt, and scotch bonnet peppers or hot sauce. Sometimes the cooking stock was strained, added to the brine, and heated with the pork pickin's. Other times, chopped cucumber and onion were added to the brine and the pork was pickled in the brine for several hours and then served cold.

Key West butchers stocked the hog parts already cut up and sold it by the pound as souse mix. And, if a housewife was too busy to prepare souse herself, she might send one of her children to the nearest restaurant, armed with a covered pot, to pick up "take out." The kids had to walk home very carefully so as not to spill their dinner on Duval Street.

ABOVE: *Key West butchers sold souse mix by the pound, ca. 1910.*
Credit: State Archives of Florida.

Noche Buena
Christmas Dinner Cuban Style

Christmas dinner in Key West has always been a tradition-packed event for the Cuban population, who consider it the most important holiday of the year. First, unlike the winter holiday up north, the weather usually is mild and balmy in December. Tables are set up in the gardens and laid with festive tablecloths, the family china, and the good silver. Brightly colored lights are strung from tree to tree. And for the entire day before Christmas, a garlicky fragrance wafts from an outdoor barbecue pit, where the star of the event—the enormous suckling pig—turns round and round, spit-roasting to a crispy, burnished mahogany.

L*echón asado*, or roast suckling pig, is the traditional centerpiece of a Cuban Christmas feast. (In Cuba, hogs were much more plentiful than beef, lamb, duck, goose, or turkey, which are popular in other cultures.) When roasted to fall-off-the-bone tenderness, the pig is placed on a bed of watercress or leafy lettuce on a large serving tray. A wreath of parsley and herbs adorns its neck, a lemon is stuck in its open mouth, and raisins replace its eyes. Surrounding the pig is an array of roasted boniatos, onions, and yuccas. The children usually fight over who will get the ears, the tail and the roasted skin, because they are crunchy and taste like crackers.

As with almost every Cuban meal, classic rice and beans also make an appearance. In a normal everyday meal, the rice and beans are served together, in one dish. Cubans call

...
The party actually begins on Christmas Eve, when friends and family gather for an evening of love, laughter, music and dancing, and holiday rum spirits.
....

this dish *Moros y Cristiano*, or Moors and Christians, referring to the conflict between the Moors, who overran Spain in the eighth century and ruled it for centuries, and the Christians, who eventually retook their homeland. On Christmas day, tradition holds that the dark-skinned Moors (beans) must be kept separate from the white-skinned Christians (rice).

The party actually begins on Christmas Eve, when friends and family gather for an evening of love, laughter, music and dancing, and holiday rum spirits. Dinner is served close to midnight, so that all revelers can greet Christmas Day and the birth of the Christ child with a smorgasbord of sugary sweet desserts. In Cuba, families did not hang Christmas stockings. Instead, on January 5, they symbolically filled a shoe with hay to feed the Wise Men's camels. Christmas trees, lights, and holy days lasted until January 6, deemed Christ's first visit from the Wise Men. Christmas gifts were exchanged on this day. (Fidel Castro outlawed the celebration of Christmas in 1969.)

ABOVE LEFT: *Roast suckling pig was the star of the traditional Cuban Christmas dinner, ca. 1958.* Credit: State Archives of Florida.

Lechón Asado (Cuban Roast Pork)

Serves 4 to 6 for dinner or 8 for Cuban press sandwiches (see Index).

The key to the flavor of Cuban roast suckling pig is that the pork marinates for 24 hours in a potent mixture of garlic, sour orange juice, and spices. Roasting a pig in a pit or in the oven at home is an arduous task, even if you can find a butcher outside of Key West, Miami, or Tampa who can supply the dressed hog. (For step-by-step instructions for doing so, however, see www.cuban-christmas.com.) The recipe below calls for marinating a pork loin roast with a mixture of the same traditional ingredients. The result is not quite authentic, but otherworldly nevertheless.

2 tablespoons minced garlic
2 teaspoons salt
1 teaspoon freshly ground black pepper
2 tablespoons dried oregano
1 cup minced yellow onions
¾ cup sour orange juice
½ cup olive oil
2 to 3 pounds pork loin roast, excess fat removed

1. Place garlic, salt, pepper, oregano, onions, and sour orange juice in a blender. Pulse until smooth. Gradually add olive oil, processing on low, until mixture is smooth.
2. Pierce entire pork roast with a sharp fork, so that it is covered with tiny holes. Place pork roast in a freezer-weight plastic zipper bag. Pour marinade over pork. Seal bag and refrigerate pork overnight, turning bag occasionally.
3. Preheat oven to 450°F. Transfer pork to a roasting pan that has been coated with vegetable cooking spray. Reserve marinade. Roast, uncovered, for 15 minutes. Reduce heat to 325°F and continue roasting, about 40 minutes, or until juices run clear when pierced with a sharp knife (an instant read thermometer should register 155° to 160°F). Remove roast from oven and allow it to rest for 10 to 15 minutes before carving. Microwave reserved marinade until it boils. Serve with sliced hot pork.

Chef Note: Sour orange is the juice of Seville oranges and is found bottled in most supermarkets in the Keys and South Florida. You can order it online at www.cubanfoodmarket.com. Or, you can make a substitution by combining 2 parts orange juice with 1 part lemon juice. In this recipe use ½ cup orange juice and ¼ cup lemon juice.

Balsamic-Hoisin Duck Breasts

Leaner than chicken, a 3-ounce skinless duck breast has only 2.1 grams of fat and 119 calories. The size of duck breasts varies greatly between breeds, but the skin of all ducks releases a tremendous amount of fat during the cooking process. Therefore, skin of the breast should be removed before cooking or the final result will be too greasy.

1 cup hoisin sauce
½ cup balsamic vinegar
3 tablespoons minced fresh rosemary
1½ tablespoons minced garlic
¾ teaspoon freshly ground black pepper
salt

3 boneless, skinless duck breasts, about 8 ounces each
1 tablespoon olive oil
3 shallots, minced
¾ cup chicken broth

1. **Up to 6 hours ahead:** Place hoisin sauce, vinegar, rosemary, garlic, and pepper in a 2-cup measuring cup. Add salt to taste. Stir to mix well. Place duck breasts in a shallow baking dish. Pour hoisin mixture over duck, turning breasts so they are completely coated with marinade. Cover and refrigerate 4 to 6 hours.

2. Place olive oil in a large nonstick skillet over medium heat. When oil is hot, add shallots. Sauté, stirring constantly, for 1 minute. Remove duck breasts from marinade, reserving marinade. Add duck breasts to the skillet. Sear duck for 2 minutes on each side. Remove duck breasts from skillet and place on a plate. Cover duck with aluminum foil.

3. Add reserved balsamic-hoisin marinade and chicken broth to skillet and bring to a boil. Reduce heat to medium-low and add duck breasts. (Sauce should continue to bubble and reduce as duck cooks.) Cook duck breasts for 10 to 12 minutes, depending upon the thickness of the breasts. Turn in sauce about every 4 minutes, until duck is medium-rare when tested with a knife.

4. Remove duck breasts from skillet and slice thinly on the diagonal. Place a pool of balsamic-hoisin sauce on each dinner plate. Fan out half the slices from one duck breast on top of sauce. Repeat with remaining duck.

CHEF NOTE: For a Keysy fruit-laced sauce, after you remove the cooked duck breasts from the balsamic-hoisin sauce, add 2 bananas, thinly sliced; or 1 apple, peeled, cored, halved, and thinly sliced; or 4 plums, pitted and cut into 6 wedges; or a combination of the fruit. Cook fruit and sauce for 1 to 2 minutes, then place a pool of sauce and fruit on each dinner plate before adding the fan of duck breast slices.

Glazed Mango-Ginger Roast Duck

 SERVES 4

1½ cups rice wine vinegar
½ cup sugar
1 tablespoon minced, seeded jalapeno peppers
1 tablespoon minced fresh gingerroot
2 cups diced mango

2 tablespoons key lime juice
2 ducks (4 to 6 pounds each)
1 large yellow onion
handful fresh thyme sprigs
salt and freshly ground black pepper

1. **One day ahead:** Place vinegar in a medium saucepan over medium heat. When vinegar is hot, add sugar and cook until dissolved, about 2 minutes. Add jalapenos, gingerroot, mango, and key lime juice. Stir to combine. Cover pan and cook for 5 minutes or until mixture just begins to froth. Remove from heat. Place mango mixture in a food processor and puree until smooth. Transfer sauce to a covered container and refrigerate overnight. (Sauce can be frozen for up to 1 month.)

2. Preheat oven to 350°F. Thoroughly wash, drain, and dry the ducks. Cut off excess skin and fat. Peel onion, cut it in half, then into wedges. Stuff the cavity of each duck with half the onion wedges. Divide the thyme between the ducks and stuff into cavities. Tie legs of each duck together with kitchen twine to close cavities. Season generously with salt and pepper.

3. Place ducks on a rack in a large roasting pan. Place in oven and bake for 2½ hours. (Pour fat from roasting pan after 1½ hours.)

4. Bring mango sauce to room temperature. Increase oven temperature to 375°F. Spoon sauce over ducks. Return ducks to oven and cook 1 hour more, basting ducks 3 more times, until skin is crisp and browned. Remove ducks from oven. Discard onions and herbs from cavities. Cut each duck in half through the breastbone and on either side of the backbone. Place half a duck on each of 4 individual plates. Heat remaining sauce for 1 minute in microwave oven, place in a small pitcher, and serve with duck.

Though commonly known as Long Island ducklings, the breed of duck most widely sold in the United States is actually the Pekin, first brought to this country from China in the 1800s. Actually, only one-third of domestic ducks are raised on Long Island itself. Midwest duck farms supply the rest of the Long Island ducklings, which are usually not more than 8 weeks old and weigh between 3 and 6 pounds.

CHEF NOTE: Substitute papaya for the mango if desired. If you like your food spicy, double the amount of jalapeno peppers called for in the glaze.

Shepherd's Pie

As American as shepherd's pie? Hardly! But dinner pies immigrated to America along with the Pilgrims to Massachusetts and then moved offshore to the Bahamas with disgruntled English Tories during the American Revolution. In the old country, the English made a potato-topped pie that contained either minced beef (Cottage Pie) or diced lamb (Shepherd's Pie). When the Bahamians settled in Key West, the penchant for dinner pies came with them. In early days, however, a Keys dinner pie would be filled with fish or seafood. Beef and lamb were delicacies rarely encountered in the islands until the advent of Flagler's East Coast Railroad Extension in 1912.

5 tablespoons butter, divided

2 tablespoons minced garlic

1 pound portobello mushrooms, black pith removed and thinly sliced

2 tablespoons flour

½ cup chardonnay

2 tablespoons tomato paste

1 (14-ounce) can beef broth

1 pound baby carrots, quartered lengthwise

1 pound frozen pearl onions or 1 pound fresh pearl onions, blanched and peeled

1 teaspoon thyme

2 tablespoons plus 2 teaspoons salt, divided

¾ teaspoon black pepper, divided

2 pounds medium-rare leg of lamb, cut into ½-inch chunks

3 pounds potatoes, cut into eighths

1 cup milk

1. Melt 2 tablespoons butter in a large skillet over medium heat. Add garlic and mushrooms and sauté until mushrooms are soft, about 5 minutes. Stir in flour, mixing well to coat. Slowly pour in wine, stirring constantly. Add tomato paste and stir to mix well. Slowly add beef broth, stirring constantly.

2. Add carrots, onions, thyme, 1 teaspoon salt, and ½ teaspoon pepper. Stir to mix well, then cover and simmer for 5 minutes. Uncover skillet, reduce heat to medium-low and simmer 10 minutes more, until sauce is thickened slightly and carrots are al dente.

3. Remove skillet from heat. Add lamb chunks and mix well. Divide lamb mixture between 2 deep-dish pie plates or place in a 13 x 9-inch baking dish that has been coated with vegetable cooking spray. Cover with aluminum foil and set aside.

4. Place potatoes and 2 tablespoons salt in a large pot over high heat. Add water to cover by 2 inches. Bring to a boil, then cover and reduce heat to medium and cook potatoes until tender, about 20 minutes. Remove from heat and drain potatoes in a colander.

5. Add milk and 3 tablespoons butter to pot and return pot to heat until butter is melted. Remove pot from heat. Place a ricer over pot. Place boiled potatoes in ricer and force potatoes through ricer into the hot milk mixture. Add 1 teaspoon salt and ¼ teaspoon pepper and stir gently to combine.

6. Spoon potatoes over lamb mixture and spread evenly with a fork, making a spoke pattern with the tines. Be sure to bring potatoes to the outer rim of the pie plate, sealing the lamb mixture beneath. (This pie can be covered with plastic wrap, then aluminum foil and refrigerated for up to 2 days before baking.)

7. **To bake and serve:** Preheat oven to 375°F. Bake for 30 minutes.

CHEF NOTE: When you make leg of lamb, buy a large enough roast so that you have 2 pounds of meat left over. This savory pie can be prepared ahead to just before the potato topping is added, then frozen for up to a month. Bring frozen pie to room temperature, then proceed with potato topping step above and bake.

Harry S. Truman's
Key West Thanksgiving

Ordered by his doctor to find someplace warm to relax and vacation, President Harry S. Truman in 1946 settled upon the naval air station in Key West. Drawn by the balmy climate of the Florida Keys and the fact that the base was protected by the navy and could accommodate his considerable entourage of secret service, reporters, attachés, staff, family, and friends, Truman returned ten times.

ABOVE: *First Lady Bess Truman and President Harry S. Truman choose from a Thanksgiving buffet.* **Credit: United States Navy; courtesy Harry S. Truman Library.**

resident Truman stayed in the naval commandant's quarters on Front Street, which became known as The Little White House. Life moved a little slower here than in Washington D.C., but, nevertheless, his sojourns—which ranged from a week to a month—were described to the public as working vacations. President Truman and his guests swam, fished, played volleyball, spent time on the beach, and even took afternoon naps.

The President usually started his day with a walk. Breakfast was taken at the convenience of staff and guests. Lunch, often served as a buffet picnic in the north garden, commenced at 1 P.M., after which President Truman retired to his room until about 4 P.M. Dinner, promptly at 7 P.M., was usually followed by a movie.

On his tenth visit in 1951, President Truman spent from November 8 to December 9 at The Little White House. His wife, First Lady Bess Truman, and a number of friends and dignitaries joined him on Wednesday, November 21 to enjoy the Thanksgiving weekend. Pumpkins, harvest corn, fall flowers, and colored leaves were flown down to the Keys from Washington to decorate the table and sideboard.

An elaborate Thanksgiving dinner was served at 2 P.M. The traditional menu, though extensive, did little to showcase the tropical bounty that surrounded the First Family and their guests:

Jumbo Shrimp Cocktail
Roast Turkey, Chestnut-Oyster Dressing,
Giblet Gravy
Cranberry Sauce

...

John F. Kennedy held a summit meeting in this southernmost city just before the Bay of Pigs action.

...

ABOVE: *Pumpkins, harvest corn, fall flowers, and colored leaves were flown down for Thanksgiving in Key West.* **Credit: United States Navy; courtesy Harry S. Truman Library.**

Candied Sweet Potatoes
Creamed Green Peas
Parkerhouse Rolls, Strawberry Preserves
Moulded [sic] Pineapple, Cottage Cheese Salad
Assorted Cheese, Crackers
Mince Pie, Pumpkin Pie
Plum Pudding, Hard Sauce
Fruit Cake
Mixed Nuts, Assorted Mints, Hard Candies, Chocolates
Fruit Punch, Demi-Tasse

"Give em hell Harry" isn't the only United States president to have been captivated by Key West. President Dwight D. Eisenhower recuperated at The Little White House for two weeks after his second heart attack. John F. Kennedy held a summit meeting in this southernmost city just before the Bay of Pigs action. And former President Jimmy Carter vacationed in Key West with his family in 1996. The Little White House is now a museum dedicated to President Truman's time in Key West.

Herb-roasted Lamb Dijon

The oldest domesticated species of meat, lamb has been raised in the Middle East for 9,000 years, but it wasn't until the completion of the Overseas Highway in the 1940s that the delicacy made it to a Keys table with any regularity. Spring lamb must be 4 months old and be slaughtered only from early March to early October. Most lamb consumed today is brought to market at 6 to 8 months old.

¼ cup Dijon mustard
1½ tablespoons soy sauce
2 large cloves garlic, minced
1 teaspoon sage

1 teaspoon oregano
1 teaspoon minced fresh gingerroot
1½ tablespoons olive oil
2 pounds boneless leg of lamb

1. **Up to 1 day ahead:** To make herb-mustard rub: Place mustard, soy sauce, garlic, sage, oregano, and gingerroot in a blender. With machine running, gradually add oil. Transfer mixture to a small bowl.

2. Place lamb on a work surface. Rub half the mustard mixture over the topside of the lamb. Starting at one long side, roll lamb, jelly roll fashion. Tie with kitchen twine in 3 to 4 places to secure. Coat the surface of rolled lamb with the remaining rub. Place lamb in a disposable aluminum baking pan. Cover with plastic wrap and refrigerate lamb overnight.

3. Preheat oven to 375°F. Roast lamb for 1 hour for medium rare. Carve roast into slices.

CHEF NOTE: An 8-pound roast serves 8 to 10 people with 2 pounds left over for Shepherd's Pie (see Index). Herb-mustard rub in this recipe is enough for a 2-pound roast. Increase proportions as necessary, depending upon the size of your roast.

Grill-Roasted Turkey with Mushroom-Herb Stuffing

 **SERVES 18 TO 20**

4 ounces butter

1 cup minced onion

1 cup minced celery

8 ounces white button mushrooms, chopped

1½ cups roasted garlic chicken broth

1¼ cups water

1 (16-ounce) package Pepperidge Farm Herb Seasoned Stuffing

18 to 20 pound turkey (not self-basting)

olive oil spray or ¼ cup olive or canola oil

salt and pepper

1. **Up to 1 week ahead:** Place butter in a large kettle over medium heat. Add onion, celery, and mushrooms and sauté for 5 minutes, stirring occasionally. Add broth and water. Bring to a boil. Remove pot from heat. Add dried stuffing and mix well. Cool in pan. Transfer stuffing mixture to a freezer-weight zipper bag. Place stuffing in freezer until day before serving. Defrost stuffing in refrigerator overnight.

2. **To roast turkey:** Preheat gas grill for 10 minutes with all burners on low heat (400°). Wash turkey and pat dry. Stuff turkey with cold Mushroom-Herb Stuffing. Coat skin of turkey with olive oil spray or brush skin with oil. Season skin with salt and pepper. Place turkey in an aluminum foil disposable roasting pan that has been coated with cooking spray. Place a tent of aluminum foil over turkey and seal tightly. Place pan on the grill rack and close lid. Cook for 3 hours (20 pound turkey), or until popper is exposed or turkey leg can be pulled away from the body.

3. Remove tenting. Baste turkey with drippings (remove 3 tablespoons drippings for gravy; see Index). Close grill lid, raise heat to medium, and cook 15 minutes more or until bird is golden brown. Remove turkey from grill. Allow bird to sit 5 minutes. Remove dressing to an ovenproof bowl and place in a warm oven until serving. Carve turkey, place on a large platter, and serve immediately.

CHEF NOTE: Try this method of cooking your Thanksgiving turkey and you'll never use your oven again! Resist opening the grill lid and peeking, because you'll cause the heat in the grill to drop significantly.

Benjamin Franklin, scientist turned statesman, was in favor of making the turkey the national bird of the United States, instead of the bald eagle. No firm evidence ties the turkey to the first Pilgrim Thanksgiving, but nevertheless, the bird is firmly entrenched in that holiday's tradition today. The wild turkey is native to northern Mexico, the Keys neighbor across the Caribbean Sea, but early island settlers usually had to settle for chicken on Thanksgiving Day. However, legend has it that some innovative cooks actually roasted a white heron, which must have produced very lean cuisine indeed.

The Cornish hen originated in Cornwall, England, but didn't become a culinary staple until its breeding was established in the United States. The Rock Cornish game hen, which is naturally small, is a cross between the Cornish and White Rock breeds of chicken. Early Keys residents raised chickens in their yards—Plymouth Rocks or Rhode Island Reds—despite an ordinance forbidding them to do so.

CHEF NOTE: If you would like to make this dish for a crowd or a buffet dinner and don't want to serve the birds whole, cut them in half, through the backbone and breastbone. Place half-hens in a large, shallow roasting pan. Double or triple the spice amounts and glaze ingredients to adjust for number of birds you are cooking.

Apple-Lime-Dijon-Glazed Rock Cornish Game Hens

2 Rock Cornish game hens
olive oil
1½ teaspoons salt, divided
½ teaspoon freshly ground black pepper, divided
½ teaspoon sugar
1½ teaspoons minced garlic, divided
1 tablespoon butter

¼ cup finely chopped sweet onions, like Vidalia
½ cup apple jelly
3 tablespoons whole grain Dijon mustard
¼ cup lime juice
2 tablespoons seeded and minced jalapeno peppers
3 tablespoons heavy cream

1. Preheat oven to 350°F. Brush or spray Cornish hens with olive oil. Season backside of hens with ½ teaspoon salt and ¼ teaspoon pepper. Coat an 11 x 7-inch baking dish with vegetable cooking spray. Place hens in dish, backsides down. Season top of hens with ½ teaspoon salt, ¼ teaspoon pepper, and ½ teaspoon sugar. Sprinkle 1 teaspoon minced garlic atop hens. Place hens, uncovered, in oven and roast for 1 hour.

2. Meanwhile, melt butter in a large nonstick skillet over medium heat. Add onions and sauté, stirring occasionally, until onions are softened, about 3 minutes. Add apple jelly and stir until jelly is melted and combined with butter. Add remaining ½ teaspoon minced garlic, mustard, lime juice, minced jalapenos, and a pinch of salt. Bring mixture to a boil and cook 5 minutes, stirring constantly, until mixture is reduced by one-third. Whisk in heavy cream. Set aside.

3. When hens have roasted for 1 hour, remove them from oven. Spoon about 2 tablespoons glaze over each hen, making sure all exposed surfaces are covered with glaze. Return hens to oven and roast for 15 minutes more. Place skillet containing remaining glaze over low heat until it is heated through.

4. **To serve:** Place one hen on each individual plate and spoon a tablespoon of glaze over top of each. Place remaining glaze in a small pitcher and serve accompanying hens.

Classic Arroz con Pollo

salt and freshly ground black pepper
3 to 3½-pound chicken fryer, cut-up
½ cup olive oil
2 sweet onions, like Vidalia, chopped
1 red pepper, chopped
2 tomatoes, peeled, seeded, and chopped
2 large cloves garlic, minced
4 cups chicken broth

1 bay leaf
¼ teaspoon ground saffron
2 cups basmati rice, rinsed until water runs clear, then drained
½ cup petite frozen peas
1 roasted red pepper, cut in strips
1 roasted orange or yellow pepper, cut in strips
¼ cup chardonnay

1. Preheat oven to 350°F. Salt and pepper chicken pieces. Place olive oil in a large skillet over medium-high heat. When oil is hot, add chicken, skin side down. Sauté chicken, turning twice, until skin is golden brown and crispy. Remove chicken from skillet and place on paper toweling to absorb grease.

2. Place oil from skillet in a large, covered casserole or Dutch oven on medium-high heat. Add onions, chopped red peppers, tomatoes, and garlic. Sauté for 5 minutes, stirring frequently. Add chicken broth, bay leaf, saffron, and 1½ teaspoons salt. Stir to mix well. Bring mixture to a boil. Stir in rice. Place sautéed chicken pieces atop rice mixture.

3. Cover casserole and place in oven. Bake for 30 minutes, or until chicken is cooked through and rice is fluffy.

4. Meanwhile, place peas in a small bowl with 1 tablespoon water. Microwave on high for 1 minute. Drain peas.

5. Remove covered casserole from oven. Sprinkle peas and roasted pepper strips evenly over chicken and rice. Drizzle with chardonnay and serve.

CHEF NOTE: To roast a pepper: Cut peppers in half lengthwise. Remove and discard seeds and membranes. Line a baking sheet with aluminum foil. Place peppers, skin side up, on baking sheet; flatten peppers with the palm of your hand. Broil 3 inches from heat for 10 minutes or until the peppers are blackened and charred. Place peppers in a freezer-weight zipper bag. Seal and allow peppers to stand 15 minutes. Peel and discard charred skins.

The marriage of chicken and rice has been a union of convenience in Spanish cultures for centuries. The Key West Cuban-American community is no exception. Arroz con pollo, a seasoned chicken-on-the-bone and rice mixture, has long been popular, usually served at midday, which on island time is the main meal of the day. Since this is a one-pot meal, the rice absorbs all the wonderful flavors of the chicken, spices, and vegetables.

Guava is one of the most popular Cuban fruits, popping up in the culture's cuisine in everything from cocktails to dessert. The guava fruit varies from the size of a walnut to that of an apple. Its rich ruby-pink flesh is imbedded with edible seeds that taste like a fusion of strawberries, bananas, and pineapple. The vitamin C content of a guava can be five times that of fresh orange juice.

CHEF NOTE: In the Keys and in South Florida you can find pureed guava in the frozen food section of most major supermarkets. If you can't find the puree, you can puree canned guava shells in a blender or food processor. Mango puree makes a wonderful substitute for the guava in this recipe.

Coconut Chicken with Island Guava Sauce

1 ½ cups unsweetened shredded coconut
1 ½ tablespoons curry powder
1 tablespoon plus 2 teaspoons cornstarch
2 ½ tablespoons water, divided
1 egg, beaten
1 cup guava puree

½ cup orange juice
2 tablespoons key lime juice
2 tablespoons honey
2 tablespoons dark rum
3 tablespoons olive oil
4 boneless, skinless chicken breasts
salt and freshly ground black pepper

1. Place coconut on a large dinner plate. Add curry powder and mix with a spoon to combine. Set aside.

2. Place 1 tablespoon cornstarch and 1 tablespoon water in a shallow bowl. Stir to dissolve. Stir beaten egg into the mixture. Set aside.

3. Place guava puree, orange juice, key lime juice, and honey in a medium saucepan over medium-high heat. Bring to a boil, then reduce heat to medium-low and simmer for 5 minutes.

4. Meanwhile, place 2 teaspoons cornstarch and 1 ½ tablespoons water in a small bowl. Stir to dissolve. Add cornstarch mixture to saucepan, stir to combine, and simmer for 1 minute, or until sauce has thickened slightly. Reduce heat to low. Stir in rum and keep sauce warm until ready to serve.

5. Place olive oil in a large nonstick skillet over medium heat. Dip chicken breasts in egg mixture, then press both sides into coconut until well coated. Season chicken with salt and pepper. When oil is hot, add chicken breasts to skillet. Sauté for 5 minutes. Turn breasts and cook 5 minutes more or until chicken is a very pale pink when cut with a knife. (Do not overcook; chicken will continue to cook when removed from skillet.) Place a pool of guava sauce topped with a chicken breast on each dinner plate.

Dijon-Dill Grilled Chicken Breasts

⅔ cup Dijon mustard

⅓ cup honey

¼ cup snipped fresh dill

2 tablespoons freshly grated orange peel

4 boneless chicken breasts

1. **Three hours ahead:** Combine mustard, honey, dill, and orange peel in a small bowl. Wash chicken breasts and pat dry. Place chicken breasts in a freezer-weight zipper bag. Pour marinade over chicken breasts. Close zipper and shake bag until chicken is well coated with marinade. Refrigerate for 3 hours.

2. Prepare gas grill. Remove chicken from marinade. Place marinade in a small bowl and microwave for 1 minute. Place chicken on grill. Cook for 5 minutes, basting with reserved marinade. Turn chicken and continue cooking for 5 more minutes, basting with marinade until chicken is opaque almost all the way through when cut with a knife. Remove chicken from grill. Chicken should be just slightly pink when you remove it from the grill. (It will continue cooking after you remove it from the heat.)

CHEF NOTE: One of the most important tools in my kitchen is the Microplane. I couldn't live without it. This long, narrow zester/grater (1-inch wide, 7-inches long with 4-inch handle) grates the zest of citrus peels in seconds. And it works well for grating chocolate, Parmesan cheese, ginger, and garlic as well. Any good comprehensive kitchen store sells the tool.

Everyone knows that oranges are a great source of vitamin C. But less touted are the beneficial properties of the oft-discarded orange peel. Scientific studies have revealed that compounds found in orange peels, called polymethoxylated flavones (PMFs), can lower cholesterol more effectively than prescription drugs, and without side effects. Another flavone in oranges, the herperidin molecule, has strong anti-inflammatory properties and has been shown in animal studies to lower high blood pressure as well.

Jamaican Chicken a la Bagatelle

Bagatelle restaurant in Key West is situated on two floors of a former sea captain's home on lower Duval Street. This is one of the premier spots from which to observe the Fantasy Fest parade, the culmination of the outrageous weeklong Mardi Gras–type celebration held every October in Key West.

¼ cup mild curry powder

1 cup flour

1½ pounds chicken, cut into ½-inch-thick strips

4 ounces clarified butter

4 tablespoons cream of coconut

1 mango, peeled, cut from the seed, and diced

2 bananas, sliced into ½-inch pieces

4 ounces dark rum

4 tablespoons (½ stick) unsalted whole butter at room temperature

4 tablespoons unsweetened grated coconut, toasted

1. Place curry powder and flour in a medium bowl. Mix thoroughly with a spoon. Dredge chicken strips in flour mixture, coating all sides well. Place chicken in a mesh strainer and shake over the sink to remove excess flour.

2. Place clarified butter in a large nonstick skillet over medium-high heat. Add chicken and sauté, shaking pan and stirring frequently, until chicken is cooked through on both sides. Add cream of coconut, mango, and bananas. Stir to combine ingredients. Add rum and flambé until alcohol burns off. Add whole butter and stir until it is melted and mixed with chicken and fruit. Divide chicken among 4 plates and sprinkle one-quarter of the coconut atop each serving.

CHEF NOTE: When the milk solids and water have been removed from butter, it has been clarified. Clarified butter has a much higher smoking point, making it better than whole butter for sautéing at higher temperatures without browning and burning. To clarify butter, melt the butter slowly in a small saucepan. Allow it to rest for a while to separate. Skim off the foam that rises to the top and gently pour the butter off of the milk solids, which have settled to the bottom. One 8-ounce stick (8 tablespoons) of butter will produce about 6 tablespoons of clarified butter.

Minted Satay Chicken with Pomegranate Yogurt Sauce

½ cup fresh lemon juice

1 cup snipped fresh mint

8 cloves garlic, minced

2 tablespoons olive oil

2 teaspoons salt

1 tablespoon freshly ground black pepper

3 pounds skinless, boneless chicken breasts

1 seeded pomegranate

2 cups plain yogurt

2 scallions, finely chopped

¼ cup snipped fresh cilantro

Traditional satay, which means "triple stacked," is the Southeast Asian answer to a kabob—marinated, skewered, and grilled meat or poultry. Chinese immigrants are credited with inventing the culinary method when they sold skewered, barbecued meat as street food. In this Conchfusion recipe, Asian satay and Middle Eastern yogurt sauce collide with a tropical pomegranate for a tasty mix of cultures.

1. **Up to 1 day ahead:** Combine lemon juice, mint, garlic, oil, salt, and pepper in a small bowl. Slice chicken across the grain into ½-inch-thick slices. Place chicken in shallow container. Pour lemon-mint mixture over chicken. Cover and refrigerate for at least 1 hour or up to 24 hours.

2. Place pomegranate seeds, yogurt, scallions, and cilantro in a medium bowl, and stir to combine. Place in a covered container and refrigerate for up to 24 hours.

3. Preheat gas grill or broiler. Remove chicken from marinade and thread onto metal skewers. Microwave marinade for 1 minute. Grill or broil chicken skewers, basting with marinade, for 2½ to 3½ minutes per side, or until no longer translucent. (Do not overcook or chicken will be dry.) Place skewers on a serving platter and serve with Pomegranate-Yogurt Sauce.

CHEF NOTE: To remove pomegranate seeds, cut crown off pomegranate. Lightly score rind lengthwise in several places. Immerse scored fruit in a large bowl of cool water and let it soak for 5 minutes. Then, holding fruit under water, break sections apart with your fingers, separating seeds from the membranes. Seeds will sink to the bottom while the rind and membranes float to the top. Skim off and discard membranes and rind. Pour seeds in a colander and drain. Transfer to paper toweling and pat dry, picking away any remaining membranes. Store seeds in a plastic zipper bag for up to 1 week.

Not Your Mama's Chicken Potpie

The origins of potpie can be traced back to medieval England, when everything from a live bird to a parchment document might be baked into a pie, much to the delight, or consternation, of the diners. Colonists brought their pie traditions to the Bahamas and on to the Florida Keys with early Conch settlers.

8 ounces raw chorizo sausage, casings removed, then crumbled

3 tablespoons olive oil

3 pounds skinless, boneless chicken breasts

1 medium red onion, chopped

3 garlic cloves, finely minced

1½ teaspoons flour

1¾ cups chicken broth

1 large potato, peeled and cut into ½-inch dice

12 baby carrots, quartered lengthwise, then cut in half

1 bay leaf

1 teaspoon salt

½ teaspoon freshly ground black pepper

¼ cup chopped green pimento olives

¼ cup chopped sweet pickle gherkins

¼ cup golden raisins

1 (2-ounce) jar pimentos, drained

2 hard-boiled eggs, diced

1 cup frozen petite green peas, thawed

1 teaspoon soy sauce

1 teaspoon red wine vinegar

1 (15-ounce) package Pillsbury refrigerated piecrusts (2 per package)

1 egg beaten with 1 tablespoon water

1. **Up to 2 days ahead:** Cook chorizo sausage in a medium nonstick skillet over medium heat, stirring often, until sausage is cooked through and the grease is rendered. Remove with a slotted spoon and drain sausage well on paper toweling. Set aside.

2. Place olive oil in a large nonstick skillet over medium-high heat. Add chicken breasts to hot oil and sauté in two batches until browned, about 15 minutes per batch. Remove chicken to a separate plate and set aside.

3. Lower heat to medium, add onions and garlic to the skillet, and sauté for 5 minutes or until onions are soft. Stir in flour; cook 1 minute, stirring constantly. Slowly add chicken broth, stirring constantly.

4. Add potato, carrots, bay leaf, salt, and pepper to skillet. Stir to combine well. Reduce heat to medium-low. Place browned chicken in skillet, cover and simmer 15 to 20 minutes or until chicken is just cooked through and no longer pink when cut with a knife.

5. Remove skillet from heat. Remove chicken to a separate plate and cool. Discard bay leaf. Add chorizo sausage to skillet mixture and stir to combine. Stir in olives, pickles, raisins, pimentos, hard-boiled eggs, peas, soy sauce, and vinegar.

6. Cut cooled chicken breasts into bite-size chunks. Fold into skillet sauce mixture and combine well.

7. Coat a 13 x 9-inch rectangular baking dish with vegetable cooking spray. (Or you can use two 10-inch deep dish pie plates.) Place chicken pie mixture evenly in dish. Cover with aluminum foil and refrigerate for up to 2 days or cover tightly with plastic wrap, then aluminum foil, and freeze for up to 1 month.

8. **To bake and serve:** Preheat oven to 375°F. Bring piecrusts to room temperature. Unfold both crusts and roll to increase diameter by about 1 inch. Place one circular crust atop chicken mixture on each half of rectangular baking dish. With kitchen scissors, trim inner circles so that crusts overlap each other in a straight line by about 1½ inches. Trim any excess crust from circles overlapping each side of baking dish and crimp edges. Roll out trimmed off dough and cut decorative shapes (i.e., leaves, flowers, geometric designs). Brush entire crust with egg wash. Add decorative shapes to top of crust and brush them with egg wash. Cut several ½-inch slits randomly in piecrust. With 2-inch-wide strips of aluminum foil, form a collar around crimped edges of piecrust.

9. Place chicken potpie in oven and bake for 35 to 40 minutes or until visible crust begins to brown. Remove foil from crimped edges and bake 10 minutes more or until entire crust is golden brown and chicken mixture is bubbling.

CHEF NOTE: This lip-smacking savory dish redefines the typical chicken potpie. Inspired by the unusual combination of ingredients traditionally used in Spanish *pastels* and Filipino *pastilitos*, this chicken potpie leaves its bland cousins far behind. For a still different twist, top the pie with prepared puff pastry, available in most supermarket freezer cases, instead of the refrigerated ready-to-bake piecrusts.

Grand Finales

7

The word "stressed" spelled backwards becomes "desserts," a little recognized fact some would say is no coincidence. Others take things a bit further, maintaining that sugar is one of the essential food groups. Whatever the reasons that people feel a meal isn't complete without something sweet to top it off, generations of Conchs, Cubans, and "strangers" in the Florida Keys have always agreed: Every meal deserves a finale.

"Here in the tropics," recalled members of the Key West Woman's Club in their 1949 cookbook, "heavy desserts are not, as the Spanish say, 'simpatico,' though we do find stubborn traces of our Bahama-English ancestry in the hearty duffs, for instance. But light creams, delicate cakes, cool sherbets and fruit ices and ice creams predominate, with the tartness of lime juice for accent, with coconut drifting to white snow across many dishes, and the perfume of pineapple and banana."

Blessed with a panoply of tropical fruits literally at their doorsteps, Keys cooks— through decades and centuries—have created confections unique to their island culture. English duff made with guava, papaya, or coconut morphed into a sort of tropical plum pudding. Traditional Cuban flans showcased fresh oranges or bananas. Ice creams were flavored with such exotic fruits as soursop, sapodilla, and sugar apple. Cakes and trifles were made with mango, passion fruit, and calamondin. And key lime pie—the quintessential Keys dessert—took on as many variations as the quirky personalities of its creators.

LEFT: *Girl with guava, ca. 1950.* Credit: State Archives of Florida.

Spiced bread pudding has been a classic Keys dessert since the Bahamian immigrants settled in Key West. Reminiscent of a light plum pudding, bread pudding usually was served at Thanksgiving or Christmas or other important holidays.

Bahamian Bread Pudding with Banana-Rum Butter Sauce

margarine or Crisco
2/3 cup evaporated milk
4 cups fresh breadcrumbs
8 tablespoons (1 stick) butter, softened
2 eggs, lightly beaten
1 cup plus 1 tablespoon sugar
4 teaspoons molasses
2 teaspoons baking soda
1 tablespoon cinnamon, divided
2 pinches ground cloves
1 1/2 cups grated fresh coconut

1 1/2 cups golden raisins
2/3 cup unsalted butter
1/2 cup light brown sugar
8 finger bananas or 4 large bananas, thinly sliced
1/4 teaspoon nutmeg
3 tablespoons Captain Morgan's spiced rum
2 tablespoons banana liqueur
3/4 teaspoon vanilla, divided
3/4 cup whipping cream

1. Preheat oven to 325°F. Grease a 2-quart baking dish with Crisco or margarine. Place evaporated milk in a large bowl. Place breadcrumbs in milk and stir until crumbs have absorbed liquid. Add 8 tablespoons butter, eggs, 1 cup sugar, molasses, baking soda, 2 teaspoons cinnamon, and cloves. Combine ingredients with an electric mixer. Add coconut and raisins and stir with a large wooden spoon until well mixed. Transfer mixture to prepared baking dish. Bake 35 to 45 minutes or until a knife inserted in the center comes out clean.

2. Meanwhile, make rum sauce: Place unsalted butter in a large nonstick skillet over low heat. When butter has melted, add brown sugar, banana slices, 1 teaspoon cinnamon, and nutmeg. Stir gently with a wooden spoon, until mixture becomes smooth and bananas soften slightly, 1 to 2 minutes. Remove skillet from heat and add rum and banana liqueur. Return skillet to heat and flambé. Shake skillet until flames subside.

Stir in ½ teaspoon vanilla and remove from heat. (If bread pudding is not yet ready, keep sauce warm over low heat. If you make the sauce earlier in the day, place it in a saucepan over low heat for several minutes, stirring occasionally, until heated through.)

3. Place whipping cream in a medium bowl. Beat with an electric mixer until cream begins to thicken. Add 1 tablespoon sugar and ¼ teaspoon vanilla. Continue beating until whipped cream holds a soft peak. Cover and chill until serving.

4. **To serve:** Divide bread pudding among individual dessert bowls. Top with rum sauce and a dollop of whipped cream.

CHEF NOTE: Liz Higgs won a *Key West Citizen* recipe contest in 2001 with a version of this bread pudding.

Goin' Bananas

Although it is widely believed that bananas originated in Southeast Asia, food historians think ancient gatherers in prehistoric times also harvested the fruit. These early bananas contained many seeds, and some experts think early man may have propagated the fruit, removing the seeds and improving its texture and taste. Indonesian and Arab traders brought the banana to Africa and Europe, and Portuguese and Spanish explorers are credited with introducing the fruit to the New World. They planted corms, or root bulbs, everywhere they landed, but, susceptible to frost, the bananas didn't grow north of the subtropics. Most Americans didn't taste bananas until the 1800s, when naval sailors encountered the tropical fruit in the Caribbean. In the Florida Keys, however, bananas had long been a dietary staple by then.

Bananas don't grow on trees, as many think, but instead are the fruit of a giant herbaceous plant, or perennial, that grows to a height of 30 feet or more. As the banana stalk grows and leaf sheaths form and unfurl, a flowering stem emerges from the top of the plant and a large bud develops. Each unfolding bud reveals a double row of small flowers, each of which becomes an individual banana called a finger. Each row has about 20 fingers, which make up a hand. Seven to nine hands develop on each stalk, called a stand, which can weigh up to 100 pounds.

...
How many bananas can a family eat?
...

Bananas are ready to harvest after nine to twelve months. They must be picked green and the stalk hung in a cool place to ripen, because if allowed to ripen on the stalk, they will split, become infested with insects, and get eaten only by birds and rodents. As the banana ripens, its skin turns from green to yellow, an indication that the starch within the banana is turning to sugar. Unfortunately, all the bananas on a stalk ripen at about the same time, which causes a frenzy of banana creations from Keys cooks harvesting their dooryard gardens.

Bananas rank as America's number one fruit. More than 300 varieties exist, but until recently few Americans outside South Florida and the Keys have tasted anything but the cardboard-tasting, overhybridized and gassed Chiquita or Dole brand bananas found in the supermarkets. Today, however, large grocery chains have begun to stock short red bananas and short, plump manzano finger bananas, which are far sweeter and more finely textured. Looking like a jumbo banana and also increasingly marketed in the U.S. is the plantain, a cooking banana that is a staple in the cuisines of the Keys, Cuba, and Latin America.

In the latter part of the nineteenth century cargo ships brought Caribbean-grown produce to northern markets in the U.S. mainland, sometimes stopping in Key West when in need of repair. As Walter H. Norman recalls in *Nicknames and Conch Tales*, this usually resulted in a banana bonanza: "Many times in my early life I can remember when we would have ships come in need of repair. These ships would always tie up at the Porter-Allen Docks. Some of these ships were on their way to United States ports to deliver their cargo, which once in a while was perishable. Those ships loaded with perishables had to be unloaded, and usually it had to be done in a hurry. That is why the captains of the banana boat would allow anyone on board for 25 cents, and one could take away as many bananas that one could carry. I used to take two pieces of rope and tie two bunches of bananas on to each end of the rope. A friend would sling these ropes over my shoulders, and I would walk, or you might say stagger, off the boat with four bunches of bananas. You could do this as many times and as long as the bananas lasted—but how many bananas can a family eat?"

Baby Bananas on a Stick

Makes about 20

The frozen bananas in this recipe taste like banana ice cream with chocolate sauce. They are so rich and yummy that kids . . . and grown-ups too . . . love them.

1 bunch baby bananas (about 18 to 20)
1 package 6-inch wooden skewers

1 (7.25-ounce) jar Hershey's Chocolate Shell Topping

1. For each banana: Peel banana and insert skewers through the center the length of the banana. Wrap banana tightly with plastic wrap. Freeze for 3 to 4 hours.

2. Place chocolate sauce in a shallow bowl. Remove bananas from freezer one at a time. Remove plastic wrap. Dip in chocolate sauce to cover (you may have to use a spoon to cover all of the surface). When the chocolate topping hardens, nearly instantly, rewrap banana tightly with plastic wrap and return it to the freezer. Repeat process with remaining bananas.

Chef Note: For a variation, roll bananas in ground macadamia nuts before chocolate hardens.

SERVES 4

Baked Rum Bananas

The Spanish carried bananas with them to the New World in the 1500s, planting the root corms in Central America and the Caribbean islands, where they flourished. With its proximity to Cuba, the Florida Keys encountered the fruit long before the mainland did. Bananas weren't formally introduced to Americans until the 1876 Philadelphia Centennial Exhibition, where, wrapped in foil, they were sold for 10 cents each.

¼ cup brown sugar
½ cup freshly squeezed orange juice
¼ teaspoon nutmeg
¼ teaspoon cinnamon

½ cup plus ⅛ cup Myers's dark rum
4 large bananas
1 tablespoon butter
vanilla ice cream

1. Preheat oven to 450°F. Place brown sugar, orange juice, nutmeg, cinnamon, and ½ cup rum in a small saucepan over medium heat. Heat until sugar is melted. Remove from heat.

2. Meanwhile, peel bananas and cut them in half crosswise, then lengthwise, forming 4 pieces from each banana. Place bananas in a single layer in a baking dish. Pour hot rum mixture over bananas. Dot bananas with tiny bits of butter, about 3 dots per banana slice. (Can make dessert up to this point just before dinner, cover, and keep at room temperature until entrée course is finished.)

3. Bake bananas 10 minutes, uncovered, basting with rum mixture occasionally. Sprinkle remaining ⅛ cup rum over bananas and bake 5 minutes more.

4. **To serve:** Divide bananas among 4 dinner plates or shallow dessert bowls. Top with a scoop of vanilla ice cream.

CHEF NOTE: If you can find baby finger bananas in your local supermarket, use them instead of ordinary bananas. They are much more flavorful. Cut each finger banana in half lengthwise. Allow 2 finger bananas per person.

Calamondin Cake

1 package Duncan Hines classic yellow cake mix

1 (3-ounce) package lemon Jell-O

⅓ cup milk

4 extra-large eggs

1 tablespoon plus 2 teaspoons lemon extract

1 cup calamondin puree, divided

½ cup canola oil

4 tablespoons (½ stick) butter

pinch salt

2 cups plus 2 tablespoons confectioners' sugar

¼ cup sliced almonds, toasted

1. Combine cake mix and Jell-O in a large bowl. Add milk. With an electric mixer on low speed, fold milk into dry ingredients. Add eggs, one at a time, beating well after each addition.

2. Place 1 tablespoon lemon extract, ½ cup calamondin puree, and canola oil in a small separate bowl and whisk until well blended. Add this calamondin mixture slowly to batter, beating constantly with an electric mixer. Grease and flour a bundt pan. Turn batter into bundt pan. (Greasing the bundt pan with Crisco is key to unmolding the cake.)

3. Bake at 300°F on middle rack for 55 to 60 minutes or until cake pulls away from sides of pan and a wooden skewer inserted in the cake comes out clean. Remove cake from oven and allow it to cool for only 5 minutes. Loosen edges with a knife. Turn cake out on serving platter and glaze while still hot.

4. Meanwhile, as the cake is baking, prepare glaze. Place butter, ½ cup calamondin puree, salt, and 2 teaspoons lemon extract in a medium glass bowl or mixing cup. Microwave on high for 1 minute or until butter is melted and puree is hot. Mix well with spoon or whisk. Sift 2 cups confectioners' sugar into calamondin mixture, stopping to mix sugar into puree about every ½ cup. Set aside.

5. Spoon glaze on top of warm bundt cake, allowing it to drizzle down sides of plate and onto serving platter. Cover all surfaces of cake with glaze. Place toasted almonds atop glazed cake. When cake is cool, sift 2 tablespoons confectioners' sugar atop cake.

Originating in China, the calamondin is an ornamental tree now widely grown in California and Florida. The orange calamondin fruits are very small (1-inch diameter) and very sour. The fruit is not sold in most supermarkets but can sometimes be found in Asian markets or specialty produce stores. In the Florida Keys, virtually every dooryard garden features a calamondin tree. Though the fruit can be used like a lemon, usually both the flesh and peel are used in dessert recipes.

CHEF NOTE: Most people blessed with a calamondin tree in their dooryard garden puree the fruit as it ripens, then freeze it in ½ cup containers until needed. To make calamondin puree: Wash fruit. Cut in half and remove seeds. Puree fruit (with peel) in blender or food processor. (Puree can be frozen until needed.)

Bagatelle, the timeless restaurant at the tip of Key West's Duval Street, created this chocolate decadence. The recipe calls for bittersweet chocolate, which should not be confused with its slightly sweeter cousin, semisweet. Actually the two types of chocolate are similar. Bittersweet chocolate, by definition, contains a minimum of 35 percent chocolate liquor, while semisweet has a maximum of 35 percent. Chocolate liquor, the basis for all chocolate, is the unsweetened byproduct of refining cocoa beans. Varying amounts of sugar, lecithin (for texture), and vanilla are added during processing to create bittersweet, semisweet, or sweet chocolate.

Chocolate Silk Pie a la Bagatelle

1 cup walnuts
¼ cup light brown sugar
4 tablespoons (½ stick) unsalted butter, melted
20 ounces bittersweet chocolate, divided
1 egg, beaten

1 teaspoon vanilla
½ cup heavy cream, scalded
10 egg whites, whipped to form peaks
1 cup whipping cream, beaten and unsweetened

1. Combine walnuts, brown sugar, and melted butter in the bowl of a food processor. Pulse to coarsely chop. Press mixture into the bottom of a 10-inch springform pan. Set aside.

2. Fill the lower pan of a double boiler with water nearly up to the level of the upper pan. Place the double boiler over medium heat. Cover and bring water to a boil, then reduce heat to low. Place 10 ounces of chocolate in top pan. Cover and allow chocolate to melt.

3. Meanwhile, place the other 10 ounces of chocolate in the bowl of a food processor and pulse to chop. Slowly add the whole egg, vanilla, and scalded cream, pulsing until mixture is smooth and glossy. Transfer to a large mixing bowl. Fold in the melted chocolate from the double boiler. Gently fold in the whipped egg whites and whipped cream.

4. Pour filling into prepared springform pan. Refrigerate for at least 3 hours or overnight.

CHEF NOTE: For a slightly sweeter pie, use a combination of bittersweet and semisweet chocolate.

Guava Custard Pie

 SERVES 8

9-inch prepared deep-dish piecrust

2 (16-ounce) cans guava shells, drained

2 extra-large eggs, beaten

1 (12-ounce) can evaporated milk

1 (14-ounce) can Eagle Brand sweetened condensed milk

6 ounces water (see instructions in recipe)

1 tablespoon vanilla

¼ teaspoon nutmeg

1. Preheat oven to 425°F. Place unbaked piecrust in a large deep-dish pie plate and crimp edges. Place guava shells in a single layer in the crust so that bottom is completely covered.

2. Place eggs in a large bowl. Beat with an electric mixer until frothy. Add milks, water (measure the water in the empty but un-rinsed sweetened condensed milk can in order to get every last drop of the sweet milk into the recipe), vanilla, and nutmeg. Mix on low speed until blended. Pour custard batter over the guava shells. Make a ring of aluminum foil about 3-inches wide. Lightly cover the edges of the piecrust, connecting the ends to form a collar.

3. Carefully place pie plate in oven. Bake for 15 minutes. Reduce oven temperature to 350°F and bake for 35 to 45 minutes or until set. Remove foil collar from piecrust edges during the final 15 minutes of baking. Remove pie from oven and cool on a wire rack.

CHEF NOTE: Pat Gibson won a *Key West Citizen* baking contest in 1997 with a variation of this recipe.

In the early twentieth century, guava shells were prepared by peeling firm, ripe guavas, then scooping out the seeds and soft pulp. Two cups of sugar syrup (2 parts sugar to 1 part water) was brought to a boil and 1 quart of guava shells was added. Heat was reduced and the shells were cooked for 3 to 5 minutes. The shells were packed, cavity surface down, in overlapping layers in canning jars and each layer covered with the sugar syrup, then processed in a hot water bath. Absent a guava tree in the dooryard garden, today most Keys cooks buy canned guava shells.

Mango
The King of All Fruits

The mango is to the Florida Keys and most of the Caribbean what the apple is to Washington State, Michigan, and the Northeast—the king of all fruits. This sweet, juicy fruit, which ancient Persians called *samarbehist*, or fruit from heaven, is believed to have originated in Burma nearly 6,000 years ago. The word mango is thought to have derived from the Tamil word "man-gay"; when the Portuguese colonized western India, they called the fruit "manga."

Thriving in year-round warm climates that have dry winters and hot summers, mangos are cultivated in more than 100 countries and five U.S. states—Florida, California, Texas, Arizona, and Hawaii. Mango trees are evergreen, growing as tall as 60 feet high and bearing fruit for up to 40 years.

Dr. Henry Perrine introduced the mango to the Florida Keys in 1833 when he planted them on Indian Key offshore from Lower Matecumbe. But in 1838 the Seminoles attacked the thriving settlement, where they massacred all the residents, including Perrine, set fire to the island, and consequently killed all the mango trees. Mangos weren't reintroduced to the Keys until 1861, when a Dr. Fletcher brought the seeds with him from Cuba.

Florida mango season is from May through September, although imported fruit is now widely available year-round in most supermarkets. Even when rock hard—the condition that most mangos are marketed—the fruit ripens in less than a week. The mango turns from green to variegated shades of yellow, orange, and red as it ripens. When fully ripe the mango emits a sweet, fruity aroma and its flesh gives a little when gently pressed with a finger.

Rich in vitamins, minerals, and antioxidants, a mango contains no cholesterol, 1 gram of fat, and only 110 calories per fruit. Mango also has a stomach-soothing enzyme, similar to the papain found in papayas. It is little wonder that a mango tree still dominates nearly every Florida Keys dooryard garden.

Mango Madness

If you are lucky enough to have a mango tree in your yard, you are lucky enough. When your crop ripens, which generally happens almost all at once, you'll need some tips of the trade to properly preserve this tropical comfort food.

To peel, pit, and chunk a mango: Use a sharp knife and cut fruit along either side of the large, flat seed. Cut ½-inch squares by scoring the mango flesh to the skin. Do not cut through the skin. Turn mango half "inside out" and cut the cubes away from the peel with a knife.

To peel, pit, and slice a mango: Place fruit in refrigerator for 30 minutes before slicing; cold fruit is easier to slice. With a sharp, thin-blade knife, cut a small slice from the bottom and top ends of the mango. Place fruit on one flat end and cut away skin from top to bottom. Cut fruit into slices lengthwise along the flat side of the pit.

To freeze mango chunks or slices: Dip sliced or chunked fruit into a lemonade bath. Place pieces, not touching, on a baking sheet. Freeze until solid. Remove with a spatula and place in freezer-weight plastic zipper bags. Return to freezer for up to one year. Serve slices partially thawed.

To freeze mango puree: Puree pitted, peeled fruit in a food processor. Add a squeeze of lime juice to the puree. Pour puree into ice cube trays (transfer to plastic zipper bags when totally frozen) or small freezer containers. Freeze for up to one year. Frozen mango puree will slice like cold butter. Cut off the portion you need to use and refreeze the rest. Use pureed mango in beverages, smoothies, baked goods, marinades, and salad dressings.

If you are not fortunate enough to have your own mango tree, don't despair. Chances are you can find plenty of mangos in your supermarket. When choosing a mango, look for fruit that already has started turning red, orange, or yellow. Sniff the stem end of the fruit. If it smells earthy, likely freshly dug potatoes, put it back. The mango should smell aromatically fruity. Ripen the fruit at room temperature until it responds to slight thumb pressure.

Frangipani Citrus Cake

The emergence of frangipani, or plumeria, flowers heralds the approach of spring in the Florida Keys. The tree's distinctive five-petal flowers are commonly used to make Hawaiian leis. The frangipani tree becomes dormant during the winter drought months in the Keys and the Caribbean, when it drops all leaves and flowers and looks completely dead. A branch broken off and stuck in the ground will start a new tree and even flower in the first season. Frangipani flowers, though inedible, are often used here to decorate elaborate desserts.

1¼ cups egg whites (about 9 jumbo eggs), at room temperature

1½ teaspoons cream of tartar

1 teaspoon vanilla extract

¼ teaspoon salt

1½ cups sugar

1 cup cake flour

4 egg yolks

1 tablespoon plus 1 teaspoon grated orange peel

1 tablespoon grated lemon peel, divided

20 tablespoons (2½ sticks) butter, softened

3 cups sifted confectioners' sugar

1 tablespoon fresh lemon juice

2 to 3 tablespoons fresh orange juice

1. Preheat oven to 375°F. Place egg whites, cream of tartar, vanilla, and salt in a large bowl. Beat with an electric mixer at high speed until soft peaks form. (Egg whites are sufficiently beaten if they stay put when you shake the bowl.) Sprinkle in sugar, 2 tablespoons at a time, continuing to beat at high speed until sugar dissolves and whites stand in stiff, glossy peaks. (Do not scrape the bowl.) With mixer speed on low, gradually fold in flour until just blended. Wash and dry the beaters.

2. Beat yolks in another large bowl with an electric mixer at high speed until yolks are thick and lemon-colored. Using a wire whisk, fold in half of the egg-white-flour mixture, 1 tablespoon grated orange peel, and 2 teaspoons grated lemon peel.

3. Drop a heaping tablespoon of the white batter into an ungreased 10-inch bundt pan. Then drop a heaping tablespoon of the yellow batter next to the white batter. Repeat, forming a checkerboard pattern, until all batter is placed in pan. Bake cake for 30 to 35 minutes or until a toothpick poked in the cake ring comes out clean. Invert cake over a cooling rack (do not remove from pan). Cool in pan for 1 hour.

4. Meanwhile prepare icing. Place butter, 1 teaspoon grated lemon peel, and 1 teaspoon grated orange peel in a small bowl. Beat with an electric mixer at medium speed until creamy. Gradually add the confectioners' sugar, alternating with lemon and orange juices, beginning and ending with powdered sugar. Beat until icing reaches spreading consistency.

5. When cake is cool, gently run a knife between the cake and the pan (both inner and outer rings). Unmold onto serving plate (if you have difficulty, gently pull cake out with your hands). Frost cake and refrigerate. Place a vase of yellow and white frangipani in the center of the frosted bundt cake for a touch of tropical spring. (Substitute tulips, jonquils, or daffodils if you don't have a frangipani tree in your northern landscape.)

CHEF NOTE: Egg whites should be at room temperature. Use a clean, dry bowl and beaters. Oily residue on the beaters or overbeating will cause stiff whites to deflate. Adding cream of tartar helps support the protein structure that is created around the millions of tiny air bubbles formed when the whites are beaten. Juicy advice: Juice the oranges and lemons after you have grated the peels. Freeze any extra juice or grated citrus peel for another use.

Key Lime Cake

Every dooryard garden in the Florida Keys has a key lime tree, but the much-coveted little yellow fruit is no longer grown commercially here. Northern supermarkets often sell key limes in their produce sections, but the limes are picked green in Mexico or Central America and, therefore, will yield little juice. Only yellow, ripe key limes are juicy. Most commercial key lime juice in the U.S. is sold as concentrate. The owners of Nellie & Joe's Key Lime Juice began bottling the liquid in their Key West kitchen in the early 1970s using fruit harvested from their dooryard garden and those of their friends. Nellie & Joe's is still the only commercial key lime juice actually processed and bottled in the Keys, although the juice itself is imported from Caribbean groves.

margarine or Crisco
1 package lemon supreme cake mix
1 small package lemon instant pudding
4 jumbo eggs
½ cup water
½ cup vegetable oil
¾ cup key lime juice, divided
2 cups sifted confectioners' sugar

1. Preheat oven to 350°F. Grease (with margarine or Crisco) and flour a bundt pan. Place cake mix, pudding mix, eggs, water, oil, and ½ cup key lime juice in a large bowl. Beat with an electric mixer on medium speed for 2 minutes. Pour batter into bundt pan. Bake for 35 to 40 minutes or until a wooden pick inserted in the center comes out clean. Invert cake on a large serving plate.

2. Place confectioners' sugar and ¼ cup key lime juice in a small bowl. Mix with a spoon until well blended. Make puncture holes in the top of the bundt cake with a wooden skewer. Drizzle sugar mixture over cake with a tablespoon, allowing sugar syrup to soak in.

3. Slice and serve cake with a scoop of vanilla ice cream.

CHEF NOTE: Unlike when making a key lime pie (see Index), fresh key lime juice and concentrate are interchangeable in this recipe. The concentrate will turn a brownish color after 4 to 6 months, although the taste is unaffected, so once the bottle is opened I recommend you freeze the juice in ¾ cup portions. Frozen juice will keep for years.

Key Lime Cheesecake

 **SERVES 10 TO 12**

1½ cups graham cracker crumbs

⅓ cup shredded unsweetened coconut

¾ cup plus 2 tablespoons sugar

4 tablespoons (½ stick) unsalted butter, melted

24 ounces cream cheese (3 8-ounce packages), softened

½ cup sour cream

3 extra-large eggs

3 tablespoons flour

¾ cup fresh key lime juice

1 teaspoon vanilla

key lime slices

1. Preheat oven to 375°F. Place graham cracker crumbs, coconut, and 2 tablespoons sugar in a small bowl. Stir to combine. Drizzle in melted butter, stirring with a fork until well mixed with the crumbs. Place crumbs in the bottom of a 10-inch springform pan. With fingertips, pat crumbs to an even layer in bottom of pan. Bake crust for 8 minutes. Remove from oven and cool on a wire rack.

2. Meanwhile, place cream cheese, ¾ cup sugar, and sour cream in a large bowl and beat with an electric mixer. Add eggs, one at a time, beating after each addition until mixture is smooth. Add flour and beat to combine. Add key lime juice and vanilla and beat until smooth.

3. Pour cream cheese mixture into springform pan. Bake for 15 minutes. Reduce oven temperature to 250°F and continue baking for 55 minutes or until center of cheesecake has set. Remove cheesecake from oven and allow it to cool on a wire rack. Cover with aluminum foil and refrigerate overnight.

4. **To serve:** Remove sides of springform pan. Garnish each piece with a slice of key lime.

CHEF NOTE: You can eliminate the coconut in the crust if any of your family or guests have allergies.

Legend maintains that cheesecake was served to Olympic athletes at the first games in Greece in 776 B.C. But anthropologists claim cheese molds date back as far as 2,000 B.C. The Romans spread the delicacy throughout Europe, and immigrants brought their recipes to America centuries later. It is no surprise that Keys cooks have "tropicalized" the classic cheesecake by adding key lime juice, so popular is the tart juice in the island chain.

Quintessential Key Lime Pie

Dubbed the official dessert of the Florida Keys, key lime pie reigns supreme in our island chain and enjoys a colorful history as well. Early pioneer settlers on the island of Key West, isolated from the mainland by a water gap until the completion of Flagler's Florida East Coast Railroad Extension in 1912, had little access to fresh dairy products. They relied, instead, on canned milk, which arrived by ship.

The Borden Company is widely credited with the innovation of the traditional, authentic key lime pie. Gail Borden invented sweetened condensed milk in 1859, which is still marketed as Eagle Brand, and the company embarked on a campaign to encourage use of the milk in pie making.

Combining eggs, key lime juice, and the Eagle Brand sweetened condensed milk, Keys cooks created a citrus custard pie filling, which was actually cooked by the high acidic content of the key lime juice.

Traditional key lime pie is not cooked in the oven, although many restaurants now bake the pie to 160°F because of modern concerns of salmonella.

Key West legend, however, maintains that credit for the very first key lime pie goes to Aunt Sally, William Curry's African-American cook. Florida's first millionaire, Curry came to Key West from the Bahamas as a young boy and made his fortune in the wrecking and salvage business.

Two key lime pie debates perpetually rage among locals in the Florida Keys: Which is the authentic crust—pastry or graham cracker crumbs? And what is the traditional topper—meringue or whipped cream? Conventional wisdom maintains that pie pastry was probably used in the nineteenth century, although graham cracker crusts are widely prevalent today. And chances are, given the dearth of fresh milk products before 1912, whipped cream was an unlikely topping. But exactly when meringue began crowning the pie is anyone's guess.

Of one fact, however, there is no doubt. Key lime pie is deep yellow in color—always! Beware of those green custard pies heralded up north as key lime pie. They are impostors.

LEFT: *Former Florida governor Bob Graham serves from giant key lime pie, ca. 1983.* **Credit: State Archives of Florida.**

Manny & Isa's Key Lime Pie

Serves 8

4 large eggs or 6 medium eggs
1 (14-ounce) can Eagle Brand sweetened condensed milk
4 ounces key lime juice
1 prepared piecrust, baked and cooled
¼ teaspoon cream of tartar
½ cup sugar

1. Preheat oven to 375°F. Separate egg yolks from whites. Put whites aside for use in meringue. Place yolks in a medium bowl. Beat with an electric mixer until frothy. Add sweetened condensed milk and mix together. Add key lime juice and mix again. Pour into baked, cooled piecrust.

2. To make meringue: Thoroughly wash and dry bowl and beaters. Place egg whites in medium bowl. Beat with an electric mixer until medium peaks form. Add cream of tartar and continue to beat. Add sugar slowly and continue beating until mixture is stiff. Spread meringue over pie, sealing it to the crust. Bake until meringue is golden brown, about 15 minutes. Refrigerate key lime pie until chilled.

Chef Note: This famous key lime pie, from the former Manny & Isa's Kitchen in Islamorada, is one of the best recipes for the traditional pastry piecrust and meringue-topping version I have ever tasted. Manny gave me the recipe in 1995 when I wrote the *Insiders' Guide to Florida Keys and Key West*. If you are using fresh key lime juice, the pie will set without refrigerating. If you are using bottled juice, you must refrigerate the pie before the filling will set.

No Fuss, No Guilt Key Lime Pie

Serves 8 small slices or 6 hearty slices

1⅓ cups graham cracker crumbs
⅓ cup butter or margarine, melted
1 (8-ounce) container nonfat Cool Whip
1 (14-ounce) can nonfat Eagle Brand sweetened condensed milk
8 ounces nonfat sour cream
½ cup key lime juice

1. Place graham cracker crumbs and melted butter in a medium bowl. Mix thoroughly with a fork. Transfer to an 8-inch pie plate and press crumbs on bottom and sides to form a piecrust. Refrigerate crust until needed.

2. Place Cool Whip, sweetened condensed milk, sour cream, and key lime juice in a large bowl. Beat with an electric mixer until smooth. Pour into graham cracker crust. Place in freezer uncovered for 15 minutes or until set. Cover pie with aluminum foil and freeze until ready to serve. Take pie out of freezer about 10 minutes before serving.

Chef Note: Although it will add some guilty calories to the dessert, you can top this graham cracker crumb based pie with whipped cream for more authenticity.

Key Lime Dessert Bars

2¼ cups flour, divided
½ cup plus 2 tablespoons confectioners' sugar
16 tablespoons (2 sticks) butter
4 eggs
2 cups sugar

pinch salt
1 teaspoon baking powder
⅓ cup key lime juice
½ teaspoon grated fresh key lime or lemon peel

At the gateway to Everglades National Park in Homestead at the top of the Keys, "Robert Is Here" lays rightful claim to being the best rare and exotic fruit and vegetable market in South Florida. Robert claims he has been in the produce business since he was seven years old, and one thing is certain, it is impossible to leave his place without trying such exotics as monstera deliciosa, mamey sapote, or atemoya. Robert Is Here will ship his fruit anywhere in the U.S., including fresh, ripe, yellow key limes. Sold by the 10-pound box, key lime orders go out on Mondays and Tuesdays, year round. The fresh limes can be juiced and frozen for future use.

1. Preheat oven to 350°F. Combine 2 cups flour and ½ cup confectioners' sugar in a medium bowl. Add the butter in ½-inch pieces and cut in with a fork until mixture has a pebbly texture. Press mixture in the bottom of a 13 x 9-inch baking pan. Bake for 25 minutes or until golden. Remove from heat.

2. Meanwhile, place eggs in a large bowl and beat with an electric mixer until pale yellow and airy. Continuing beating at high speed, slowly adding sugar, salt, ¼ cup flour, baking powder, key lime juice, and grated peel, until well mixed.

3. Pour batter over warm crust. Return baking pan to oven and bake 20 to 25 minutes more or until top is golden. Place 2 tablespoons confectioners' sugar in a small sieve. Remove baking pan from oven and immediately dust top of dessert bars with confectioners' sugar. Allow dessert bars to cool. Cut into 2-inch-square bars.

CHEF NOTE: To find Robert Is Here, turn right at the first stop light on U.S. Hwy. 1 southbound, after exiting Florida's Turnpike in Florida City. After about 1 mile you will see a rooftop with enormous letters painted on it: ROBERT IS HERE. You can't miss it. And if you stop, don't miss trying one of Robert's fantastic fruit shakes, made with fresh sugarcane. Mango, key lime, and coconut are my personal favorites.

Mandarin-Pineapple-Coconut Cake

 **SERVES 12 TO 15**

margarine or Crisco

1 package Duncan Hines classic yellow cake mix

1 (11-ounce) can mandarin oranges with juices

8 tablespoons (1 stick) unsalted butter, melted

¼ cup canola oil

4 extra-large eggs

1 (8-ounce) can crushed pineapple, well drained and juices reserved

2 cups heavy cream

1 package unflavored gelatin

1½ cups sweetened shredded coconut

1. Preheat oven to 350°F. Grease two 9-inch-round cake pans with margarine or Crisco and dust them with flour.

2. Place cake mix, mandarin oranges with juices, butter, oil, and eggs in a large bowl. Beat with an electric mixer until well blended. Divide batter between the 2 baking pans. Bake 27 to 30 minutes or until a wooden toothpick inserted into the center of each cake comes out clean.

3. Remove cakes from pans and cool them on a wire rack. While cake is still warm, poke holes all over the top of each cake layer. Brush top of cakes with pineapple juice, dividing the juice between the 2 layers.

4. Place heavy cream in a medium bowl. Whip cream with an electric mixer until it can hold a stiff peak. Using a large spoon or wire whisk, gently fold gelatin and pineapple into whipped cream.

5. Place 1 cake layer on a serving platter. Spread whipped cream mixture over the top of the cake with a rubber spatula. Place the second layer atop the cream. Spread cream over sides and top. Sprinkle top of cake generously with coconut and press coconut onto all side surfaces. Refrigerate at least 1 hour before serving.

Serving coconut cake to special guests is a Key West tradition. Among the dignitaries who enjoyed such a confection over the years were Secretary of State John Foster Dulles and Presidents Harry Truman and Dwight D. Eisenhower.

CHEF NOTE: Conchs believe only freshly grated coconut should be used in a true Key West coconut cake, but frozen grated coconut is the next best thing. This recipe calls for the more universally available sweetened, shredded coconut. If you have access to fresh or frozen grated coconut, by all means substitute it, but add some sugar, to taste, to the whipped cream frosting first.

SERVES 8

Orange Flan

The Spanish first created flan, which is popular in virtually every Hispanic culture around the globe. Cubans brought the dessert—a classic baked custard with a caramelized sugar topping—to the Florida Keys, where the recipe has evolved through the centuries.

3 tablespoons sugar
3 whole eggs plus 2 egg whites
1 (12-ounce) can evaporated milk
1 (14-ounce) can Eagle Brand
sweetened condensed milk

1 cup fresh orange juice
1 teaspoon vanilla

1. Preheat oven to 350°F. Place sugar in a metal or aluminum 9-inch pie plate. Heat sugar on medium-low heat, stirring constantly, for 3 to 4 minutes, until sugar dissolves and caramelizes. Swirl caramel around pie plate, coating the bottom and sides. Set aside to cool.

2. Place eggs and egg whites in a large bowl. Beat with an electric mixer until frothy. Add milks, orange juice, and vanilla and whisk to mix. Allow mixture to rest 5 minutes. Spoon off bubbles. (If these remain they will cause large holes to develop in the flan.)

3. Place ½-inch hot water in a 10-inch round baking dish. Place 9-inch pie plate inside dish atop the water. Slowly pour custard batter into pie plate so that additional bubbles don't form. Spoon out any bubbles that do form. Carefully transfer pan to oven.

4. Bake for 45 to 50 minutes or until a knife inserted near the center comes out clean. Cool in refrigerator for at least 1 hour. Run a knife around edge of pie plate. Spray serving dish with vegetable cooking spray. Invert serving plate over pie plate, grasp both plates firmly, and turn them over. Shake gently to release flan. Refrigerate until serving.

CHEF NOTE: Much-coveted flan recipes have been handed down through generations of Conchs. Ilianna Flagg's mother taught her how to make flan following this recipe. I have substituted orange juice for the whole milk called for in the original, creating a tropically light, updated version.

Queen of All Puddings

margarine or Crisco
5 eggs, yolks and whites separated
1 cup sugar, divided
1 tablespoon butter, softened
2 (12-ounce) cans evaporated milk

1 (14-ounce) can Eagle Brand sweetened condensed milk
12 Uneeda biscuits, crumbled
1 teaspoon vanilla
11 ounces guava paste (half a 22-ounce tin)

1. Grease a 3-quart soufflé dish with margarine or Crisco. Preheat oven to 350°F. Place 5 egg yolks and one egg white in a large bowl. Beat with an electric mixer until frothy. Add ½ cup sugar and the butter and mix well. Add evaporated and sweetened condensed milks and beat until mixed. Fold in crumbled biscuits. Stir in vanilla. Pour batter into soufflé dish and bake until custard is set, about 1 hour.

2. While custard is baking, cut the guava paste into small pieces. Place a small pan over low heat and add guava paste and 3 to 4 tablespoons of water. Melt guava paste and mix with water to form a thick syrup.

3. About 10 minutes before custard is finished, place 4 remaining egg whites in a medium bowl. Beat with an electric mixer until stiff. Add ½ cup of sugar, 2 tablespoons at a time, beating after each addition, until all sugar has been mixed into the egg whites.

4. When custard is set (a knife inserted in the center comes out clean), remove custard from oven. Reduce heat to 300°F. Pour guava syrup over custard and then spread meringue on top, sealing edges to soufflé dish. Return custard to oven and bake 15 to 20 minutes or until top of meringue is golden. Remove pudding from oven and allow it to cool. Serve at room temperature or chilled.

CHEF NOTE: Many variations of Queen of All Puddings have developed over the centuries. This recipe, unearthed by Jerry Wilkinson of Florida Keys Historical Society, most closely resembles the original Queen of All Puddings. Staying as true to the 1800s recipe as possible, I have adapted it for the twenty-first century. If you can't find Uneeda biscuits, substitute coarse, hard crackers, such as Gilda brand, or hard, stale French or Cuban bread. If you can't find guava paste, substitute guava preserves or jelly.

Early Conchs brought this special pudding to Key West from the Bahamas. Adapting the recipe for Queen Pudding, a classic English meringue custard dessert, to the limitations of their tropical climate, the Conchs substituted crackers for breadcrumbs and guava paste for raspberry jam. They called their new creation Queen of All Puddings, which they served as a traditional Christmas dessert or special occasion treat. Uneeda biscuits—thick, square biscuits developed by the National Baking Company in 1898 (later Nabisco)—were the crackers of choice. Guava paste is a guava marmalade that has been cooked until all the water has evaporated. It is commercially produced in Central and South America and imported into the U.S., sold in tins or boxes.

Cracking the Coconut

The mainstay of tropical cultures for centuries, the coconut originated in Asia. Blessed with a buoyant, waterproof shell, the coconut floated to far away places, including the tropics, where it planted itself on small islands. Tropical cultures have long used all parts of the coconut palm: wood to build homes and furniture; leaves to thatch roofs and fences; coconut shells to carve into plates, bowls, and spoons; and from the nut itself, coconut oil, meat, and water for consumption.

s subtropical islands with a tropical climate, the Florida Keys, too, have always been a coconut culture. As the Keys became more inhabited, more and more land was planted in coconut palms. Locals called it the "cocoa-nut boom." The shallow-rooted palms grew in a minimum of soil and required little or no care once they were planted. The palms were planted with the expectation that the coconut harvest would prove lucrative, but there is no documentation that the venture ever proved profitable. Nevertheless, the palms greatly improved the appearance of the

starkly barren landscape of the Keys and provided a dietary staple for settlers, which remains an integral part of islands' cuisine today.

But the proliferation of fruit from the "cocoa-nut boom" had its drawbacks, as one local Conch observed: "The cocoa-nuts [sic] shed its fruit when ripe, endangering the heads of those passing. Parents having children who play under the trees are constantly uneasy, as a full-grown cocoa-nut [sic], falling forty feet, would nearly annihilate a child. They are gathered by means of long poles, attached to the end of which is an iron hook—some-

...

Fresh, ripe coconuts sound sloshy when shaken, are dry and free from mold, and have three clean eyes.

...

times with ladders and ropes."

The coconut goes through three stages in its ripening process. A drinking nut is an immature coconut that is mostly liquid. Called coconut water, this liquid is pure and sweet, drinkable right from the coconut. (The water should be drained from the nut, by piercing its eyes, before the nut is cracked.) As the coconut matures, the liquid forms into a soft, jellylike meat called spoon meat, which was popularly used to flavor early Keys ice cream. These immature coconuts are called jelly nuts. When totally ripe, the jelly turns into a thick white meat around the inside of the shell and a smaller amount of liquid remains in the middle of the nut. Mature nuts are just simply called coconuts or cocoas.

Fresh, ripe coconuts sound sloshy when shaken, are dry and free from mold, and have three clean eyes. To harvest a coconut, choose a mature nut that contains a large amount of liquid (shake nut to determine the amount of liquid). Place a sharp wooden or metal stake securely in the ground. To remove the greenish outer husk, hold the coconut on the stake and in three or four locations near the stem end of the coconut, apply downward pressure and a twisting motion. The husk should fall away.

Then pierce the eyes with a nail or ice pick and drain out the liquid. (Save and refrigerate.) Tap the shell with a hammer to crack it and loosen the meat. Remove meat in pieces with a sturdy kitchen table knife. Wipe coconut meat with a damp, clean cloth. Peel off brown layer with a sharp knife. Grate coconut or roughly chop it in a food processor. Tightly cover coconut meat with cling wrap and refrigerate it or sprinkle meat with a little sugar, place in freezer-weight zipper bags and freeze.

Fresh Coconut Milk

Makes 2 cups

An integral ingredient of tropical cuisines all over the world, including today's Conchfusion cuisine of the Florida Keys, coconut milk can be made from the meat of any fresh coconut, even those purchased in the supermarket.

4 cups grated or finely chopped fresh coconut meat
2 cups boiling water

1. Place coconut meat in a large bowl. Pour boiling water over meat and mix well with a spoon. Allow mixture to stand 20 minutes. Place a double thickness of cheesecloth over a strainer, then place strainer over a large bowl. Place coconut mixture in strainer, pressing on the coconut meat to remove all the liquid. Store coconut milk in the refrigerator until ready to use. Discard coconut meat.

Chef Note: When cooking with fresh coconut milk be careful not to allow it to boil or it may curdle.

Ricotta, which in Italian means "cooked again," is made from the by-products of the production of such cheeses as mozzarella and provolone. Soft, smooth, fresh, and unripened, ricotta is a combination of whey and whole, low-fat, or skim cow's milk.

CHEF NOTE: Freshly squeezed orange juice and grated orange peel are essential in this recipe. Jumbo cupcake tins can be found at a kitchen supply store. You can make the cupcakes with traditional tins, but the effect won't be as dramatic.

Ricotta-Orange Jumbo Cupcakes

1 package Duncan Hines orange supreme cake mix

1 1/3 cups plus 2 tablespoons freshly squeezed orange juice

1/3 cup canola oil

5 large eggs

16 ounces ricotta cheese

6 tablespoons sugar

1 teaspoon orange extract

2 (3-ounce) packages cream cheese, softened

5 cups sifted confectioners' sugar

1/4 cup finely grated orange peel, divided

1. Preheat oven to 350°F. Place cake mix, 1 1/3 cups orange juice, canola oil, and 3 eggs in a large mixing bowl. Combine ingredients with an electric mixer at slow speed. Increase speed to high and beat 2 minutes.

2. Place 2 eggs in a medium bowl and beat with a wire whisk until frothy. Add ricotta, sugar, and orange extract and beat with a wooden spoon until well blended. (Do not beat with mixer.)

3. Place cupcake papers in each cupcake tin. Fill each tin two-thirds full with orange batter. Drop ricotta mixture by spoonfuls evenly on top of the batter until cupcake tin is nearly full. (Do not mix ricotta into batter.) Bake for 40 to 45 minutes for jumbo cupcakes or 25 to 30 minutes for regular size cupcakes or until a toothpick inserted in the center comes out clean. (When cupcakes are done, the ricotta filling will go to the bottom and the cake will rise to the top.) Remove cupcakes from tins and cool on a wire rack.

4. Meanwhile, prepare frosting. Place cream cheese and 2 tablespoons orange juice in a medium bowl. Beat with an electric mixer until smooth. Slowly add sifted confectioners' sugar, beating constantly. Beat in 3 tablespoons grated orange peel. Refrigerate until ready to frost cooled cupcakes.

5. Frost cupcakes and sprinkle each with a little of the 1 tablespoon reserved grated orange peel. Refrigerate until ready to serve. Place on a 3-tiered platter to serve.

Stuffed Guava Shells

 SERVES 4 TO 6

8 ounces cream cheese, softened
1 tablespoon milk
2 tablespoons orange juice
1 tablespoon key lime juice

1 tablespoon sugar
2 (16-ounce) cans guava shells, chilled
thin salted sesame crackers

1. Place cream cheese in a small bowl and beat with an electric mixer. Add milk, orange and key lime juices, and sugar and beat until smooth. Drain guava shells, reserving guava syrup. Fill each guava shell with cream cheese mixture. If shells are small, place 4 to 6 on an individual dessert plate. If shells are large, serve only 2 per serving. Drizzle guava syrup over cream cheese and shells. Garnish with several crackers.

CHEF NOTE: Modern variations for serving guava shells abound: Fill the shells with ice cream and garnish with nuts; top shells with sour cream and sprinkle with nutmeg; or, for a tangier dessert, drizzle the shells with Goat Cheese Dressing (see Index).

The most popular dessert in Key West in the late nineteenth century was guava shells and cream cheese. Guava shells can be home-made by peeling fresh guavas and scooping out the seeds and soft pulp with a spoon, then cooking the shells in sugar syrup and canning them. However, a red-fleshed guava is needed to make guava shells, a variety not often found in the Florida Keys. Cuban factories prepared and canned the guava shells in the early days of Key West. The shells are now imported from Mexico.

Tres Leches—Three Milk Cake

The Cuban-American community has adopted as its own this unusual cake, which actually originated in Central America. Tres Leches is a classic yellow cake that, once baked, is saturated with more than 4 cups of liquid—a mixture of three kinds of milk. The result is a remarkably light, sweet, moist confection.

1 package Betty Crocker Super Moist yellow cake mix (with pudding)
1 ¼ cups water
⅓ cup canola oil
3 eggs

1 (12-ounce) can evaporated milk
1 (14-ounce) can Eagle Brand sweetened condensed milk
1 cup heavy cream
¼ cup sweetened flaked coconut

1. Preheat oven to 350°F. Place cake mix, water, oil, and eggs in a large mixing bowl. Beat with an electric mixer on low speed for 30 seconds. Increase speed to medium and beat 2 minutes more, scraping bowl occasionally.

2. Coat the entire inside of a bundt pan with vegetable cooking spray. Pour cake batter into pan and bake for 38 to 43 minutes or until cake pulls away from sides of pan and a wooden skewer inserted in cake comes out clean. Remove to a wire rack to cool for 5 minutes, while preparing the milk mixture.

3. Place evaporated milk, sweetened condensed milk, and cream in a medium bowl. Whisk to mix well. Invert bundt cake onto an oversize round serving platter. With a wooden or metal skewer, poke holes all over cake. With a flatware tablespoon, spoon milk mixture over cake, allowing it to absorb into the cake. Some of the milk mixture will pool around the cake and in the center of the bundt. Keep spooning this mixture over cake, adding new holes occasionally, until all liquid has been absorbed. (This will take about 30 minutes.) Sprinkle cake with coconut. Refrigerate cake until completely chilled, about 1 hour, before serving.

CHEF NOTE: The neutral flavor of this cake encourages experimentation. Variations are endless: Substitute sweetened coconut milk for ½ cup of the sweetened condensed milk. Add ¼ cup rum, brandy, Irish cream, peach schnapps, or chocolate syrup to the milk mixture. Bake it as a sheet cake or a layer cake. Frost the cake with vanilla whipped cream or fluffy white icing. Top it with a medley of fresh seasonal fruits. But because of the preponderance of milk in this cake, be sure to keep it refrigerated until ready to serve.

Tropical Fruit Sorbet

3 ripe bananas

2 cups cubed mango

1 cup fresh cubed pineapple

3 ounces fresh key lime juice

1½ cups sugar

1 ounce dark rum

1 cup mango nectar

1½ cups fresh orange juice

1. Place bananas, mango, and pineapple in a blender. Process fruit until smooth. Add key lime juice and sugar and process until well blended. Mix rum, mango nectar, and orange juice in a large measuring cup. Remove half the fruit mixture from blender. Add half the juice and process until smooth. Remove mixture to a large bowl. Place other half of fruit in blender. Add remainder of juice and process until smooth. Add to mixture in bowl. Stir to blend well.

2. Transfer tropical fruit puree to a 13 x 9-inch baking dish. Place in freezer. Stir mixture every hour for 4 hours or until mixture is frozen. Transfer sorbet to a covered freezer container.

CHEF NOTE: You can eliminate the rum in this sorbet if you'd like a non-alcoholic version to use in breakfast smoothies. The sorbet will freeze more solidly, so take the sorbet out of freezer 5 to 10 minutes before using.

How do you pick a ripe pineapple? Actually, pineapples are ripe when they are harvested. The pineapple's color does not indicate maturity or ripeness. Shell color is divided into seven categories—from zero, all green, to number six, all yellow. The pineapple can be any gradation from green to yellow and still be ripe. To spot a pineapple that has been harvested at the peak of its flavor, look for fresh, green leaves at its crown. Next check its eyes. Eyes of a pineapple are flattened and the size of a nickel when ripe. And trust your nose, it knows. If the pineapple smells sweet, it is on its way to fermentation. Pass it by. And if it feels soft to the touch, it is already rotten.

Pure Guava
A Taste of the Tropics

A favorite Keys fruit, guava came to the islands with Cuban immigrants. Today seldom seen fresh in supermarkets because its susceptibility to fruit fly infestation has caused an importation ban, the guava is an oval yellow-green fruit, ranging in size from a walnut to an apple. The fruit's pinkish-red pulp, which is peppered with a mass of tiny edible seeds, has been described as tasting like strawberries, bananas, or pineapple, but the fruit really has a unique flavor and intense aroma all its own.

ABOVE: *Guava tastes like a unique blend of strawberries, bananas, and pineapples.* **Credit: State Archives of Florida.**

A staple of Cuban cuisine, guava paste, a concentrated guava jell, is produced and packaged in round tins. It traditionally has been used in place of guava jelly on bread, waffles, and pancakes, not only because it tastes good, but also because it costs a lot less than the jelly.

Guava shells are also staples of Cuban-American cuisine. Cuban factories peel and halve guavas, scoop out the seeds and then stew and can the remaining shells in heavy syrup. These shells used to be exported to the U.S., but because of the U.S. government trade embargo with Cuba, the canned fruit as well as guava paste now comes from Central and South America.

Guava duff has been one of the most popular Keys desserts since the early 1800s, often served at Christmas or on a special occasion. A steamed pudding cake, the duff was put in a small flour sack, boiled until firm, and served with a sweet egg sauce.

In *Lore of the Wreckers*, Brise Shepard relates Mary Cappick's *Key West Story* tale of Captain Amos Sauls' affinity for guava duff: "Captain Amos Sauls, a New Englander, came to Key West in 1830. He sailed a smart wrecking schooner and lived alone in a small cabin down near the waterfront. The captain was a God-fearing man and went to church on Sundays, dressed in his best shore-going clothes. Occasionally after church he was the guest of some hospitable family for dinner. It may have been in this way that he acquired a taste for guava duff, a delectable dessert, served hot with sugar and brandy sauce. So irresistible was the pudding that he learned to make it for himself. Each Sunday,

Guava Duff

Serves 6 to 8

Conchs preferred to leave the guava seeds in the duff but claimed "strangers" liked the duff better if the seeds were strained out. As a stranger I agree. The seeds add an unpleasant hard bite to the otherwise unusual and tasty dish.

4 tablespoons (½ stick) softened butter, divided

1¾ cups sugar, divided

3 eggs, beaten and 1 egg separated

2 cups fresh guava pulp, sieved to remove seeds, or diced canned shells

3 cups flour

4 teaspoons baking powder

½ teaspoon salt

1 to 3 tablespoons hot water

1. **For the duff:** Place 2 tablespoons butter and 1 cup sugar in a large bowl. Cream with an electric mixer. Add 3 beaten eggs and guava pulp and beat until smooth.

2. Place flour, baking powder, and salt in a small bowl. Stir to mix. Add flour mixture to the guava pulp a little at a time, beating continually until mixture is stiff. Spray a medium-size lidded tin with vegetable cooking spray or grease with Crisco. Pour guava batter into tin and cover firmly with lid. Immerse tin in a pot of water that comes two-thirds up the side of the tin. Place pot over medium heat and bring water to a bubbling simmer. Steam duff for 2 to 3 hours or until a wooden skewer inserted in the center comes out clean.

3. **Meanwhile, prepare the egg sauce:** Place 2 tablespoons butter and ¾ cup sugar in a medium bowl. Cream with an electric mixer. Add egg yolk and beat to combine. Beat egg white in a separate bowl until stiff but not dry. Fold into butter mixture. Add hot water, a tablespoon at a time, stirring to make a smooth sauce. Because of today's salmonella concerns, place sauce in a small saucepan and cook over medium-low heat stirring constantly until mixture is heated through and just about to bubble, about 2 minutes. Remove from heat and cool.

4. Remove duff from hot water. Slide a thin knife around edge of tin to loosen duff. Unmold on a platter. Slice duff and serve with topped with egg sauce.

Chef Note: Egg sauce can be transferred to a covered container and refrigerated for up to two days. Place in a saucepan over low heat and stir constantly until sauce is heated through, about 2 minutes.

---

when not invited out, he would return to his house, change his shore clothes for seafaring garb and whip up a guava duff, letting it boil several hours on his charcoal-burning cookstove.

"One Sunday the guava duff had just begun to boil on the captain's stove when the cry of 'Wreck asho-o-re!' rang down the street. Key West did not tolerate fishing or sponging on the Sabbath, but a shipwreck couldn't very well be put off till the next day. Captain Sauls hesitated. It was not so much his religious convictions that bothered him: it was the guava duff. He paced the floor in shameful indecision as his cronies trotted down the street to the wharf. A few minutes later, as the alarm died away, neighbors watching the race from their porches on Front Street rubbed their eyes and looked again. Among the running men headed for the waterfront was a figure staggering along with a burden almost too heavy for him to carry. It was Captain Sauls, both arms clasped around the lower portion of a sheet-iron stove in which a fire burned brightly—and on top of which a pot of guava duff sat steaming merrily, on its way to the wreck."

Tri-Berry Tart

A member of the rose family, the strawberry is indigenous to the Americas, Asia, and Europe. The strawberry is the only fruit that grows with its seeds on the outside. In the Florida Keys, the best straw-berries come from local strawberry farms, like Knaus Berry Farm, in Homestead at the top of the Keys. The berries, planted in October, ripen in the dead of winter—peak harvest is in February.

1 cup flour
1/4 cup confectioners' sugar
8 tablespoons (1 stick) butter, softened
5 teaspoons cornstarch
1 cup pineapple nectar
1 teaspoon lemon juice

1/2 cup plus 1/3 cup granulated sugar
8 ounces cream cheese, softened
1 teaspoon vanilla
1 pound strawberries
6 ounces blueberries
6 ounces raspberries

1. **To make the crust:** Preheat oven to 325°F. Place flour in a medium bowl. Sift confec-tioners' sugar into bowl. Add butter and cut in with a fork until mixture forms a pebbly dough. With clean hands, form dough into a ball and knead between hands until it is smooth.

2. Place dough ball between two 15-inch-square sheets of parchment paper. Roll dough with a rolling pin to form an 11-inch circle-like shape. Invert a 10-inch dinner plate over the top parchment paper, and cut a circle through parchment and dough with a sharp paring knife, following contour of dinner plate. Remove and discard excess parchment and dough. Transfer the 10-inch circle of parchment and dough to a baking sheet. Place in refrigerator for 5 minutes to firm up.

3. **To bake:** Remove top parchment from dough crust and place on a baking sheet in oven. Bake for 15 minutes or until crust is light brown. Remove baking sheet from oven. Using two large spatulas, carefully transfer crust to serving platter and allow it to cool.

4. As crust is baking, prepare glaze. Place cornstarch and 1 tablespoon pineapple nectar in a small saucepan over medium heat. Stir to form a paste. Add rest of pineapple nec-tar, lemon juice, and 1/2 cup sugar. Stir to mix well. Cook pineapple mixture, stirring fre-quently, for 6 minutes or until thick and bubbling. Remove glaze from heat. Place a piece of plastic wrap on top of glaze surface to prevent a skin from forming. Allow glaze to cool slightly while assembling the pizza.

5. Place cream cheese, 1/3 cup sugar, and vanilla in a small mixing bowl. Beat with an electric mixer until smooth. Carefully spread mixture over cooled crust. (Crust will be like a crisp sugar cookie so use a light hand.)

6. Cut 3 strawberries in half and place, cut side down, in center of the tart like daisy petals. Place a whole strawberry in the center. Cut remaining strawberries into thin slices. Place raspberries around perimeter of tart. Sprinkle remainder of tart with blueberries. Place strawberry slices upright, in the spaces between the blueberries, forming a freeform circular pattern. Spoon cooled glaze over fruit. Place in refrigerator and chill for 2 hours before serving. (Do not leave tart at room temperature for more than a few minutes before serving. Glaze will unset a bit and become runny.) Carefully cut tart into 12 wedges and serve.

CHEF NOTE: Strawberries do not ripen after they are picked, so be sure to choose firm, bright-red berries. They are very susceptible to mold, so do not wash them until you are ready to use them. Store strawberries on a single layer of paper towels in a shallow container in the refrigerator.

They All Schemed for
Ice Cream

Before the turn of the twentieth century, ice was hauled to the Florida Keys from Maine in coastal sailing schooners. The ice was transported covered with sawdust and was weighed in Key West before it was either stored in a thick-walled icehouse in Key West or reloaded onto smaller vessels and taken to the nearest wharf up the Keys. There the perishable cargo was transferred again, this time to sloops that delivered the ice to its final destination. Inevitably, the searing tropical sun had melted the ice to half its original size!

LEFT: *McDuffie's Snowball and Ice Cream Shop, Key West, ca. 1975.* Credit: State Archives of Florida.

n *A Key West Companion*, Christopher Cox relates the childhood recollections of making ice cream in Key West. When a ship docked at the wharf in Plantation Key where he grew up, the family of a man known only as Mr. Mackey would sometimes get ice from the crew. They packed a big wooden tub (formerly filled with lard) with ice and rock salt. Then they placed a smaller tub inside and filled it with cream, sugar, and fruit, such as coconut, mango, or guava. Mackey's mother put an "apronful of silverware" into the mixture and then tied a rope around the tub with two pieces of rope extending off to either side. It took two people to make the ice cream: They would sit on either side of the tub, hold the ropes, and pull the tub back and forth. When the silverware stopped clunking, the ice cream was ready to eat.

With the eventual availability of affordable ice from ice plants established in Key West, ice cream became one of the most popular desserts on the island. Residents held ice cream socials in their homes, where they created rich homemade frozen custards from the jelly of half-ripe coconuts and the fruit of their dooryard gardens. By 1949 ice cream parlors had sprung up on Duval Street. Adults and children visited nearly every day, purchasing delicately flavored ice creams and fruit ices. Ingredients ranged from green coconut and ripe tamarind to soursop, sugar apple, and sapodilla. The ice cream was often eaten with fried green plantains, which were thinly sliced and looked like potato chips.

Ice cream parlors still pepper Duval Street, attracting residents and visitors alike with their homemade concoctions. Flamingo Crossing, 1107 Duval Street, makes 150 different flavors, offering 32 choices on any given day.

Conch Ice Cream

Makes about 4 cups

Conchs used sugar apple, soursop, guava, sapodilla, banana, mango, pineapple, and even canned fruit salad or cherries to make this simple homemade ice cream.

1 cup finely chopped fruit pulp
1 (12-ounce) can evaporated milk
1 (14-ounce) can Eagle Brand sweetened condensed milk
squeeze of lime (optional)

1. Place all ingredients in a large bowl and mix together with a wooden spoon. If the fruit is very sweet, add a squeeze of lime. Put mixture in an 11 x 7-inch baking dish or freezing tray. Place in freezer. Stir mixture every hour until frozen through. Transfer to a covered container. Place at room temperature a few minutes before serving.

Tropical Trifle

The trifle is an English tradition that crossed the big pond in fine form. Although its name—trifle—means something of little importance, this classic dessert evolved into fare fit for the king. The essential ingredients of a classic trifle were sponge cake soaked in sherry or white wine, rich custard, fruit or jam, and whipped cream, layered in a glass dish in that order. The cream was often decorated with almonds, cherries, or angelica. Keys cooks have reinterpreted this elaborate-looking dessert to showcase the fruits of the tropics.

1 (3-ounce) package Island Pineapple flavor Jell-O
1 cup boiling water
1 cup mango nectar
1 prepared angel food cake
1 (17-ounce) jar mango jam
2 cups fresh papaya, cut in one-inch cubes
1 quart fresh strawberries, washed, patted dry, and thinly sliced

2 cups sliced Cuban or finger bananas
2 cups fresh mango, cut in one-inch cubes
2 tablespoons coconut rum
2 cups 2% milk
2 (2.9-ounce) packages Jell-O Americana custard
1 (8-ounce) carton Cool Whip

1. **One day ahead:** Place Jell-O in a medium bowl with 1 cup boiling water and stir until Jell-O is dissolved. Add 1 cup mango nectar and stir well to combine. Cool to room temperature.

2. Meanwhile, break or cut angel food cake into 3-inch chunks. Spread mango jam on all sides of each piece. Tightly line the bottom of a large glass bowl with cake pieces.

3. Place papaya in an even layer atop cake pieces. Place 2 cups strawberries in an even layer atop papaya. Then add a layer of bananas and then a layer of mango. Sprinkle fruit with rum.

4. Pour Jell-O over fruit and cake, cover bowl with plastic wrap, and refrigerate until Jell-O is set, about 1 hour.

5. While Jell-O is setting, make Americana custard according to package instructions. When custard is thick and creamy, remove from heat. Transfer custard to a glass or ceramic bowl and cover surface of custard with a piece of plastic wrap so that a skin doesn't form. Allow custard to cool to room temperature, about 30 to 45 minutes. (Custard should be cool enough not to melt the Jell-O when added to the trifle but should not be allowed to completely set.)

6. When custard is cool, pour it into the trifle bowl over Jell-O/fruit layers. Place trifle in refrigerator for at least 3 to 4 hours, preferably overnight.

7. Just before serving: spread Cool Whip over top of trifle. Top with reserved ½ cup strawberries. Refrigerate trifle until serving.

CHEF NOTE: For a more decadent dessert, substitute a pint of whipped heavy cream for the Cool Whip. For a more tradition English-style trifle, make these substitutions: strawberry Jell-O for pineapple Jell-O; pineapple juice for mango nectar; seedless raspberry jam for mango jam; sweet sherry for rum. Instead of the tropical fruit called for in the recipe use 1 pint fresh raspberries, 3 ripe kiwis, sliced; 3 ripe peaches and 3 ripe pears, peeled and sliced; 1 quart strawberries, sliced. Or, for an all-berry trifle, substitute all berries—raspberries, blueberries, strawberries, blackberries—for the amounts of fruit called for in the recipe.

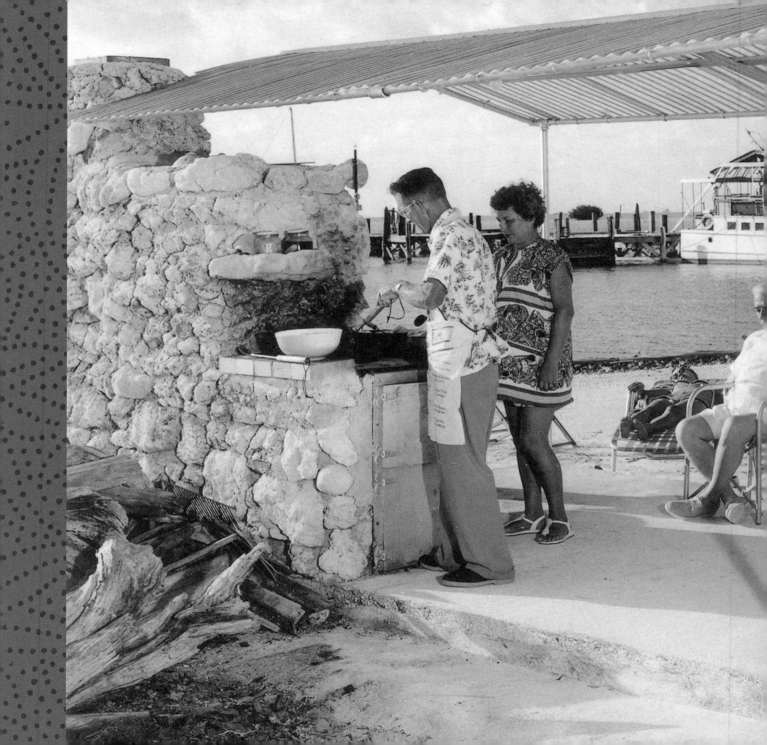

Bread *and* 🌴 8
Breakfast

In the early days of the Florida Keys, breakfast often was simply a thimbleful of strong Cuban coffee or a café con leche and a buttery toasted piece of Cuban bread. Some liked getting up early, having coffee, and then having a "proper" breakfast of grits and grunts or stewed fruit a little later in the morning. Still others preferred to sit on a shady porch, enjoy a slice of fresh papaya with a squeeze of lime, a fluffy omelet with just a pinch of oregano, and a cup of English tea.

Fast forward to the twenty-first century, where even in the Florida Keys, breakfast is often taken on the fly—on the way to work, school, fishing, diving, water sports, golf, or tennis. The winter season, however, finds residents inundated with house-guests from up north, snowbirds who wing their way south for a little fun in the sun. And with these vacationing visitors, for several days a week at least, breakfast turns into a very proper meal indeed—a leisurely, substantial repast that can sustain folks until dinner.

LEFT: *A fish fry at a tourist court in Tavenier, ca. 1955.* **Credit: State Archives of Florida.**

Dooryard Garden Breakfast Bread

This tasty bread was designed with innovation in mind. Any variety of fruit or vegetable can be substituted for the 2 cups pureed mango in this recipe. Dooryard garden tropical favorites such as papayas, coconuts, and bananas, and traditional Cuban-American choices such as sweet potatoes or ripe plantains, are just the beginning. Try grated carrots, finely chopped figs, grated apples, applesauce, drained crushed pineapple, pumpkin puree, finely chopped rhubarb, coarsely grated zucchini, or other seasonal produce. For even more variation, use 1 cup each of two different ingredients, such as grated coconut and mashed bananas. You'll never need another recipe for breakfast bread.

3 cups flour
1 teaspoon salt
1 teaspoon baking soda
½ teaspoon baking powder
3 eggs

1 cup canola oil
2 cups sugar
2 cups pureed fresh mango
3 teaspoons vanilla
margarine or Crisco

1. Preheat oven to 325°F. In a medium bowl, sift together flour, salt, baking soda, and baking powder. Set aside. Place eggs in a large bowl and beat with an electric mixer. Add oil and sugar and cream well. Add mango and vanilla. Mix together on low speed. Slowly add dry ingredients until well mixed.

2. Coat two loaf pans generously with margarine or Crisco. Divide batter evenly between the two pans. Bake for 60 to 80 minutes, or until a toothpick inserted in the center of a loaf comes out clean. Remove bread to wire racks and cool. (When cool, bread can be wrapped tightly in cling wrap, placed in a freezer-weight zipper bag, and frozen for up to 2 weeks.)

CHEF NOTE: If you'd like a cinnamon taste to the bread, add 3 teaspoons cinnamon to dry ingredients, but beware. The cinnamon may overpower the flavor of the fruit or vegetables in this bread. If you prefer nuts in your breakfast bread, add 1 cup of your choice of chopped nuts to the final batter.

Guava and Cream Cheese Pastelitos

1 package (1 pound) ready-to-bake
  pre-sliced puff pastry
10 ounces guava paste
4 ounces cream cheese

1. Preheat oven to 400°F. Place the 8 squares of puff pastry dough on top of parchment paper or wax paper. Cut guava paste and cream cheese into ½-inch dice. Place 8 pieces of guava and 8 pieces of cheese in the center of each square. Working 1 square at a time, use a pastry brush to moisten the edges of the dough square with water. Fold dough, corner to corner, over filling to form a triangle, being careful not to puncture the dough. Crimp and seal edges with a fork. (Make sure edges are completely sealed or filling will ooze out during baking.)

2. Transfer filled pastry triangles to a nonstick baking sheet, leaving at least ½ inch between each one for expansion. Bake 18 to 20 minutes or until pastry is flaky and golden brown. Remove pastelitos from baking sheet with a spatula and cool on a wire rack.

CHEF NOTE: Authentic pastelito pastry dough is complicated and time consuming to make, but this pre-cut prepared puff pastry makes a good, easy-to use substitute. Guava paste is sold in round tins or oblong logs in Keys supermarkets.

The Cuban pastry known as pastelito or pastelle resembles an American-style turnover. Flaky pastry dough encases a variety of fillings, and the type of filling determines the pastelito's shape. Guava and cream cheese together—*guayaba y queso*—is triangular, while guava or coconut is square, and cream cheese alone is long and thin. Round pastelitos usually encase savory or spicy meat fillings. Authentic pastelitos are available at Cuban bakeries in Key West and up the Keys.

Cuban Bread

Baked in 3-foot-long loaves that are about 3-inches wide and 2½ inches high, Cuban bread is white, light, and airy on the inside and a crispy golden brown on the outside. Four or five times a day, Cuban-Americans in old Key West baked this bread, serving it hot right out of the oven and consuming it all at one meal, down to the last crumb.

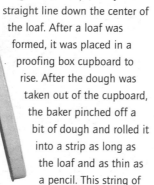

Though the mixture of ingredients—flour, sugar, salt, water, and yeast—is simple, the traditions involved in creating this bread are anything but. It was of utmost importance that the last fold of dough formed a perfectly straight line down the center of the loaf. After a loaf was formed, it was placed in a proofing box cupboard to rise. After the dough was taken out of the cupboard, the baker pinched off a bit of dough and rolled it into a strip as long as the loaf and as thin as a pencil. This string of dough was dipped in water to moisten it slightly and then carefully placed down the centerline formed from that last fold of dough.

The crucial string formed an expansion joint that allowed the loaf to crack slightly as it baked. Some bakers inserted the spine of a palm leaf or banana leaf instead of the dough string, which occasionally resulted in a bit of green foliage baked into the bread. Today's bakers have eliminated the centerline string of dough, opting instead to cut the top of the dough loaf with a sharp knife or razor blade before it goes into the oven. The heat of the oven caus-

...

Legend has it that an entrepreneurial old man known only as Luis bought Cuban bread wholesale from Molina's for 3 cents a loaf.

...

es the top to open like the petals of a flower.

Bakeries sprouted in Key West in the early 1900s and flourished throughout the century—Molina's on Margaret Street, Perez Brothers on White Street, Matchett's on the corner of Duval and Olivia Streets, and Brothers on Fleming Street buzzed with activity. Legend has it that an entrepreneurial old man known only as Luis bought Cuban bread wholesale from Molina's for 3 cents a loaf. He filled big baskets with the bread and sold them door to door for 5 cents each. By 1965 a loaf of Cuban bread cost 17 cents, still less than a penny an inch.

Cuban Bread

5 to 7 cups all purpose or bread flour
4 packages dry yeast (3 tablespoons)
1 tablespoon salt

2 tablespoons sugar
2 cups warm water (105 to 115 degrees)

1. Place 4 cups of flour in a large mixing bowl. Add yeast, salt and sugar. Stir dry ingredients with a spoon until they are well blended. Pour in water and beat with 100 strong strokes or use an electric mixer with a dough hook. Gradually work in remaining flour, ½-cup at a time, until the dough takes shape and is no longer sticky.

2. Sprinkle work surface with flour. Knead the dough, keeping a layer of flour between the dough and the work surface. Knead for about 6 minutes, incorporating as much flour as needed until dough is smooth and elastic.

3. Coat a large bowl and a piece of plastic wrap with vegetable cooking spray. Place dough in bowl, cover with plastic wrap, and place in a warm place (80-85 degrees) until doubled in bulk, about 15 minutes. (To test if it has risen, poke your finger into the dough. If a dent remains, it is ready.)

4. Punch down the dough, turn it out on the work surface, and cut it into 2 pieces. Knead each 30 seconds to squeeze out the bubbles. Shape into 2 long, French-style loaves, each about 1½-inches in diameter. Place both loaves on a greased baking sheet, allowing space between the two. With a sharp knife or razor blade, cut a deep line down the center of the length of the loaf.

5. Place the baking sheet on middle shelf of a cold oven. Place a large pan of boiling water on the shelf below the bread and set oven temperature at 400°F. (The bread will rise while the oven is heating.) Bake 50 minutes or until the bread is a deep golden brown. To test if bread is done, thump bottom crust; if it sounds hollow and hard, it is done.

6. Place bread on a wire rack to cool slightly. Serve warm.

Chef Note: Also known as Cuban water bread, this bread rises rapidly because the yeast-to-flour ratio is double that of other breads. Use all-purpose flour and active dry yeast that has been stored in a cool, dry place for no longer than one year. Eat Cuban bread within a day. Because it contains no shortening, it gets stale quickly. To make Cuban cokers, which are like dinner rolls, cut each of the 2 dough loaves into 8 pieces, 3- to 4-inches long, with a sharp knife. Form into rolls and fold ends under.

Savory Johnnycake

As the recipe for sweet Johnnycake (see next page) attests, the classic Key West cornbread feud has never been resolved. This recipe calls for buttermilk and uses no sugar. Conchs, Cubans, and "strangers" alike have their own preferences. Judge for yourself!

1½ cups yellow cornmeal
½ cup flour
1½ teaspoons baking powder
½ teaspoon baking soda
½ teaspoon salt

margarine or Crisco
1 cup buttermilk
2 eggs, beaten
¼ cup canola oil
1 (14.75-ounce) can cream-style sweet corn

1. Preheat oven to 425°F. Place cornmeal, flour, baking powder, baking soda, and salt in a large bowl. Stir to mix. Make a well in the center.

2. Grease an 8-inch-square or a 9 x 7-inch glass baking dish with margarine or Crisco. Place in oven.

3. Add buttermilk, eggs, and oil to the well in the dry ingredients. With a wooden spoon, briskly stir all ingredients until smooth. Add corn and stir until smooth. Pour mixture into hot baking dish. Bake for 20 to 25 minutes or until bread pulls away from sides of pan and edges begin to crisp. A wooden skewer inserted in the center should come out clean. Remove from oven and cool on a wire rack.

CHEF NOTE: For a variation, add ¼ cup shredded cheddar to the batter or sprinkle the cheese atop the cornbread during the last 5 minutes of baking.

Sweet Johnnycake

 **SERVES 6 TO 8**

½ tablespoon margarine or Crisco

1 (8.5-ounce) box Jiffy Cornbread Muffin Mix

1 extra-large egg

¼ cup whole milk

1 cup creamed canned corn

1-2 tablespoons diced canned jalapenos

3 tablespoons chopped roasted red peppers

1. Preheat oven to 400°F. Place margarine in an 8 x 8-inch baking pan. Put baking pan in the oven so that margarine melts and pan preheats.

2. Meanwhile, place cornbread mix, egg, and milk in a large bowl. Combine ingredients with a spoon or an electric mixer (batter will be slightly lumpy). Add creamed corn, jalapenos, and roasted peppers. Mix until all ingredients are combined.

3. Swirl melted margarine to coat all sides of baking pan. Pour cornbread batter into pan. Bake 20 to 25 minutes, or until top is golden and sides pull away from the sides of the pan slightly.

CHEF NOTE: Johnnycake is traditionally made in a black, well-seasoned skillet, which not everyone has these days. If you substitute such a skillet, be sure you add the margarine or Crisco and preheat it in the oven first, as instructed above. The hot skillet (or baking pan) gives the johnnycake a crisp bottom. If the skillet is large, cut the baking time or double the recipe. For slight variations, use Mexican canned corn instead of creamed corn, increasing milk to ⅓ cup.

Its name thought to be a corruption of a bread called "journey cake," because it was easily prepared by travelers, johnnycake made quite a journey—from New England and the southern states to the Bahamas and on to the Keys with the original Conch settlers. In the 1949 *Key West Woman's Club Cookbook*, Mabel B. Whitley noted, "The world is divided into two schools of thought on cornbread: the sweet'ners and the non-sweet'ners." This classic Key West cornbread feud appeared to be between a savory bread that used buttermilk, but not sugar or other sweetener, and a cornbread that called for whole "sweet" milk, sugar, and sometimes coconut.

Asparagus-Pepperjack Quiche

Although quiche is thought to be classically French, it actually originated in medieval Germany in the kingdom of Lothringen, which the French later renamed Lorraine. The word *quiche* is believed to have come from the German word *kuchen*, meaning cake. The dish became popular in England after World War II, making its way to the United States in the 1950s. You could expect to find this updated classic at one of Key West's charming guest house inns.

1 frozen piecrust, defrosted
small bunch asparagus
1 cup shredded pepperjack cheese
½ cup diced prosciutto
2 heaping tablespoons finely minced sun-dried tomatoes
½ cup snipped fresh basil
3 extra-large eggs
1½ cups half-and-half
⅛ teaspoon white pepper

1. Preheat oven to 350°F. Coat a quiche pan with vegetable cooking spray. Place piecrust in pan. With fingertips, press crust into curves of pan and along bottom, making sure the crust has no open seams. With a fork, prick holes in bottom and along the sides of pan. Bake crust for 10 minutes or until golden. Remove crust from oven and cool.

2. Meanwhile, clean asparagus and snap off woody ends. Place asparagus in a shallow skillet and cover with water. Steam asparagus over medium-high heat until crisp-tender, about 3 minutes. Drain asparagus, rinse with cold water, and drain again. Place asparagus on paper toweling and pat dry. Cut into ½-inch pieces (should have about 2 cups).

3. In a small bowl, mix together cheese, prosciutto, sun-dried tomatoes, and basil. Set aside. In a medium bowl, whisk eggs. Add half-and-half and white pepper and whisk to combine.

4. Place asparagus in quiche crust in an even layer. Sprinkle cheese mixture over asparagus layer. Pour egg mixture over the other ingredients in the crust. Bake for 40 to 50 minutes, or until knife inserted into the center comes out clean.

CHEF NOTE: Pepperjack cheese adds a bit of a bite to this quiche, but you can substitute any one of your favorite cheeses from the jack, cheddar, or swiss families if you like.

Dilled Breakfast Pockets

 SERVES 4

1 tablespoon butter or margarine

¼ cup minced red onions

1 large plum tomato, seeded and finely chopped

1 tablespoon snipped fresh dill, divided

6 eggs, beaten

salt and freshly ground black pepper

1 package (8) 8-inch flour tortillas

1½ cups shredded Italian cheese (mozzarella, provolone, Asiago, and Romano mix)

4 slices bacon, cooked crisp and crumbled

1. Preheat oven to 250°F. Melt butter in a large nonstick skillet over medium heat. Add chopped onions, tomatoes, and 2 teaspoons dill. Cook, stirring often, for 2 minutes. Add beaten eggs and salt and pepper to taste. Scramble the eggs until set. Meanwhile, place tortillas in a plastic zipper bag and microwave on high for 45 seconds or until soft. Remove eggs from heat.

2. **To assemble breakfast pockets:** Fold tortilla in half, then in half again, forming a tortilla wedge with two pockets. Into each pocket, place about a tablespoon of shredded cheese. Sprinkle with crumbled bacon. Divide one-eighth of the scrambled egg mixture between the 2 pockets. Top each pocket with another tablespoon of shredded cheese and a sprinkling of dill. Place filled tortilla pocket in a heatproof dish in oven to keep it warm. Repeat this process with the other 7 tortillas, keeping filled pockets warm in the oven.

3. **To serve:** Place 2 Dilled Breakfast Pockets on each individual plate.

CHEF NOTE: Be sure to have all ingredients ready before you start filling the tortilla pockets. Serve pockets accompanied by a fresh fruit compote and offer bottled hot sauce on the side if you'd like to add a spicy kick to this breakfast.

The corn tortilla has been a staple in the cuisines of Mexico and Central and South America since before the Spanish arrived in 1519. By the 1700s, native populations began moving north into what are now the states of California, Arizona, and Texas. Finding a dearth of corn in these areas but a plethora of wheat flour, the settlers invented the flour tortilla. The elastic ingredient gluten in the flour tortilla allows the leak-proof wrapper to stretch so that this tortilla can hold even more filling than its corn cousin.

Café Cubano

Cubans like their coffee strong . . . and often! Breakfast, mid-morning pick-me-up, after lunch, mid-afternoon pick-me-up, and after dinner, this Cuban tradition—brought to Key West with the immigrant population—demands specialty beans that are roasted almost to the point of being burned. The roasted beans are then very finely ground in small quantities to almost a powder.

In the mid-1900s, two coffee mills in Key West regularly blanketed the port city with the enticing aroma of roasting beans. Triumph Coffee Mill operated at a location on Truman Avenue, between Olivia and Polhaski Streets. Star Coffee Mill was on the corner of Greene and Ann Streets. In the 1990s, Baby's Coffee began roasting beans in Key West. They still offer a number of Key West specialty beans, including Baby's Cuban Roast, from their location on U.S. Hwy. 1, at mile marker 15. Because of the ongoing trade embargo with the island nation, real Cuban coffee beans are not available for purchase in the United States today, but Jamaican espresso beans make a good substitute.

To make Cuban coffee in Key West's early days, boiled water was poured over ground coffee beans that were encased in a small flannel bag. The bag was suspended from an iron tripod and the coffee filtered into a heatproof pot. The pot was placed on the stove and reheated as often as necessary. The flannel bag was then carefully washed and hung by the kitchen door in the sun to dry.

This traditional way of preparing Cuban coffee gave way to a small inexpensive stove-top espresso maker that locals called a Silex or driplator. Today, Italian-made steam-pressure espresso-brewing machines, which can brew fresh individual servings, have largely replaced the old ways of making *café cubano*.

Double the strength of regular American coffee, *café cubano* is served in small portions with lots of sugar (about 1½ teaspoons) in espresso cups or *tacitas*, which are smaller

...

Drinking a "jolt" of Cuban coffee—which Cuban-Americans call "*un buchito*," or "a mouthful," and early Conchs called a *bouchie*—is more like downing a shot of tequila.

...

Café Cubano

Put 1 to 1½ teaspoons sugar per serving into a metal cup large enough to hold all servings of coffee. Prepare coffee according to manufacturer's instructions for your espresso maker. As coffee begins brewing, pour just enough coffee into the metal cup to moisten the sugar. Stir the coffee and sugar briskly, until it becomes a light paste. When coffee is done, pour it slowly into the metal cup, gently stirring it into the sugar paste (an acquired skill, when done correctly a sugary foam forms). Pour coffee into *tacitas* or espresso cups.

Café con Leche

In a saucepan over low heat, warm whole milk in an amount equal to the *café cubano* you are brewing. Fill a regular coffee cup two-thirds full with warm milk. Pour in an espresso cup of sugared *café cubano* and stir to combine.

LEFT: *Pepe's Coffee Shop, Key West, ca. 1984.* **Credit: State Archives of Florida.**

than demitasse cups. This is not coffee to be slowly sipped. Drinking a "jolt" of Cuban coffee—which Cuban-Americans call *"un buchito"* or "a mouthful" and early Conchs called a bouchie—is more like downing a shot of tequila.

For generations, Key Westers have started the day with *café con leche*—in reality more milk-with-coffee than coffee-with-milk—and a buttered piece of toasted Cuban bread. From breakfast onward, however, any event is an excuse for a bouchie break.

Frituras de Papas

This Cuban-influenced breakfast dish had its beginnings in old Key West. Technically translated as "potato fritters," these actually are mashed potato cakes. Conch cooks were very adept are recycling leftovers into a tasty entrée for another meal.

2 cups cold mashed potatoes

2 eggs, beaten

½ teaspoon Sambuca liqueur or anise flavoring

4 tablespoons (½ stick) butter or margarine, divided

maple syrup

1. Preheat oven to 250°F. Place mashed potatoes in a medium bowl. Add eggs and Sambuca and mix thoroughly with a spoon. Melt 2 tablespoons butter or margarine in a large nonstick skillet or griddle over medium-high heat. With a flatware tablespoon place a mound of potato mixture in skillet and flatten it so that it forms a patty about 3 inches in diameter. Repeat process until skillet is full. Cook mashed potato cakes until golden brown, about 2 minutes per side. Remove potato cakes to a heatproof platter and place in the oven to keep them warm. Add remaining 2 tablespoons margarine to skillet and repeat process with remaining potato mixture. Serve with butter and maple syrup.

Uptown Spinach Grits and Grunts

Serves 8 to 10

1 cup quick grits
6 ounces sharp cheddar cheese, shredded
2 eggs
2% or whole milk
10 ounces fresh spinach, steamed, drained, and squeezed dry
1 package dried onion soup mix
1 tablespoon butter or margarine
¼ cup grated Parmesan cheese

1 cup low-fat buttermilk
1 cup flour
½ teaspoon garlic powder
¼ teaspoon white pepper
½ teaspoon dried thyme
2 teaspoons sage
2 pounds dolphinfish, cut into 1½-inch by 4-inch fingers
2 tablespoons olive oil, divided

1. To make spinach grits: Preheat oven to 350°F. Cook grits per package instructions in a large pot. Remove from heat and add cheddar cheese to grits. Mix well to combine.

2. Break eggs into a 1-cup measuring cup. Beat lightly with a fork. Add milk to make 1 cup. Add this egg mixture to grits and stir. Add spinach to grits. Mix well with a wooden spoon. Add onion soup mix and stir to combine.

3. Grease a large casserole with margarine. Transfer spinach grits mixture to casserole. Sprinkle with Parmesan cheese. Place casserole in oven and bake for 1 hour.

4. Meanwhile, place buttermilk in a shallow dish. In a small bowl mix together flour, garlic powder, white pepper, thyme, and sage. Spread evenly on a dinner plate. Dip both sides of each fish finger in buttermilk, then press into flour mixture, coating all sides. Place floured fish on another dinner plate. Repeat process with all fish fingers.

5. Place 1 tablespoon olive oil in a large, nonstick skillet over medium-high heat. When oil is hot, place half the fish fingers in skillet. Cook 2 minutes or until underside is golden. Turn fish fingers and cook 2 minutes longer or until fish flakes when pierced with a fork. Remove fish to a platter. Add remaining 1 tablespoon oil to skillet and repeat process with remaining fish fingers. Serve fish finger "grunts" with spinach grits.

Chef Note: You can assemble Spinach Grits the day before, cover with plastic wrap, and refrigerate until ready to bake. Bring to room temperature before baking. You can substitute any firm, white fish for the dolphinfish fingers, even grunts if you can find them.

Egg and Sausage Flatbread

Legend has it that Darius the Great, king of the Persian Empire at its height (521–486 B.C.), and his soldiers baked flatbread on their shields and covered them with cheese and dates. Keys cooks have taken this innovation one step further, creating a hearty breakfast meal that can be eaten on the fly or while doing battle with a sailfish or blue marlin.

1 (8-ounce) can refrigerated French bread dough

12 ounces turkey breakfast sausage, removed from casings and crumbled

1 cup shredded hash brown potatoes, thawed

1 cup shredded cheddar cheese

¼ cup 2% or whole milk

½ teaspoon salt

⅛ teaspoon freshly ground black pepper

4 eggs

2 tablespoons grated Parmesan cheese

1. Preheat oven to 375°F. Press refrigerated dough evenly onto a pizza pan or baking sheet, forming a slightly higher crimped rim of dough around the edges.

2. Place crumbled sausage in a large nonstick skillet over medium heat and sauté it until browned and cooked through. Drain on paper toweling.

3. Sprinkle cooked sausage atop dough. Then sprinkle potatoes and cheese atop flatbread. In a small bowl, whisk together milk, salt, pepper, and eggs. Pour egg mixture over flatbread toppings. Sprinkle with Parmesan cheese.

4. Bake for 25 minutes or until crust is browned and eggs are set. Cut into large squares or narrow wedges to serve.

CHEF NOTE: For easy early morning preparation, cook sausage the day before and refrigerate it in a covered container until needed.

Fancy Egg Scramble

8 tablespoons (1 stick) butter, divided
1 pound white button mushrooms, thinly sliced
1 cup diced ham or Canadian bacon
¼ cup chopped scallions
12 eggs, beaten

2 tablespoons flour
½ teaspoon salt
½ teaspoon pepper
2 cups 2% or whole milk
1 cup shredded Mexican-style cheese
2½ cups soft breadcrumbs

1. Melt 1 tablespoon butter in a large skillet over medium-low heat. Sauté mushrooms until soft, about 5 minutes. Drain mushrooms in a colander and set aside.

2. Melt 3 tablespoons butter in same skillet on medium-high heat. Add ham and scallions and cook until scallions are tender, about 5 minutes. Add eggs and scramble until just set. Set aside

3. In a 4-quart saucepan over medium heat, melt 2 tablespoons butter. Stir in flour, salt, and pepper. Gradually add milk, stirring constantly, until mixture is bubbly, about 2 minutes. Remove from heat. Add shredded cheese and stir until melted. Fold reserved mushroom and egg mixtures into cheese sauce.

4. Coat a 13 x 9-inch baking dish with vegetable cooking spray. Transfer egg mixture to baking dish.

5. In a small pan over low heat, melt 2 tablespoons butter. Add breadcrumbs and stir to coat. Sprinkle mixture atop eggs. Cover baking dish with aluminum foil and refrigerate at least 30 minutes or overnight.

6. Preheat oven to 350°F. Remove foil and bake egg mixture, uncovered, for 30 minutes or until a knife inserted in the center comes out clean and egg mixture is heated through. (Mixture will fit in an 11 x 7-inch baking dish, but increase baking time by 15 to 20 minutes.) (You can cover the dish securely with plastic wrap, then aluminum foil, and freeze for up to 1 month. Defrost completely before baking.)

The breed of hen determines the color of an egg's shell. For instance, hens with white feathers and ear lobes lay white eggs; those with red feathers and lobes lay brown eggs. A hen takes 24 to 26 hours to produce an egg, and after only a 30-minute rest, she starts all over again. No wonder chickens were a cherished part of early Keys households. Some of their descendants can still be seen running around the outdoor patio tables at Blue Heaven restaurant in Key West.

CHEF NOTE: Alternately buy white eggs and brown eggs, so you can tell which eggs in your refrigerator are the oldest. To determine if an egg is fresh, place two teaspoons salt in a cupful of water, and place egg in the cup. If the egg sinks, it is fresh. If it floats, discard it.

Stocking the Tropical Pantry

Fish and Seafood

Florida Keys fish and seafood can be easily shipped fresh from our islands. To order frozen ground, tenderized conch; frozen, tenderized conch steaks; littleneck clams; dry/diver scallops; spiny lobster; stone crabs; grouper, snapper, tuna, dolphinfish, and more, contact:

Islamorada Fish Company
(800) 258-2559
www.ifcstonecrab.com

Keys Fisheries
(866) 743-4353
www.keysfisheries.com

Key West Seafood
(800) 292-9853
www.keywestseafood.com

Fresh Choice Seafood
(305) 498-8500
www.freshchoiceseafood.com

Ethnic Sauces, Seasonings, and Spices

The international aisles of large supermarket chains carry an increasing number of pan-ethnic products from around the globe. Asian, Middle Eastern, and Latin markets also are good sources. Or, contact the sources listed below to find these recipe ingredients and more: Busha Browne's spicy hot pepper sherry, Asian hot chili sauce, Asian sweet chili sauce, sambal oelek (Thai chili sauce), hoisin sauce, tahini (ground sesame paste), Thai sweet chili sauce, mirin, Thai chile garlic paste, fish sauce, chili garlic sauce, Penzey's 4/S Seasoned Salt, ground annatto (achiote seed), saffron, ground chipotle peppers, lemongrass, canned chipotles, bird peppers, prepared wasabi, wasabi powder, pickled ginger, star anise, Szechuan peppercorns, coriander seeds, black sesame seeds, Japanese breadcrumbs (Panko), rice papers, rice stick noodles, basmati rice.

The CMC Company
(800) 262-2780
www.thecmccompany.com

Penzey's Spices
(800) 741-7787
www.penzeys.com

Hot Sauces

For hot, hot, hot, try some of our southernmost city's "homemade" hot pepper sauces:

Peppers of Key West
(800) KWSAUCE or (800) 597-2823
www.peppersofkeywest.com

Key West Island Style
(305) 853-0707
www.keywestislandstyle.com

Tropical Fruits, Vegetables, and Cuban Ingredients

The essentials of the tropical pantry are readily available in the supermarkets of the Florida Keys. But even if you live up north, you can easily order the tropical and Cuban ingredients for this book's recipes online. Find these ingredients from the sources listed below: Cuban vegetables, such as calabaza squash, malanga, bonianto, plantains, and yucca; fresh and frozen fruit pulp, such as papaya, mango, pineapple, guava, and grated coconut; mango and guava nectars; coconut milk, cream of coconut, coconut cream; guava paste and guava shells; Gilda scooped crackers; empanada pastry; chorizo sausage; Cuban-style coffee beans and Cuban coffee makers; Cuban bread; tropical dressings, marinades, grilling sauces, mustards, and chutneys; bottled key lime juice; mojo sauce and Badia sour orange juice marinade.

El Latinazo Online Latin Supermarket
(877) 628–8887
www.ellatinazo.com

Cuban Food Market
(877) 999–9945
www.cubanfoodmarket.com

Robert is Here
(305) 246–1592
www.robertishere.com

Nellie and Joe's
(800) LIMEPIE or (800) 546–3743
www.keylimejuice.com

Miscellaneous

POM Wonderful pomegranate juice is marketed in many of the large grocery chains. It can also be ordered online: www.pomwonderfulstore.com.

Baby finger bananas have begun to appear in supermarkets and Latin markets in recent years. You can also find them at: Exoticland Fruits (Columbia, S.A.), www.exoticlandfruits.com.

Hazelnut flour and many other specialty flours are available online at: Bob's Red Mill, www.bobsredmill.com, or call (800) 349–2173.

To find a paella pan and jumbo cupcake tins, recommended for use in two of this book's recipes, and for every other gadget your culinary heart may desire, contact: The Restaurant Store in Key West, (800) 469–7510, www.keywestchef.com.

Uneeda Biscuits are still marketed but are difficult to find. They are available at Publix Supermarket in Marathon, (305) 289–2920. Or try the Net Grocer at www.netgrocer.com.

Gourmet Gardens Herb Blend Pastes are produced in Australia. You'll find them in the produce sections of many major supermarkets in the U.S., like Harris Teeter. Look for them online: www.gourmetgarden.com.

Tamarind syrup can be ordered from: G. B. Russo and Sons, (800) 767–8776, www.gbrusso.com.

Superfino Carnaroli Arborio-style rice is available from Roland, Global Experts in Specialty Foods, www.rolandfood.com.

Raditore and other specialty pastas can be found at Foodservicedirect, Inc., (800) 425–4679, www.foodservicedirect.com.

Suckling pig, as well as a wide variety of cuts of beef, port, veal, lamb, and chicken can be ordered from Pete the Butcher, (860) 529–6865, www.petethebutcher.com.

Boneless duck breasts are offered by Maple Leaf Farms, (800) 348–2812, www.mapleleaffarms.com.

Order artisan breads from Cole's Peace Artisan Bakery in Key West (next to the Restaurant store, 1111 Eaton Street), www.colespeace.com.

Calamondins are not a commercial fruit crop, so they remain one of the few dooryard fruits that must be sampled while visiting the Keys. Though not marketed as harvested fruit, the calamondin is sold as an ornamental fruit tree. It grows well indoors in a large pot in northern climates and is cold tolerant to northern Florida. Order from Four Wind Growers, www.fourwindgrowers.com.

Metric Conversion Tables

Approximate U.S.–Metric Equivalents

LIQUID INGREDIENTS

U.S. Measures	Metric	U.S. Measures	Metric
¼ tsp.	1.23 ml	2 Tbsp.	29.57 ml
½ tsp.	2.36 ml	3 Tbsp.	44.36 ml
¾ tsp.	3.70 ml	¼ cup	59.15 ml
1 tsp.	4.93 ml	½ cup	118.30 ml
1¼ tsp.	6.16 ml	1 cup	236.59 ml
1½ tsp.	7.39 ml	2 cups or 1 pt.	473.18 ml
1¾ tsp.	8.63 ml	3 cups	709.77 ml
2 tsp.	9.86 ml	4 cups or 1 qt.	946.36 ml
1 Tbsp.	14.79 ml	4 qts. or 1 gal.	3.79 lt

DRY INGREDIENTS

U.S. Measures	Metric	U.S. Measures	Metric
17⅗ oz.	500 g	2 oz.	60 (56.6) g
16 oz.	454 g	1¾ oz.	50 g
8⅞ oz.	250 g	1 oz.	30 (28.3) g
5¼ oz.	150 g	⅞ oz.	25 g
4½ oz.	125 g	¾ oz.	21 (21.3) g
4 oz.	115 (113.2) g	½ oz.	15 (14.2) g
3½ oz.	100 g	¼ oz.	7 (7.1) g
3 oz.	85 (84.9) g	⅛ oz.	3½ (3.5) g
2⅘ oz.	80 g	1/16 oz.	2 (1.8) g

Index

A

B

D

About the Author

Far from the culture shock she expected upon moving to Duck Key in 1993, Victoria Shearer discovered that island life opened the window on a tropical wonderland of sun, sea, and the sweeping bounty of Mother Nature. An avid traveler and no stranger to the wonders of the world, Vicki concluded that the Florida Keys reign in a class by themselves. So, like the Bahamians and Cubans who adopted the islands centuries before her, she stayed.

A University of Wisconsin graduate, Vicki wore several professional hats—elementary school teacher, advertising agency account executive, magazine copy-editor—before combining her passion for food and travel with her love of writing. A member of the Society of American Travel Writers, she now writes feature articles for newspapers and magazines across the country. She is author of ten editions of *The Insiders' Guide to the Florida Keys and Key West* (The Globe Pequot Press), as well as *Walking Places in New England* (OutThere Press, 2001).

Vicki divides her time between Duck Key and Chocowinity, North Carolina, where she lives with her husband Bob. No day is complete without puttering in the kitchen, but she also loves to play tennis, needlepoint, and quilt. And while the titles of "author" and "cook" are quite nice, Vicki's most cherished monikers are "Mom" (Brian and Lisa, Kristen and John) and "Gram" (Christopher, Bethany, Bobby, Ashleigh, Nicholas, and Leia).

Notes 🌴